COLOR CORRECTION FOR
DIGITAL PHOTOGRAPHERS ONLY

**Ted Padova and
Don Mason**

WILEY

John Wiley & Sons, Inc.

Color Correction For Digital Photographers Only

Published by
Wiley Publishing, Inc.
111 River Street

Hoboken, N.J. 07030
www.wiley.com

Copyright © 2006 by Wiley Publishing, Inc., Indianapolis, Indiana

Published simultaneously in Canada

Library of Congress Control Number: 2006922423

ISBN-13: 978-0-471-77986-5

ISBN-10: 0-471-77986-5

Manufactured in the United States of America

10 9 8 7 6 5 4 3 2 1

1K/RZ/QV/QW/IN

about the authors

Ted Padova first began his interest in amateur photography as a Peace Corps Volunteer in Venezuela. He toured five Latin American countries, collecting shoeboxes of slides he hopefully will one day sort out. Upon completion of his two-year Peace Corps tour, he attended the New York Institute of Photography in Manhattan when it was a resident school, earning a diploma in Commercial Photography. He worked his way through undergraduate and graduate school professionally shooting weddings and portraits. Although many people laugh at his Honeywell Strobonars, he realizes he could never have completed his higher education without them.

In 2004 he retired from his Digital Imaging Service Bureau and Custom Photo Finishing Lab after 15 years of owning and operating three facilities. He has authored over 20 computer books on Adobe Acrobat, Adobe Photoshop, Adobe Photoshop Elements, and Adobe Illustrator. Today he spends his time writing and speaking nationally and internationally on Acrobat PDF and digital imaging. When not writing or speaking he can be found walking the beaches or sailing around his home in Waikiki in Honolulu, Hawaii. Ted can be reached at `ted@west.net`.

Don Mason is a graduate of Brooks Institute of Photography in Santa Barbara, California. He has been a professional photographer for more than three decades and works in virtually every aspect of commercial photography. Don first started using a computer in 1999 when he didn't believe that digital imaging would ever replace his wing lynch system used for processing all his E-6 film and his darkroom where he made his own C-prints. After four years of intensive work in Adobe Photoshop, he abandoned his analog film lab and went completely digital. Today he divides his time between shooting professional commercial photography and printing art prints for a wide range of clients on his two oversized Epson inkjet printers. Don can be reached at `Dmason5849@aol.com`.

credits

Acquisitions Editor
Tom Heine

Project Editor
Tim Borek

Technical Editor
Michael Sullivan

Copy Editor
Kim Heusel

Editorial Manager
Robyn Siesky

Business Manager
Amy Knies

Vice President & Executive Group Publisher
Richard Swadley

Vice President & Publisher
Barry Pruett

Project Coordinator
Adrienne Martinez

Graphics and Production Specialists
Jennifer Click
Amanda Spagnuolo
Ron Terry

Quality Control Technician
Charles Spencer

Proofreading and Indexing
Lisa Stiers
Ty Koontz

I would like to dedicate this work to all the wonderful people at my former Digital Imaging Service Bureau and Photo Finishing Center, the Image Source of Ventura California, who continue to work on the front lines, color correcting and printing digital camera images every day. For Jim Davis, my former partner, Stephanie Hogue and some of their most able staff, Chris Breedlove, Hugo Viveros, Jenny Frovarp, Tony Cuevas, Vicki Lewis, David Meyer, John Johnson, and Theresa Davis.

— Ted Padova

I would like to dedicate this work to those who sent me on my journey to learn the craft of photography, and to those who showed me that the magic never ends, as long as you strive to keep learning: Bertil Brink, the world-class instructors at Brooks Institute, and Ted Padova.

— Don Mason

preface

I'm excited about this book, not because I had a part in writing it, but because it gives me an opportunity to introduce you, and hopefully a good part of the Photoshop community, to my coauthor Don Mason.

Don is about as close to John Travolta's character in the film *Phenomenon* as anyone I've ever met. No, Don hasn't yet tried to learn the Portuguese language in 20 minutes as did Travolta's character, but he has learned various versions of Photoshop through the years by reading manuals and offering advice to his graphic artists and professional advertising clients. Not so extraordinary, you say? Well, Don managed to do it without ever touching a keyboard or mouse! That's right. His clients for many years frequently called in desperation asking for advice on working through problems in Photoshop. Don would always ask, "Does it have some kind of manual or guide? Okay, just drop it off at my studio before you go home tonight." And, as the story goes, the next day Don provided his clients with step-by-step instruction over the phone on how to solve complex Photoshop problems without the benefits of seeing or working on a computer.

I met Don in late 1998 when I opened my third digital imaging and photofinishing lab in Don's hometown of Bakersfield, California. Don dropped by and asked a lot of questions. He frequently made trips to my lab with spectrometers and devices to measure luminosity on monitors. We engaged in conversations about color that were off the scale to me; and I was always in awe of Don's understanding of color and the physics behind it, and how he could always explain what must be going on with the computer without ever touching one.

After many a conversation with Don, in early 1999 he finally purchased his first computer — an Apple iMac. He was still processing his own E-6 chromes and didn't think the computer would help him professionally that much, so he opted for the low-end model. A few years later Don dumped his processing equipment, enlargers, and most of his film cameras in favor of digital tools throughout his studio.

When my senior acquisitions editor at Wiley called and asked me to write this book, I told him I would only be interested if I could bring along a coauthor, and Don Mason was my only choice. As Don and I discussed this project, we wanted to bring to you a book that demonstrates some real-world methods of editing a huge array of different kinds of photos. We wanted to talk to both the professional photographer and the amateur. We wanted to avoid all the definitions of RGB vs. CMYK color gamuts that you've heard a thousand times. Rather, we wanted to provide you with more of a handy reference where you can look at an image similar to one you need to edit and go right to the steps to achieve your results.

You'll find in the chapters ahead some methods for obtaining results such as sharpening images, masking, and some other techniques that are not original, and certainly similar methods are addressed by many Photoshop professionals who have written other books. However, we believe we have some fresh new content covering many methods that perhaps you haven't seen covered elsewhere. Hopefully we've integrated the old and the new to provide you with a resource guide that can be of help in your studio when color correcting images and making tonal adjustments.

All the photography in this book is our own with the exception of a few images provided by some talented photographers. The *amazing* photos you see throughout the book are Don's own creations. The hardest part of writing this book for us was creating some photos that needed intense editing. Don is a professional photographer who typically sets up his shots with all the proper lighting controls to simplify his editing in Photoshop. For the really bad photos, we used a few of my own and then proceeded to create some shots to demonstrate extreme tonal corrections methods just in case you encounter similar images in your work.

For the professional photographer, we added a chapter where we tried to cover some studio and assignment shots from shooting aerials to location shooting. As an afterthought, we decided to add a special chapter for snapshots and the types of photos the novice photographer frequently encounters — and this chapter I'm particularly excited about. It covers some problems with photos that all of us at one time or another have taken and deemed beyond repair. We went out on a limb with this and included some images needing correction you don't often see in other Photoshop books because the originals are so poor.

As you thumb through the pages ahead, you'll find other chapters covering different topics, but the central point is that the content is wrapped around color and tonal corrections. If this is your area of interest, we sincerely hope that you find much value in this publication and that it can be of help to you in all your Photoshop editing sessions.

— Ted Padova

from Waikiki, Hawaii

acknowledgments

The authors would like to thank our production team at Wiley Publishing for all their dedicated hard work to help bring this publication to completion. Special thanks to our senior acquisitions editor, Tom Heine, for his support and confidence in asking us to write this book and aiding us throughout the project, and Tim Borek, who helped keep our progress moving and assisted in refining our manuscript. A special thank you is also extended to our technical editor, Mike Sullivan, for keeping an eye on the accuracy of our claims.

We would like to thank Patrick Smith of onOne Software, Inc. (www.onOnesoftware.com) for support with using Genuine Fractals Print Pro 4.1 and Roy Harrington for assistance with Quad Tone Rip (www.quadtonerip.com).

The authors shot all the photos in this work, with the exception of some pieces that were generously contributed by some extraordinary photographers. We would like to thank PJ Leffingwell (www.photosbypj.com), and Schaf (www.schafphoto.com) for their contributions.

In creating this book, we used as many actual commercial images shot for our clientele as we possibly could. For some of the other examples, we enlisted clients and friends as our subject matter. Without their gracious help and cooperation, this book wouldn't have been possible. We want to especially thank, Lisle Gates, Carol Murphy, Ryan Gates, Heather Gates, Bonnie Creasy, Courtney Creasy, Paul Showalter, Terry Gilson, Rosario Gilson, Gary Obermeier, Andrew Mason, Danielle Wolf, Pat Griffin, Sharon Casey, Beth Ramone, Nicole Saint John, Claudia True, Alexis Cambell, Betty Jo Sheperd, Jennifer Randall, Calico Randall, Cody Randall, Ed Hill, Joe Colombo, Mike and Cindy McBride, Bruce Maclin, Cheri Zendarski, Pat Bianchi, and Al Rose.

And a very special thank you to Mercy Hospital and the following dedicated Physicians: Nirav Naik, M.D., Hormuz Irani, M.D. Selwyn Kay, M.D., and Donald Loos, M.D.

resources

As you work through some of the steps contained in this book, it might be helpful to have sample files with which to work. You'll find a number of files we used in this book online at http://www.wiley.com/go/colorcorrection. Files are organized in folders according to the chapters in which they appear in the book. In some cases, a file may appear in more than one chapter. You can find such files in the folder respective to the first occurrence of the figure in the book. Download the fileGuide.pdf document and open in Adobe Reader to see a thumbnail view of the files contained on the Web site.

contents at a glance

contents

chapter 2 Setting Up Your Color Environment   27

chapter **3 Camera Raw Color Correction 45**

Part II Image Corrections 89

chapter **4 Tone and Brightness Corrections 91**

chapter 5 Correcting Color Problems 139

chapter 6 Editing Studio and Location Shots 175

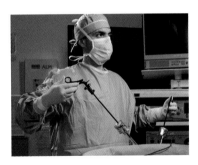

chapter 7 **Fixing Snapshots** 207

Part III Digital Darkroom Techniques   247

chapter 8 **Photocopying** 249

chapter 9 Black-and-White Photo Editing   283

chapter **10 Lens Effects 317**

chapter **11 Printing 339**

Contents

GETTING COLOR RIGHT

Part I

Chapter 1

UNDERSTANDING COLOR

*"In my mind's eye, I visualize how a particular . . .
sight and feeling will appear on a print. If it excites
me, there is a good chance it will make a good photograph. It is an intuitive sense, an ability that comes
from a lot of practice."* — Ansel Adams

We've all heard about a hundred different definitions
of color as it pertains to digital images and computer
monitors, and what's not needed is another chapter to
rehash all the stuff you already know. But just in case
we aren't in sync with our definitions, let's talk a little
about some of the more important aspects of color in
images and a little about general color management
that we should clearly understand together. Beginning
with creating the best color correction environment to
some basic understanding of digital images, let's
move forward to get a handle on a few basic principles. Pull up a chair next to the fireplace, grab a latte,
and let's sit down and agree on some understanding
of color and how to manage color in Photoshop.

UNDERSTANDING WHAT YOU NEED FOR GOOD COLOR HANDLING

Without getting into the technical aspects of viewing color, looking at reflective versus subtractive
color, examining the anatomy of your eye and all the
other scientific rules and axioms related to color viewing, there are some essential ingredients you need to
become familiar with when it comes to color viewing,
color correction, and printing correct color.

Quite simply, the most important of these ingredients
include

> **Controlled lighting.** One of the most commonly
  overlooked areas related to good color viewing
  conditions is carefully setting up your viewing
  environment (see Figure 1-1). If you work on a
  super professional color monitor, have your monitor tweaked with a $5,000 color calibrator, and
  use the most sophisticated color profiles, you're
  only halfway to color correction. If light coming
  through your window and your overhead lights
  results in a colorcast on your monitor, you're not

working in an optimum viewing environment. The
first consideration you need to make is controlling
the lighting of your workplace.

> **Monitor calibration.** You've heard it all before,
  and we repeat it here — you need to be certain
  your viewing device reflects the best possible
  brightness and gray balance that you can get. On
  the low end, you can purchase some inexpensive
  calibration equipment; on the high end, you can
  purchase some very sophisticated calibration
  tools. At some point, you need to use a device to
  get your monitor to display the best you can get
  in terms of brightness and gray balance, as we
  explain in Chapter 2.

> **Color profiles.** You have options for using source
  color profiles, viewing profiles, and output profiles.
  Getting your color translated from one device to
  another is always an important consideration when
  getting color right.

PIXELS AND RESIZING IMAGES

Since you've been around pixels for a long time,
you pretty much have an understanding that those
tiny little squares all bunched together ultimately comprise the makeup of a digital photograph. You know
that the number of pixels in one way or another relate
to image quality. Furthermore, you're certain that no
matter how many pixels you have in an image, the
quantity of those tiny little dots doesn't have a darn
thing to do with improving color. We have to manipulate, finesse, and mess around with those pixels to
balance the color.

PIXELS AND DOTS

Wouldn't it be a great world if an input dot, a viewing
dot, and an output dot were all at a 1:1 ratio? In other
words, you see a bright red pixel, you shoot a photograph and capture the hues precisely, you see the
same bright red color on your monitor, and you print
the photo resulting in a print that shows that red pixel
exactly as you saw it before taking the picture.

1-1

Unfortunately, digital life is not so easy, and a caveat is always thrown into the mix. The imbalance of dots related to different devices is one of many factors that confuse us when it comes to image color correction and preparing files for various output devices.

You might have a color printer capable of rendering 1440 pixels per inch (ppi) of resolution. Your input image (obtained from a scanner or digital camera) might be a 300-pixel-per-inch image file. When it comes time to open your image in Photoshop, you're working on a 72-pixel-per-inch display. What's more confusing is that the output resolution on your printer is really a lie. Take an Epson color printer, for example, that renders a 1440 ppi resolution. Does that mean you need 1440 pixels in your image to take full advantage of your printer? The answer is definitely NO. The reason being is because the printer fires off microscopic droplets of ink in at least four colors (Cyan, Magenta, Yellow, and Black) or more to give you the illusion of continuous-tone color. These many droplets define each pixel in terms of color and brightness.

If you prepare images for commercial printing on film setters and plate setters, resolutions of the equipment can exceed 2500 pixels per inch. Again, your image file at 300 ppi is plotted in dots, and each dot is formed by many smaller dots to create all the gray tones needed to reproduce the file at a specified halftone frequency.

X-REF

For a little more understanding of what we mean by gray tones in color images, see the section later in this chapter "RGB Color."

Digital cameras are marketed, with among many other features, the total number of pixels the camera's sensor is capable of capturing. You hear numbers such as 6.3 megapixels, 7.2 megapixels, 11 megapixels, and so on. These figures describe images captured with the total number of pixels per image. When you first open a digital camera image, the resolution of the image may be 72 ppi. As a result, you need to resize the image to the correct proportions for your desired output; when you do, the image resolution increases proportionately.

NOTE

Some digital cameras saving in *JPEG* format default to 72 ppi at dimensions producing the total pixels captured by the camera sensor. Cameras capable of saving files in Camera Raw format typically save with higher resolutions also at the dimensions that produce the total pixels captured by the camera sensor.

As an example, follow these steps to resize an image without affecting the resolution:

1. Open an image taken with a digital camera in Photoshop CS2.

2. Choose Image ➪ Image Size or press Command/Ctrl+Option/Alt+I to open the Image Size dialog box (see Figure 1-2).

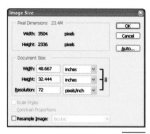

1-2

3. Type a new number in the Resolution box to change the resolution. Leave the Resample Image checkbox deselected when changing the image size. As you increase the amount in the Resolution text box, the values change proportionately in the Width and Height text boxes. The more resolution you add to the Resolution text box, the lower the values appear in the Width and Height text boxes.

Individually resizing images works well when color correcting a single image or maybe just a handful. However, if you've filled up your memory card and need to size many files, it's best to use an automated *Action* when files need to be the same size.

CREATE AN ACTION FOR RESIZING IMAGES

To create an Action for resizing images, follow these steps:

1. Open an image taken with a digital camera in Photoshop CS2. Start with one image open in Photoshop to create the action.

2. Choose Window ➪ Actions if the Actions palette is not currently open.

3. Click the right-pointing arrow to open the Actions palette menu and select New Action (see Figure 1-3).

4. Choose Image ➪ Image Size or press Command/Ctrl+Option/Alt+I to open the Image Size dialog box.

5. Type the resolution value you want for a batch of images and then click OK in the Image Size dialog box.

6. Choose File ➪ Save As and select the format you want to use for the file from the Format drop-down menu. Click Save to save the file.

7. Close the file by clicking on the Close box or choosing File ➪ Close.

8. Click the Stop playing/recording button in the Actions palette. At the bottom of the Actions palette you see a row of tools. The first tool in the palette, represented as a square, is the Stop playing/recording button.

1-3

PLAY AN ACTION

When it comes time to use your action, follow these steps:

1. Choose File ➪ Automate ➪ Batch to open the Batch dialog box shown in Figure 1-4.

1-4

PRO TIP

You can create a new group and nest all your own custom actions in the group. First, select New Set from the palette menu and the Name dialog box appears. Type a name for your new group and click OK. The new group appears as a folder in the Actions palette. To nest a new action below the folder name, click the new group folder to select it. Open the palette menu and choose New Action when you want to create an action. All your actions can then be grouped together in your new folder apart from the default actions Photoshop provides you.

After you click the Stop playing/recording button the Action is listed in the palette and ready to use on a folder of files. Be certain to copy all your files from your memory card to your hard drive and place them in a single folder.

2. From the Set and Actions drop-down menus, select your Set (if you created one) and select the new action you created to resize images.

3. Click Choose under the Source item in the Batch dialog box to open the Choose a folder dialog box.

4. Navigate your hard drive in the Choose a batch folder dialog box to locate the folder where you saved the images from your media card. Select the folder and click Choose to return to the Batch dialog box.

5. Click Choose in the Destination area. Follow the procedures in step 4 to specify the folder where you want to save the resized images.

   If you need to create a new folder for your saved images, you can click Choose and click New Folder in the Choose a batch folder dialog box.

6. Click OK.

   Photoshop automatically opens files in the source folder, resizes images according to settings you supplied when you created the action, saves the results to the destination folder, and closes each file after saving.

RESAMPLING IMAGES

Going back to the Image Size dialog box, if you select the Resample Image check box you change the number of pixels in an image to a value higher or lower than the total pixels you started with depending on what values you type in the Resolution box. For example, if you size an image at 6 x 4 inches with the Resample Image check box deselected, the resolution may increase to 600 pixels per inch. At this point, the total pixels in your image remain the same. Check the Resample Image check box and change the resolution to 300 ppi. When you click OK, half the pixels in the file are tossed away and the image is said to be *downsampled*, which means the resolution is lowered.

Ideally, plan on downsampling images to the optimum resolution of your output device. In terms of color printing on continuous-tone devices, 300 ppi can generally be applied to most color printers.

Quite often you'll need to downsample digital photo images. When you select the Resample Image check box in the Image Size dialog box, the drop-down menu adjacent to the check box offers five resampling modes. The default is Bicubic, and for most of your continuous tone images, this is the mode to choose. In Figure 1-5 you can see the results of using the Bicubic method compared to using Bilinear and Nearest Neighbor.

X-REF

For more information on working with moiré patterns, see Chapter 8.

Bicubic   Bilinear   Nearest Neighbor

1-5

The other two options, Bicubic Smoother and Bicubic Sharper, are helpful when sampling images such as portraits or photos that need some sharp detail. Use Bicubic Smoother when downsampling portraits where facial features are rendered a little smoother. Use Bicubic Sharper when you want sharper detail like when shooting aerials or architecture.

PRO TIP

When in doubt, however, use Bicubic and be done with it. Other modes use different algorithms to calculate new pixel values, but none works better overall as a default than the Bicubic method. Bicubic is always superior to Nearest Neighbor or Bilinear for general use with photographic images

UPSIZING IMAGES

As a general rule, upsizing images by adding more resolution to a file often produces undesirable results. Too much upsampling can make your image look like mush. Photoshop uses an algorithm to calculate new pixels based on the values of the original pixels and at best produces a guess at what those pixel values should be. Sometimes the result of the guesswork is a less-than-desirable image.

There are some circumstances, however, where upsizing images can be helpful. The results may or may not be desirable, so you have to run tests and print samples to see if your resampling efforts are satisfactory. A good example might be a digital camera image that needs to be printed as a large poster. If the output of the original file is pixelated, you can try to upsample the image and print a small area of the photo to test the results.

NOTE

Photoshop's algorithm for resampling images has improved over the years and offers you some impressive results. In Photoshop CS2, the Bicubic method of resampling is more impressive than found in earlier versions of the program.

For a more sophisticated approach to resampling, you can acquire a Photoshop plug-in designed to resample images. Genuine Fractals is a product developed by onOne Software (www.ononesoftware.com) designed exclusively for the purpose of upsampling images. In Figure 1-6, you can see the results of upsampling an image 400 percent using Genuine Fractals. The original image appears in the center

GF PRINT PRO UPSAMPLED 400%   P.S. BICUBIC SHARPER 400%

1-6

inset. On the right is a close-up of the file upsampled in Photoshop using Bicubic resampling, and Genuine Fractals upsampling on the left.

Whether you use Photoshop or a plug-in like Genuine Fractals, don't expect to take a wallet size image at 72 ppi from your Web page and upsample the image. You need to start with a file that is at least a 4 x 6 inches at 300 ppi or greater for best results and keep the resizing of the image to within certain sizing limitations such as 800 percent or less.

UNDERSTANDING COLOR MODES

Photoshop supports working in, converting to, and saving files in a number of different color modes. For digital photographers, the default and most popular color mode is RGB. In addition to RGB, you can convert to other color modes for editing images or submitting files to clients for various types of output.

You don't need to be concerned with every color mode Photoshop can handle. Most often you'll work with one of four color modes that include RGB, CMYK, Lab, or Grayscale.

RGB COLOR

You're probably familiar with the standard RGB color mode that you see when viewing color images on your monitor, take color photos with your digital camera, or scan pictures with your scanner. RGB is the default color mode for working on color images and correcting color.

Color in Photoshop is represented in channels. In an RGB color image, you have three channels — one for red, one for green, and one for blue. When you open the Channels palette and look at each of the three RGB channels, you see various levels of gray. The RGB composite channel is seen as color, but the three individual channels are seen as white, gray, or black depending on the color represented in the composite channel (see Figure 1-7).

1-7

Each of these three channels can be changed for color value and brightness. Whatever change is made on the individual channels is reflected in the composite image. If you use Photoshop tools for correcting color and brightness, most of your correction tools offer options for selecting the composite image where you make changes to all three channels simultaneously, or you can make changes to a selected channel. In Figure 1-8, a curves adjustment is made on the Red channel.

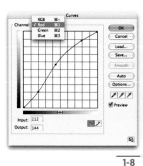

1-8

You have options for adjusting individual channels in other dialog boxes, too, such as Levels and Channel Mixer.

CMYK COLOR

CMYK color is process color using mixes of Cyan, Magenta, Yellow, and Black. If your digital photography is limited to output for photo prints and Web graphics, you don't need to be concerned about CMYK. However, if you prepare files for commercial printing at print shops, CMYK is something you need to understand.

Whereas RGB encompasses a large color *gamut* representing more that 16 million colors on your color monitor, the CMYK model offers you fewer colors that can be seen on your monitor and reproduced on a printed piece. Regardless of whether you output RGB or CMYK files, your working environment stays in RGB color and all your color correction is performed on RGB images.

What is important when editing images for CMYK output is to be certain you see the color as closely as possible to what will be rendered in CMYK. While editing in RGB mode, choose View ➪ Proof Setup ➪ Working CMYK. Your monitor then displays colors more closely to the CMYK color gamut.

LAB COLOR

Lab color, like RGB color, represents color images in three channels. These channels are L or Lightness channel, and the *a* channel and the *b* channel. The L (Lightness) channel represents all the brightness in your image while the a and b channels represent all the color. The entire color spectrum is split in half with each of these two channels taking one-half of the full color spectrum.

When it comes to editing Photoshop images for color and brightness, you can use Lab color when you want to make changes without affecting the color in the image. For example, you might convert an RGB image to Lab color and select the L (Lightness) channel in the Channels palette (see Figure 1-9) or press Command/Ctrl+1. After selecting the Lightness channel, you might sharpen an image using the Unsharp Mask filter. Doing so sharpens the image without changing color.

1-9

GRAYSCALE

Grayscale images are single-channel files with only a Gray channel. Grayscale images have no color, and in order to add a color tint to an image, such as a

---

Color Correction in Photoshop versus Photoshop Elements

Throughout this book are screen shots and references to Adobe Photoshop with little mention of Adobe Photoshop Elements 4. Elements is a truly great image-editing tool that provides an abundant number of features for editing and printing your digital photographs. Many cameras ship with Elements on a CD-ROM so you may get the program free with the purchase of your camera.

Unfortunately, Photoshop Elements doesn't have some critical editing tools for correcting color and brightness that are available in Photoshop. Among other features, Elements does not provide you a Channels palette where you can edit individual channels. The channels are there and visible when you open a dialog box like the Levels

dialog, but you can't edit individual channels with other editing tools. Nor does Elements support a Curves dialog box that provides you with more brightness control than you get with the Levels dialog box.

In addition to the lack of editing features for channels and curves, Elements does not support much in the area of color profiling. You only have two choices when managing color using either the Adobe RGB (1998) color space or sRGB. Custom profiling is not part of the program.

Due to the lack of these critical tools, we recommend that all serious digital photographers who want the most out of color correction avoid using Elements and stick to Photoshop.

sepia tone, you need to convert the grayscale image to RGB color.

If you are printing a black-and-white photo, you may get better results on some equipment by first converting the grayscale image to RGB color. On some other printers, you might be best leaving the image in Grayscale mode.

X-REF

For information on working with grayscale images, see Chapter 8. For information on printing grayscale images, see Chapter 11.

UNDERSTANDING BIT DEPTH

As we previously explained, your color images are represented in three channels. Each of these channels contains a level of gray to express any given color. Essentially, the gray values block out or hold back light. A level of 0 in each channel means no light passes through each channel resulting in a black image. Conversely, a level of 255 is wide open and lets all light pass through resulting in a pure white image.

NOTE

The number 255 is a figure you want to remember. Because 0 (zero) is a number, too, there are a total of 256 levels of gray in an image.

When you work with 256 levels of gray for each channel, you are working on an 8-bit image. If you take 256^3 (256 x 256 x 256), the result is a number in excess of 16 million, which is the total number of colors in the RGB color gamut. When it comes time to reproduce your images on a printer, the printer outputs your file from 8-bit images in an effort to reproduce as many of those possible 16.7 million colors as it can.

If you use a digital camera capable of capturing *Camera Raw* images, your camera sensors are likely

to capture 12-bit or higher images — the most common higher bit being 16-bit. A 16-bit image has 4096 levels of gray per channel. This extra data permits you to decide which 256 levels of gray ultimately are used on your final printed piece. In Figure 1-10, for example, the Levels dialog box is opened on an 8-bit image. The left side of the histogram reports no data showing on this side, which means there is no detail in the darker areas of the image.

1-10

Because your printer can only print 8-bit images, the extra image data is tossed during printing. However, when you edit an image for brightness and color correction, you want to perform as much of your editing as you can while in a higher bit mode. Having the extra data in an image lets you decide which 256 levels of gray from the 4096 levels will be used when printing the image.

Figure 1-11 shows the Levels dialog box for a 16-bit image with data across all 256 levels of gray. You can skew the input sliders on this image to the left or right to pick up a little more detail in either the highlights or shadows. In essence, you are telling Photoshop which levels of gray you want to reproduce.

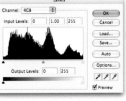

1-11

X-REF

For more information on using the Levels dialog box to adjust brightness and contrast, see Chapter 4.

UNDERSTANDING DYNAMIC RANGE

*D*ynamic range is the measure of capturing data in the highlights and shadows. If your images are clipped (showing no data on either end of a histogram), the dynamic range is much less than a photo captured where you see a histogram containing data at both ends and all through the midtone areas.

Input devices such as cameras and scanners are categorized in terms of dynamic range as well as output devices. Looking at a digital camera, you can find many point-and-shoot models that boast more than 7 or 8 megapixels that cost less than $500. You can also find digital cameras in the 4- to 6-megapixel area that cost more than $2000. One of the primary differences between the cameras is the dynamic range of the sensors. Obviously, the more costly cameras provide you a greater dynamic range, which means you see much more detail in the shadows and highlights.

ADDING MORE IMAGE DATA

If you use a digital camera capable of capturing images at higher bit depths with a dynamic range sufficient for capturing details in shadows and highlights, you can't always get all the necessary data you need to produce a good quality print. You have to consider lighting conditions and the amount of available light you have to work with. At times, there won't be enough light to get all the detail you want in shadow areas, and the light may be too much to get any detail in highlights.

If you do photo reproduction and copy work, you're stuck with the dynamic range as it exists on your source material. Old photographs that may be washed out don't provide you with a good quality image to obtain a quality copy no matter how good your camera may be.

Photoshop has a few tricks that can help you improve dynamic range and add more data to a file. In the case with photocopy work, take an antique or aged photo that appears washed out and shoot the print with your digital camera. To add more data, follow these steps:

1. Open an image that appears washed out in Photoshop.

2. Open the Layers palette and drag the Background layer to the New Layer icon to duplicate the layer.

3. Open the Layers palette mode menu and select Multiply (Figure 1-12).

   The top layer appears darker as the Multiply mode takes all the black on one layer and adds it to all the black on the second layer. Note that you can change the Opacity on the top layer to control the amount of darkening you want in the composite image by dragging the Opacity slider left and right.

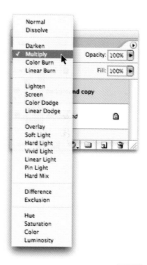

1-12

PRO TIP

Using the AutoContrast adjustment when working with 16-bit images can accomplish similar results as described in these steps. If you have 8-bit images, follow the steps outlined here.

4. Open the palette pop-up menu and select Flatten to flatten the layers.

5. Adjust Levels and Curves to optimize the brightness.

6. Compare the results of the edited image to the raw image you opened in Photoshop.

In Figure 1-13, you can see a comparison of the image before and after following the steps outlined here.

1-13

X-REF

For information on using Levels and Curves, see Chapter 4.

PRO TIP

If you have a portion of an image that needs to be darkened, use the Lasso tool and create a selection where you want to improve contrast. Choose Select ⇨ Feather to open the Feather dialog box. Type a value to add a large feather to the selection. The amount of the feather depends on your image size and resolution so you may need to test it a few times. Start with at least 20 pixels for your feather radius. Click OK and press Command/Ctrl+J to duplicate the selection as a new layer. Select Multiply from the Mode pop-up menu and only the selection is darkened.

IMPROVING CAPTURED DYNAMIC RANGE

In a controlled shooting environment, you have another option for adding more data that will improve the dynamic range in your photos. This method requires you to use a tripod, and your subject matter should be still with no visible motion such as people walking, automobiles passing, or sporting events action shots.

A super-wide captured dynamic range cannot be reproduced on any known hardcopy output device, but this option retains all the captured tonal data, allowing the user to manipulate it later in the editing process to fit the output device, without clipping shadows or highlights.

To improve dynamic range where the lighting conditions may not be optimum to capture sufficient detail in shadows and highlights, you need to take three to five photos of the exact same image at different exposures then merge them together in Photoshop. Follow these steps to see how to do it:

1. Take a photo using your tripod, then change the Exposure Value (EV) one to two stops to over- or underexpose the image and take a second photo. Repeat the process of changing EV to one to two stops again in the opposite direction producing at least one underexposed and one overexposed photo along with your original photo.

   The photos you use can be either 8-bit or 16-bit images. The Merge to HDR command ultimately creates a 32-bit image after you run the command. If you reduce the image bit depth after converting to 32-bit, some clipping is likely to occur and you lose a little tonal range when dropping the bit depth.

2. Add your photos to Adobe Bridge so you can clearly see the thumbnails of each photo.

3. In Adobe Bridge, choose Tools ⇨ Photoshop ⇨ Merge to HDR (see Figure 1-14).

   You can also use the Merge to HDR command in Photoshop if you don't have the files displayed in Adobe Bridge. Choose File ⇨ Automate ⇨ Merge to HDR.

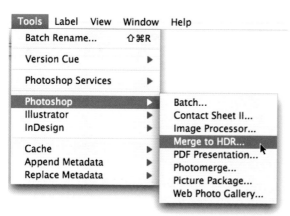

| Tools | Label | View | Window | Help |

Batch Rename...   ⇧⌘R
Version Cue   ▶
Photoshop Services   ▶
Photoshop   ▶   Batch...
Illustrator   ▶   Contact Sheet II...
InDesign   ▶   Image Processor...
                              Merge to HDR...
Cache   ▶   PDF Presentation...
Append Metadata   ▶   Photomerge...
Replace Metadata   ▶   Picture Package...
                              Web Photo Gallery...

1-14

4. Wait a few minutes for Photoshop to process your image and view the results in a new Photoshop document window. Photoshop merges all the data from the individual images and effectively increases the dynamic range. If you expose for shooting shadows, shoot for properly exposing highlights, and the third shot for the midtone ranges, the Merge to HDR command combines the dynamic range from the images to provide you with ample data in the shadows, highlights, and midtone areas. In Figure 1-15, you can see the five images we started with and the end result after merging the photos.

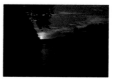

1 second@F-22   1/4 second@F-22   1/15 second@F-22   1/60 second@F-22   1/250 second@F-22

1-15

Don captured the river scene in Figure 1-15 with a 12 f-stop range from bright sun to deepest shadows. This type of capture is near impossible with negative film, but Photoshop's Merge to HDR ultimately creates a composite image with a rich tonal range. The overall image sharpness suffers a little because a slight breeze moved the trees a bit. Printed at 5 x 7, it's hardly noticeable, but larger prints show a slight lack of crispness in the trees.

USING COLOR PROFILES

You have two major issues to deal with when it comes to managing color. One is your eye and how you see color, and the other is your hardware and how color is seen and interpreted by all your devices. When it comes to you seeing color, you need to be concerned with controlling light and setting up your monitor for the best viewing conditions. With respect to devices, you need to be concerned with the capture device — in this case, your digital camera — and the output device.

X-REF

For viewing color and setting up your color-viewing environment, see Chapter 2.

Color is managed on devices through the use of *color profiles*. Color profiles are data files used by your devices, and color profiles in your Photoshop images are lines of code added to the image files. One of the most important uses of color profiles is for translating colors from one device to another so that you are assured of, as closely as possible, colors ultimately appear the same across all your equipment. The operative here is translation, and it's important to know that quite often you need to convert color from one source to another.

MONITOR COLOR PROFILES

You've probably read much about the fact that color viewing and management is not an exact science and you can't expect to get color precisely the same between your monitor and your output. This is true, but what we expect is to get things pretty darn close where the anomalies between various sources handling color are very subtle and have little effect on how you properly view and manage color.

When it comes to viewing color, the viewing device needs to be calibrated, and the result of your calibration efforts is creating a monitor profile. Essentially, this means quite simply that when you turn your computer on, your operating system loads the monitor color profile with all the settings used to calibrate your monitor into memory so you see the same monitor brightness each time you start working in Photoshop.

A monitor color profile doesn't have a direct impact on your Photoshop image and printing the file. Monitor profiles are simply used to be certain that your monitor has the correct brightness, absence of colorcasts and color tints, and displays your photos on-screen with colors as true as possible.

X-REF

To learn how to create a monitor color profile, see Chapter 2.

CRT VERSUS LCD MONITORS

LCD (liquid crystal display) monitors are the rage today and with prices continually dropping, more people are discarding their traditional CRT (cathode-ray tube or television-type) monitors in favor of the much smaller footprint of the LCD monitors.

If you want the best viewing conditions for correcting color in Photoshop, resist the temptation to purchase an LCD monitor. The color clarity of CRTs cannot be matched by any LCD screen produced today. Among other things, you have a number of different adjustments you can make on CRT monitors for changing contrast, brightness, and hues. The end result is that CRT monitors are better able to represent actual document colors. In many cases you can purchase a super-quality CRT monitor at much less cost than an average-priced LCD monitor.

If you're a color professional, stay away from the LCDs (see Figure 1-16) and buy a good-quality CRT display. It's the tool of choice for color specialists.

For more on CRT monitors, see Chapter 2.

COLOR WORKSPACES

If there's a monkey wrench in the color-management process, it's the confusing idea of knowing that you have a monitor color profile and a color working profile. Color working profiles define your color workspace that impacts how your image color is translated between different color monitors and viewing conditions. If, for example, you want to exchange a file with another user, you embed (or save your profile) with the color workspace you use. The recipient of your file may use another color workspace, in which case the user might convert your image from your color workspace to his or her workspace. Through this conversion, the color is translated as near as possible to maintain as much of the same color from your original workspace to the converted color workspace.

Photoshop provides you with two primary color workspaces when you install the program. In Photoshop, choose Edit ⇨ Color Settings. The Color Settings dialog box appears. Click the RGB item in the Working Spaces area of the dialog box, and you see preinstalled color profiles as well as any custom profiles you create or import (see Figure 1-17).

> **Adobe RGB (1998).** The first of the two primary workspaces used by most photographers and artists is Adobe RGB (1998). This workspace is popular with anyone who prepares images for some form of print output. This workspace provides a wide range of RGB colors that theoretically can be reproduced on a printing device.

1-16

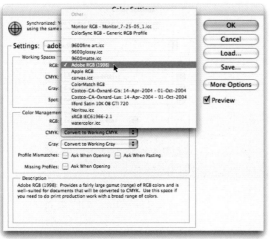

1-17

CAMERA COLOR PROFILES

Digital cameras can also capture your images while embedding a color profile. The Canon 20D is capable of embedding either Adobe RGB (1998) or sRGB when capturing files saved as JPEG. The Canon 20D lets you choose between the two profiles by adjusting the camera's settings.

If you want to quickly check to see if your camera saves files with a color profile, open Adobe Bridge and select a thumbnail of a photo taken with your camera. Take a look at the Metadata pane, and you should see Color Profile if your camera supports it. Figure 1-18 shows how the Metadata shows the selected image has the sRGB color profile embedded in the image.

> **sRGB.** The official name for this profile is sRGB IEC61966-2.1, but most of us commonly refer to it as simply sRGB. This workspace is designed for use with images displayed on monitors such as Web viewing or images intended for screen pre-viewing. The color gamut can display some colors that may not be reproduced on some printing devices.

You may hear some people recommend that you stay away from sRGB when preparing files for print. However, don't completely dismiss this workspace when sending your files off to a photo lab. Some photo-reproduction equipment that prints in RGB (not CMYK) may take advantage of the full sRGB color gamut.

1-18

OUTPUT PROFILES

Output color profiles are used by equipment to print your photographs. Assuming you have set up your working environment with the proper lighting, calibrated your monitor for the proper viewing of your images on-screen, and identified your color workspace in Photoshop's (or Adobe Bridge's) Color Settings dialog box, you are viewing colors as true as possible that can be reproduced on some device. Your color then needs to be converted properly to the output device so the entire range of colors as best as possible can be output when you print your pictures. This is where the output profile comes in. Output profiles are used to match the color you see on your monitor to the printed piece.

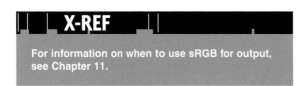

X-REF

For information on when to use sRGB for output, see Chapter 11.

Color Settings Adjustments in Adobe Bridge

Users of two or more of the CS2 applications may want to open Adobe Bridge and choose Edit ⇨ Creative Suite Color Settings. When the Suite Color Settings dialog box opens, you can select a Settings option that defines all your color workspaces. When you make a selection in the Suite Color Settings dialog box, colors across all your Adobe CS2 applications are synchronized, meaning you use the same workspaces when working in Photoshop, Illustrator, InDesign, and Adobe GoLive. Making your choice for color settings in Adobe Bridge eliminates the need to choose Edit ⇨ Color Settings in Photoshop and all the other CS2 programs.

Output color profiles are available to you in one of three forms:

> **Developer profiles.** The printing device manufacturer may provide color profiles created specifically for your equipment or equipment used by your photo lab. You might acquire the profiles through the developer's Web site or directly from your photo lab or service center.

> **Custom profiles you create.** If you have available to you equipment capable of creating color profiles directly from test prints on your equipment, you can use your calibration equipment to create your own custom profiles. This is particularly helpful when printing to desktop printers.

> **Custom profiles developed by a service.** You can purchase color profiles for your equipment from sources that you can find on the Internet. For a small service fee, the service creates a profile for you and sends you the profile in an e-mail attachment.

X-REF

For information on creating profiles and using services to purchase custom profiles, see Chapter 2.

What's important for you to know before you plunge into the other chapters in this book is that you need to address all the issues here related to viewing environment and color profiling. Attempting to print your photos on any output device is a shot in the dark if you don't use color profiles and understand the need for managing color throughout your workflow.

EMBEDDING COLOR PROFILES

When you edit a Photoshop image using a color workspace that you established in the Color Settings dialog box, you want to embed the working-space profile in your image. Embedding a profile has several advantages. First, if you exchange files with other users or work between a Mac and a Windows machine, your images can be converted to color workspaces on other computers. Second, when outputting a photo to a printing device, your workspace color can be converted to the device profile. Finally, if you eventually upgrade to another version of Photoshop where newer profiles are introduced, you can convert your workspace in legacy files to the newer profiles.

Photoshop offers you three options for embedding a color profile in a image:

> **Use the Save As dialog box.** First, identify your color workspace in the Color Settings dialog box, then choose File ⇨ Save As to open the Save As dialog box. Select the check box for Embed Color Profile: (name of color profile to embed), as shown in Figure 1-19. If you don't see the check box, you don't have a Format selected from the Format drop-down menu that supports saving your file with an embedded profile.

> **Use the Assign Profile dialog box.** With an image open in Photoshop, choose Edit ⇨ Assign Profile to open the Assign Profile dialog box. The second radio button reflects your current RGB workspace. In Figure 1-20, the workspace is Adobe RGB (1998). If you want to temporarily use another color profile while working on the file, click the drop-down menu adjacent to Profile shown in Figure

1-20. A list of all profiles appears in the menu. You might use the Profile option and select a profile different than your current workspace. For example, suppose you work in Adobe RGB (1998) and you want to edit a file for Web hosting. You can select sRGB from the Profile menu and click OK.

1-19

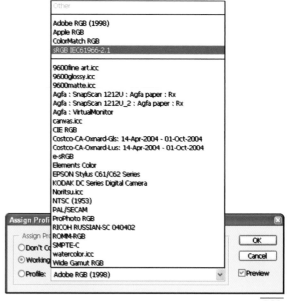

1-20

The assign profile dialog box should be used with caution. Its main purpose is to assign a profile to a color file that was saved without a profile. If you always use the Ask When Opening option in the Color Settings dialog box, you'll be aware of the lack of a color profile when you open your file. To change the color profile, use the convert option. Assigning a profile that is not correct is a sure way of ruining the color accuracy of your file.

> **Use the Convert to Profile dialog box.** Your third option is to choose Edit ⇨ Convert to Profile. The Convert to Profile dialog box shown in Figure 1-21 opens where you can see the current profile assigned in Photoshop in the Source Space area, and you can choose from the Profile a destination space from the drop-down menu. Whereas Assign Profile changes the current workspace and has nothing to do with embedding the profile in your document, this option actually changes the profile in the document. You use the dialog box to actually convert the pixels in your file to the destination profile. When you choose File ⇨ Save As, the destination profile appears by default in the Save As dialog box. When you click Save, the profile is embedded.

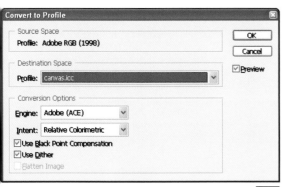

1-21

CONVERTING COLOR

When you identify a color workspace and open a file where another workspace is embedded in the file, a color mismatch occurs. You have a number of differ-ent options for handling color mismatches that are established in the Color Settings dialog box (refer to Figure 1-17). In the Color Management area of the Color Settings dialog box are three drop-down menus for handling RGB color, CMYK color, and Gray conversions. Below the drop-down menus are three check boxes used to determine how color mismatches are handled by Photoshop.

For RGB color, which is our primary concern in digital photography, the drop-down menu offers three options that include:

> **Off.** This turns off all color management. Don't select this item because you'll defeat the purpose for managing color.

> **Preserve Embedded Profiles.** Select this if you know you work on images that have different profiles assigned for different purposes and don't want to mess with them.

> **Convert to Working RGB.** More often than not, this is your best choice for all your Photoshop work. Any image you open is converted to your current color workspace.

Below the drop-down menus are check boxes for how to handle the options you select in the pull-down menus. These include:

> **Ask When Opening.** If you see an annoying dialog box appear each time you open an image in Photoshop, it's because this check box is selected. You're being prompted for making a choice for converting color. If the check box is not selected and you select Convert to Working RGB, Photoshop automatically converts your color without you knowing it. To stay informed and know what's happening with your color conversions, keep this box selected.

> **Ask When Pasting.** This check box performs the same action as Ask When Opening when you copy pixels from one Photoshop file and paste them into another file. Check this box to be prompted if you copy data from a file where a mismatch occurs.

> **Ask When Opening (Missing Profiles).** This option relates to any images where no profile is embedded in the document. You might have a collection of Photos taken with your digital camera where no profile is embedded. If this is the case, selecting this check box prompts you upon opening each file. In a production environment where you need to open many files and you know you want them all converted to your current workspace, do not select this check box.

If you select Convert to Working RGB from the pull-down menu in the Color Management area of the Color Settings dialog box and you select the Ask When Opening check box, you are prompted in the Embed Profile Mismatch dialog box each time you open a file. The dialog box, shown in Figure 1-22, provides you with three choices that include:

> **Use the embedded profile (instead of the working space).** This option preserves the current embedded color profile. You can use this option if you edit a number of images you want to output for Web use while your current workspace is set up with Adobe RGB (1998).

> **Convert document's colors to the working space.** By default, this is the selection you want to use. If this selection is made, you convert the embedded profile in a document you open to your current color workspace.

> **Discard the embedded profile (don't color manage).** This option again defeats the purpose for color management. As a matter of rule, don't select this option.

1-22

PHOTOSHOP'S COLOR AND TONAL CORRECTION TOOLS

If you travel back in time to Photoshop 1, 1.7, or later in Photoshop 3 when Layers were introduced, you find some essential correction tools that are still present in the latest version of Photoshop. Your correction tools for adjusting brightness and contrast and correcting color that were available in the first release of Photoshop were Levels, Curves, and Hue/Saturation. These three tools are your most important assets when it comes to correcting your digital camera images.

In later versions of Photoshop, we saw the introduction of some tools that were intended to make the job of color correction easier such as the Auto tools (Auto Levels, Auto Contrast, Auto Color), Match Color, Replace Color, Selective Color, Channel Mixer, Photo Filter, Shadow/Highlight, Exposure, and Variations.

Are these newer tools better for handling brightness and color adjustments with your digital photos? Quite simply, let us put it this way. If you gave us Photoshop 3, we could correct just about any photo using only Levels, Curves, and Hue/Saturation. (We could perform all these corrections in Photoshop 1, but having Layers makes the job much easier). These three tools are incomparable when it comes to balancing color and making brightness/contrast corrections in Photoshop. Upon occasion, you can get a little help from some of the newer tools, but nothing is better for any given adjustment in Photoshop than the three staple tools. Throughout this book, we show you various techniques using these three tools for just about all corrections made on images with a wide range of problems.

Some of the essential basics for color correction involve using:

> **Levels.** Your first step in correcting any image involves observing the Levels dialog box. Press Command/Ctrl + L to open Levels. As shown in Figure 1-23, you see a histogram containing 256 levels of gray and the frequency for each gray

level represented by the peaks in the graph. You can adjust the tone levels by moving the Input sliders for the composite RGB channel, or you can select a channel from the Channel drop-down menu where adjustments are made to individual channels.

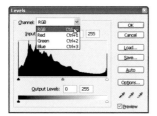

1-23

The spikes at either end of the histogram show data clipping. In the histogram in Figure 1-23 some of the highlight and shadow data is clipped, meaning there is data loss in these areas of the photo, perhaps because the camera's sensor was unable to capture the full dynamic range of the image.

On the left, you find the black point, on the right is the white point, and the middle slider is the midtone adjustment. You also find three Eyedropper tools that can be used to sample an area in a photo (by selecting an Eyedropper and clicking in the background photo) to set the black point, midtones, and white point.

PRO TIP

For information on using the sliders and buttons in the Levels dialog box, see Chapter 4.

> **Curves.** Your single most important correction tool in Photoshop is the Curves dialog box. You can adjust brightness and contrast as well as perform color correction all within the Curves dialog box. Many of the adjustments you make in Curves can also be handled in Levels, but the Curves

dialog box provides you an easier, more intuitive method for corrections once you become familiar with how to use Curves.

As is the case with the Levels dialog box, you also find a Channel drop-down menu where adjustments can be made to the composite RGB channel or the individual channels as shown in Figure 1-24. You also find a tone curve representing all the 256 levels of gray and you make adjustments by clicking on the diagonal line to plot points and move them along the tone curve.

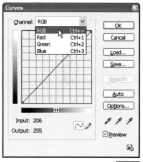

1-24

We talk about using the Curves dialog box throughout this book. The first thing you'll want to do is set up the Curves dialog box to make it easy to follow our mention of using Curves. You press Command/Ctrl + M to open the Curves dialog box and press the Option/Alt key and click on the grid. The grid changes from a default view of four horizontal and vertical gridlines to ten horizontal and vertical gridlines. Keep the Curves dialog box set to ten gridlines for easier manipulation of the tone curve.

Another adjustment you want to make in Curves is to change the direction of the curve. By default the curve begins with the white point and extends to the top right corner to the black point. This direction is opposite the Levels dialog box where the tone curve runs from black to white. To change the direction so black appears in the lower left corner and white appears in the top right corner, click one of the arrows on the gradient bar below the grid. The direction is changed and matches the same direction as the Levels dialog box.

You'll note that the Curves dialog box also includes three Eyedropper tools. These tools are used the same as when working in Levels to set white point, midtone, and black point.

> **Hue/Saturation.** The Hue/Saturation dialog box opens when you press Command/Ctrl + U. From the Edit menu in the Hue/Saturation dialog box, you can target colors for adjusting the Hue, Saturation, and Lightness by moving the respective sliders as shown in Figure 1-25. You also find three eyedropper tools used for sampling areas in the photo where colors can be identified for making adjustments within a range of a given color.

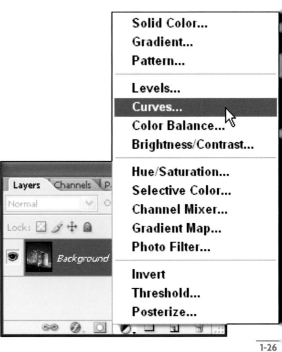

1-26

1-25

> **Adjustment layers.** Quite often a single Levels, Curves, or Hue/Saturation adjustment may not be enough to color balance or correct brightness in images. Once you make an adjustment, you may want to return to a dialog box and make some changes to the settings applied in the dialog box. Handling these options is best performed using an Adjustment layer. You can create many adjustment layers and you can return to any adjustment layer to change the settings.

Adjustment layers are created by clicking the Create new fill or adjustment layer icon in the Layers palette and selecting the adjustment you want to make from the drop-down menu as shown in Figure 1-26.

You can also apply a blend mode to an adjustment layer. You can make a change from the Normal blend mode to any one of the other blend mode options after creating an adjustment layer or you can choose to select the blend mode you want at the time an adjustment layer is created.

Many times throughout this book we use the Luminosity blend mode to apply corrections to the brightness values in an image. Luminosity doesn't disturb the color balance when using any of the correction tools when you make tonal adjustments. To change the blend mode when you create an adjustment layer, press the Option/Alt key when you select an adjustment layer menu item from the Create fill or adjustment layer drop-down menu. After making a menu selection, the New Layer dialog box opens as shown in Figure 1-27.

In Figure 1-27 we pressed the Alt key down and selected Curves from the Create a new fill or adjustment layer drop down menu to open the New Layer dialog box. From the Mode drop-down menu we can select a blend mode before the Curves dialog box opens. As we make adjustments, the image preview is applied to the background image using the blend mode we choose in the New Layer dialog box.

> **Layer masks.** You may often find images needing color balancing and/or tonal corrections applied independently to different areas of an image. Backgrounds and foregrounds, for example, may require different adjustments. When you make a selection in an image, then create an adjustment layer, you additionally create a layer mask. The layer mask enables you to make adjustments to only the selected area without affecting the unselected portion of your image.

To create a layer mask, first create a selection. While the selection is active, create an adjustment layer. In Figure 1-28 we created a selection and chose Hue/Saturation from the Create new fill or adjustment layer drop-down menu. The Hue/Saturation dialog box opened. In the Layers palette, the white area in the layer mask is the only area that will be affected by our edits in the Hue/Saturation dialog box.

Upon occasion we use a few other tools in Photoshop to perform color and tonal corrections; however, many of the other tools are used in combination with the three basic correction tools you'll find used throughout this book. Once you learn how to effectively use Levels, Curves, and Hue/Saturation dialog boxes and you understand all the blend modes and masks used in adjustment layers, you can use the full potential in Photoshop to correct any image.

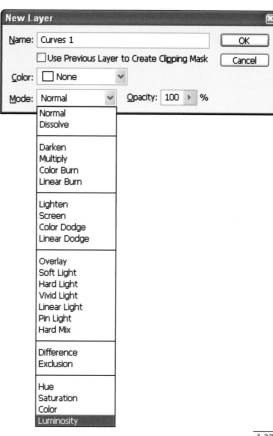

1-27

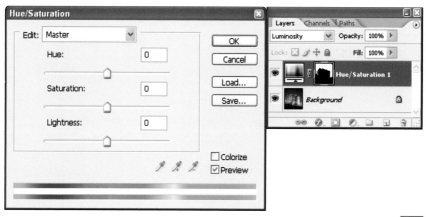

1-28

25

Q & A

Why don't I get 16-bit images with my digital camera?

You may be saving pictures in JPEG format, and Photoshop doesn't support 16-bit in JPEG format. Try changing the capture mode to saving Camera Raw format. Another reason might be that your camera doesn't support Camera Raw and capturing 16-bit images. Consult your camera's manual to see what formats and bit depths are supported.

If all you have to work with are 8-bit JPEG images, either because your camera doesn't support shooting Raw or because you have files where only JPEG is used in a photo shoot, you can convert 8-bit images to 16-bit as explained in Chapter 4.

Why does a dialog box open when I try to use Merge to HDR informing me that my images don't have enough dynamic range?

There is not enough total dynamic range (exposure difference) in the bracketed image files being used to create a 32-bit file. Try using wider camera exposure variations for the files to be merged to HDR.

If you shoot images with a one-stop difference, try changing your EV (Exposure Values) to more extreme differences such as two or three stops. At first you'll see radical over/underexposures; but when you use the Merge to HDR command, Photoshop is likely to create the merged file.

Why don't I embed my monitor color profile after I calibrate my monitor?

Your monitor profile is used for correcting views on your monitor and doesn't have anything to do with the file you are editing and saving from Photoshop. The color working space affects your image and should be embedded in your photos so the color can be converted to other monitor workspaces and output profiles.

If I print files to my desktop color printer, do I need to set up my CMYK color workspace and convert to CMYK color?

Everything depends on the printing equipment you use. In most cases, desktop color printers are designed to print RGB files. Although these printers have CMYK inks and variations thereof, many take advantage of the larger RGB color gamut.

When printing files to your printer or using service centers, read the printer manual documentation or ask the technicians printing your photos what color mode is preferred for the device that ultimately prints your photos.

Chapter 2

SETTING UP YOUR COLOR ENVIRONMENT

"Pictures, regardless of how they are created and re-created, are intended to be looked at. This brings to the forefront not the technology of imaging, which, of course, is important, but rather what we might call the eyenology (seeing)." — Henri Cartier-Bresson

Correcting color in digital images requires you to optimize your working conditions for the best possible viewing environment as well as make sure all your equipment is calibrated properly. Getting color precise with absolutely no discernible differences is not completely possible when viewing color images on monitors and printing photos on a wide range of output devices. Therefore, what we strive for is to control the variables as much as possible to bring our color viewing and printing together as close as we can. If you skip one variable in the process, you move just a little farther away from an ideal color matching system.

In this chapter you learn the important aspects related to color viewing and equipment calibration. Before you plow into Photoshop's tools for adjusting color and brightness, be certain you take some time to understand what this chapter explains in terms of optimizing your color viewing environment.

CONTROLLING LIGHTING

Accurate and consistent color editing requires full-spectrum lighting, with a color temperature reasonably matched to the monitor color temperature setting, so that both the viewing area and monitor view are consistent with one another. Most quality full-spectrum lighting used today is fluorescent-type lighting fixtures that utilize special lamps with a sophisticated phosphor mix that yields a full white-light spectrum.

USING BALANCED LIGHTING

The color quality of the light is rated as the *CRI* (color rendering index) in percentage values. A CRI of 100 percent is a perfect match to natural daylight;

although, the best lamps available are rated around CRI 98 percent — a very close match to natural daylight. A standard Cool White fluorescent lamp has extremely poor color quality and is rated at about CRI 60 percent.

Full-spectrum lights fit in standard fluorescent fixtures and are also available in the new Spiralux form that fits in a standard lightbulb fixture.

Ideally, the *Kelvin* rating (color of the lamp) should match closely to your monitor color temperature setting. A 5000K lamp (daylight balance) should ideally be used with a 5000K monitor setting. We find that the lamps seem a bit cooler (bluer) in color than the same monitor setting, at least on a CRT monitor, so we use 5000K lamps with a 5500K monitor setting. Your mileage may vary. Prices for these lamps are usually about three times or more in price than an inexpensive Cool White lamp. The good news is they last for years, and some are very reasonably priced.

Don's studio uses standard 96-inch fluorescent fixtures that are fitted with Sylvania Sun Stick lamps that are rated at 5000K and a CRI of 92. Cost is about $8 per tube. Sun Stick lamps can be found at your local home improvement store. The homemade viewing booth shown in Figure 2-1 uses a pair of 48-inch Triten 50 full-spectrum tubes. Color temperature is 5000K, with an awesome CRI of 98 percent. Cost per tube was $6. To purchase the Triten 50 full-spectrum tubes visit www.1000bulbs.com. This vendor also stocks Spriralux full-spectrum lamps. Just look for "Full Spectrum" links on the vendor Web site.

Keeping the lighting consistent is very important, also. The lighting in a room with large windows varies a great deal during the day. For viewing purposes, a windowed room should have good curtains or shades to keep ambient light levels consistent at all times. Visual monitor calibration is based on the viewing environment. In a windowed room, monitor calibration is like a broken clock — it's always correct once a day!

2-1

BUILDING A VIEWING BOOTH

All the nice balanced lights you purchase won't mean much if you put your monitor against a bright yellow and orange wall. What you need is an area encased in a neutral gray environment. For a makeshift viewing booth, follow these steps:

1. Purchase an 18 percent gray card. You can find 18 percent gray cards at photo suppliers.

2. Purchase a paint that matches the color of the gray card. Take your 18 percent gray card to your local paint store and ask for a flat paint that matches the color of your gray card when the paint dries. Most hardware and commercial paint stores will be happy to provide exactly what you need.

3. Construct your booth. Using particleboard or unfinished plywood, construct the booth encased on the sides, above, and the desktop.

4. Prime and paint the booth.

5. Set up your monitor. If using a CRT monitor, you can cut a hole in the back of the booth (see Figure 2-2) and push the monitor back to provide more surface area for your keyboard.

2-2

UNDERSTANDING MONITORS

Computer monitors come in two flavors —CRT and LCD. As mentioned in Chapter 1, LCD monitors, although now more prolific and newer in the marketplace, just don't match the color clarity you find in CRT monitors.

In addition to improved color clarity, CRT monitors also cost much less than LCDs. A Dell Trinitron 21-inch display as of this writing sells for $179 at online reseller outlets — try: www.tigerdirect.com. There is a downside to CRTs, however. In addition to their large footprints, overall bulkiness, increased power consumption, and the excess heat they produce, they are becoming increasingly scarce. Many CRT manufacturers have discontinued entire lines of CRTs in favor of the newer LCD technology.

If you find a good value on a CRT monitor, be careful and find out when the monitor was made. If you purchase an older used monitor, it may have exceeded its useful life. You can expect to get about three to five good years out of a CRT before it starts loosing definition and color clarity. There is no magic formula, however, as monitors vary greatly in fidelity and life expectancy.

If you have an LCD monitor now, keep your eye on product reviews and current literature. The LCD technology is new and continually advancing. CRTs used on computers have been around for more than 20 years with 20 years of continued research and development and improvement. As time goes on, we expect LCD monitors to advance and ultimately render even better color clarity than the best CRTs of years past.

CALIBRATING YOUR MONITOR

Your monitor needs to be calibrated to adjust the gamma and brightness, correct any color tints or colorcasts, and generally get your monitor to display as accurately as possible colors contained in any given image. You have a few choices for what tool you can use to adjust your monitor brightness ranging from expensive calibration equipment of $3000 or more, to a low-cost hardware device costing less than $300, or skip the hardware completely and use tools provided by Adobe or your OS developer to set up your monitor depending on which platform you use.

HARDWARE CALIBRATION DEVICES

We'll skip the high-end costly devices and suggest that at the very least one valuable purchase you make for creating a monitor profile is a hardware profiling system. Our choice for a low-end device with superb capabilities is the GretagMacbeth Eye-One Display 2 (www.gretagmacbeth.com) costing $249 as of this writing.

Eye-One Display 2 is an easy-to-use profiling tool that works with CRT displays, LCDs, and laptop computers. You attach the suction cup to your monitor (see Figure 2-3), click a few buttons in the software application accompanying the hardware, and Eye-One Display 2 eventually prompts you to save a monitor profile. The profile you create is automatically used by your operating system when you start up your computer. When the profile kicks in, your monitor is balanced using the settings determined when the calibration was performed by the device.

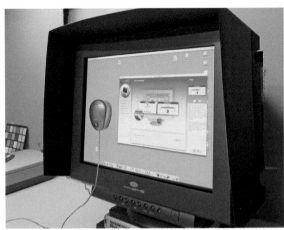

2-3

CALIBRATING MACINTOSH DISPLAYS

If you haven't purchased a calibration tool, you can use the Macintosh Display Calibrator Assistant that comes free with your OS X installation. Although we highly recommend using a tool like Eye-One Display 2, this option is available to you until you gather the funds to make a purchase for a calibration device.

NOTE

If you calibrate your monitor using a hardware device, don't follow guidelines here for calibrating your monitor.

For a down-and-dirty calibration effort on the Macintosh using the Macintosh Display Calibrator Assistant, follow these steps:

1. Open your System Preferences by clicking System Preferences in the Dock.

2. Click Displays in the System Preferences dialog box.

3. Click Color in the display pane.

4. Click Calibrate and the first of several panes opens, as shown in Figure 2-4. Each pane provides a description for making adjustments as you progress through the Display Calibrator Assistant. When you finish making adjustments in a pane, click Continue to advance to the next pane. Descriptions in the panes are intuitive and easy to follow.

5. When you arrive at the Name pane, a text box appears where you type a name for your profile. Type a descriptive name and click Continue to advance to the last pane.

6. The Conclusion pane provides you a description of the profile attributes (see Figure 2-5). Review the summary and then click Done to complete the creation of your new profile.

2-4

2-5

CALIBRATING WINDOWS DISPLAYS

For Windows users, Adobe provides a software utility to calibrate your monitor. The Adobe Gamma application has been around for some time and discontinued on the Mac when OS X was introduced. However, on Windows it remains the utility to use when you don't have a hardware calibrator. Like the Macintosh Display Calibrator Assistant, Adobe Gamma enables you to determine attributes for monitor adjustments that are eventually saved as a monitor profile.

To use the Adobe Gamma device, follow these steps:

1. Open your Control Panels by clicking the Start menu and choosing Settings ⇨ Control Panel.

2. Double-click Adobe Gamma in the Control Panels folder to open the Control Panel. The Adobe Gamma dialog box appears.

3. Click Wizard to use the Adobe Gamma Wizard.

4. Type a name for your profile and click Next. The first pane in the Wizard asks you to name your profile. Type a name in the text box for the profile name (see Figure 2-6).

5. Adjust the brightness and contrast controls on your monitor. Follow the description in the Wizard to make your monitor adjustments.

6. Select the Phosphors for your monitor. Click Next in the Wizard and you arrive at a pane where you can select options for monitor phosphors from a drop-down menu. By default, Adobe Gamma supplies a choice. If you know the phosphors for your monitor to be different than what is selected from the menu, open the menu and select another item. Generally, accepting the default works with most monitors.

7. Adjust the gamma. Click Next and you arrive at the gamma settings (see Figure 2-7). By default, the View Single Gamma Only check box is selected. Deselect the option and the pane displays individual gamma adjustments that can be made for Red, Green, and Blue. To adjust the gamma for each of the three colors, squint your eyes slightly and move the slider below each setting. Try to blend as close as possible the outside square with the inside square by moving the slider back and forth.

After making the slider adjustments, select a gamma choice from the Gamma drop-down menu. For Windows machines, select 2.2 for the gamma.

8. Select the Hardware White Point. Click Next in the Wizard, and you arrive at a pane where hardware white point is selected. This setting defines the general colorcast on your monitor. You can choose between 5000 degrees Kelvin resulting in a slight red cast to 9300 degrees Kelvin that produces a cooler colorcast. Your target should be 6500 degrees, which generally comes close to natural daylight.

9. Create the profile. Click Next and you arrive at an option to change the white point for your working conditions that is different than your hardware white point. Click Next and leave the white point set to Same as Hardware. Click Finish in the last pane, and the profile is created.

2-6

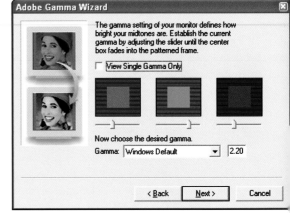

2-7

PROFILING FOR PRINTING EQUIPMENT

In a best-case scenario you would use a low-end calibration device costing over $1,000 and a high-end device costing more than $3,000 to create printer profiles for all your output devices. What these devices do for you is create custom profiles from test prints you output to your target printer. A test page containing an array of colors is measured by a spectrometer you drag across rows and columns of printed color swatches. After completing the color assessment, a profile for that specific printer is created.

GretagMacbeth (www.gretagmacbeth.com) offers the Eye-One Photo system, a low-cost solution for a proofing system that includes calibration equipment and software to calibrate your monitors, RGB and CMYK output devices, digital cameras, scanners, and digital projectors for screen displays. This system is available for a list price of $1,595 as of this writing. If you want to knock out digital cameras from the equipment, you can purchase the Eye-One Proof system for a suggested list price of $1,395.

If you decide to purchase a calibration system for your output device, be careful to purchase the right system for the kind of output you produce. Some devices are designed to create profiles for CMYK-only printers. That's fine for some inkjets and prepress proofing systems; however, devices such as mini-photo labs are RGB output devices and won't benefit from a CMYK profiling system.

ACQUIRING DEVICE PROFILES

If you send your photos to commercial photo labs and print vendors, you can often find color profiles available on vendor Web sites specifically created for the output equipment and papers used. For your own personal desktop printers, you can sometimes find output profiles available on developer Web sites or on the CD that shipped with your printer.

When you download a profile off the Web or copy a profile from a CD, the color profile needs to be installed in the proper directory to make it useable by Photoshop. If the profile is copied without an installer application, you need to manually copy the profile to the correct folder.

INSTALLING PROFILES ON THE MAC

On the Mac, open the Library folder on your installer hard drive — don't open the user Library folder. Look for the Application Support folder and open it. Inside that folder is an Adobe folder. Open the Adobe folder, then open Color\Profiles\Recommended. The complete directory path is `Macintosh HD\Library\Application Support\Adobe\Color\Profiles\Recommended`. If you use a command in Photoshop, such as Convert to Profile, and you are prompted to select a profile, the items in the Recommended folder appear in a subsection in the menu where profiles are selected. In Figure 2-8, we choose Edit ⇨ Convert to Profile and open the Profile drop-down menu. You can see all the profiles we have

Using Developer Profiles

Commercial print vendors often create color profiles for their equipment and ship the profiles on a CD accompanying the output device. These profiles are quite generic in nature and don't account for differences between computer platforms, inks, and papers used with the printer. More often than not, the profiles you receive from a printer manufacturer won't get you close to a good color match from your monitor to your printer. The ideal would be to have a custom color profile developed for each device, each time the consumables change, and for each paper you use.

currently stored in our Recommended folder between the two horizontal lines appearing above 9600fine art.icc and below watercolor.icc.

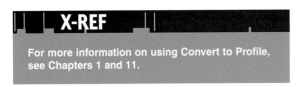

For more information on using Convert to Profile, see Chapters 1 and 11.

2-8

INSTALLING PROFILES ON WINDOWS

On Windows XP, open the Windows folder on your hard drive. The directory path for color profiles in Windows is `C:\Windows\system32\spool\drivers\color`. Copy your profiles to this directory, and the output profiles are logically grouped together when you open a drop-down menu to select a profile (see Figure 2-9).

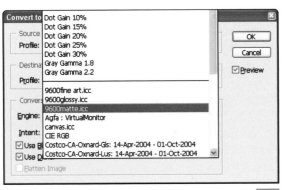

2-9

PURCHASING CUSTOM PROFILES

If you have a desktop color printer or large-format printer and you want to have a profile created, you can use a custom service that creates the profile for you. Rather than spend a lot of money on a calibration device you may use for only a few printers, you can commission a provider such as Dry Creek Photo (www.drycreekphoto.com) to create a custom ICC Profile for you for as little as $50 per paper stock. You can also get a year's worth of support and free upgrades for $99.

At Dry Creek Photo, log on to the Custom ICC Profile page at www.drycreekphoto.com/custom/customprofiles.htm. Download a profiling package by clicking on a link respective to your platform (both Mac and Windows are supported). After downloading the kit that contains a profiling target image in TIFF format, print the target image on your printer using the paper material you want calibrated.

The target print is submitted to Dry Creek Photo's highly sophisticated calibration equipment, which creates your profile. The profile is then sent to you by the Dry Creek technicians. Load the profile in the proper folder on your hard drive.

Color Profiling in Photoshop Elements

Just in case you haven't evolved to Photoshop and you are using a copy of Photoshop Elements that came with your digital camera, the folks at Dry Creek Photo provide a useful utility that can be used for profile embedding for Elements users. The tool is only available for Windows users and it's a free download from the Dry Creek Web site.

To download the ICC Profile Converter, log on to www.drycreekphoto.com/tools/profile_converter/, where you'll find a link to download the small converter application. Photoshop Elements supports only two profiles: sRGB and Adobe RGB (1998). If you want to embed a printer profile in your images, you need to use a tool like the Dry Creek Photo ICC Profile Converter to convert your current workspace to the device profile.

The tool is easy to use. Save your file in TIFF format (the ICC Profile Converter only supports TIFF). Open the ICC Profile Converter and click on the ellipsis for Source Image and Source profile to identify the source profiles, and click on the ellipsis for Destination Image and Destination Color Profile to identify the profiles you want to convert to. If you want the profile embedded in the resultant document, select the Embed profile in image check box. Click Convert to convert the profiles from source to destination.

You can open the converted image in Photoshop Elements and save the file as a JPEG if you need to supply JPEG files to your print vendor. Inasmuch as Elements won't let you convert a profile or select a profile for embedding, it preserves any embedded profile found in an image you open in the program.

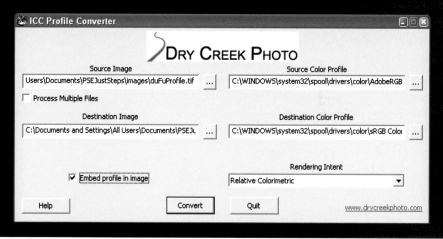

Using Color Output Profiles

Once you acquire or create an output color profile, you need to use that profile when printing to your desktop printer or somehow manage to get the color profile used with a commercial printer. You have two options for converting your RGB workspace color to an output profile:

> Embed a color profile in your images.

> Assume a profile when printing.

Embedding a color profile in an image adds some code to the image and the profile essentially becomes part of the image. Assuming a profile is like linking to a file. The color in the image is not actually converted. The color conversion when using assumed profiles occurs at the time the file is printed.

Each option has advantages and disadvantages. If you embed a color profile, you can tweak the color during edit mode in the color space in which your file is ultimately printed. Embedded profiles help you automate your workflow without needing to make decisions at the time of output. If assuming a profile, you have more manual methods to employ because you need to select the profile manually when you print your images. Also, if for some reason you need to use different profiles for several images, you can embed different profiles in different images and print the files together on the same output; for example, using a layout program where several images are imported on the same page. If assuming profiles, you are restricted to using only one RGB and one CMYK profile for each print.

Embedding color profiles in RGB images requires little memory added to your image. CMYK files, on the other hand, grow significantly when color profiles are embedded in them.

PRO TIP

As a standard rule of thumb, choose to embed color output profiles in your RGB images and use assumed profiles when printing CMYK images.

Converting color to an output profile

Assuming all the ingredients in your color management system are up to date, the final step before printing a file is to convert your color workspace to the output workspace. Even though you do most of your color correction and editing in your RGB color workspace, you generally need to do some tweaking of color in the final output color space. The first step is to convert the color and then do your final edits. When you save the RGB files, you embed the color space for the output device. Here's how:

1. Open a file in your default RGB color workspace. Choose Edit ⇨ Convert to Profile. The Convert to Profile dialog box, shown in Figure 2-10, appears.

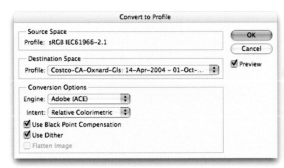

2-10

2. Select a destination profile. From the Profile pull-down menu, select the output color profile you want to embed in your RGB image.

3. Select an Engine. The color engine handles the color conversion, and you have some options from which to choose in the Engine pull-down menu. Depending on what platform you work, your options for the color engine are different:

> **Adobe (ACE).** The Adobe Color Engine was developed by Adobe to work with the Adobe applications — particularly the Adobe Creative Suite programs. Whereas other programs rely on color engines developed by the OS

developers, Adobe created this engine to help develop consistent color management when using the Adobe programs. If you are a CS2 user or you prepare images for others who use the Creative Suite, use this engine as your default. Even if you work exclusively in Photoshop, use the Adobe (ACE) option.

> **Apple Color Sync and Apple CMM (Mac only).** These are the other two options in the Engine pull-down menu on the Macintosh. Application software developers rely on color engines developed by the OS developers. Developers rely on color management models when writing code for APIs (Application Program Interfaces). On Macs, the default engine is Apple Color Sync. You have a selection in the Convert to Profile dialog box for using this model or the Apple CMM engine when converting color. As a matter of practice, when using any Adobe program, rely on the tried and true Adobe (ACE) option.

> **Microsoft ICM.** The Microsoft ICM option (see Figure 2-11) is the Windows counterpart to Apple's ColorSync. You can associate devices with profiles in Windows using the Advanced Display settings and the Color management tab. As a rule, use the Adobe (ACE) engine on Windows as a default.

2-11

4. Select an Intent. When you convert color, some information will be lost in the conversion. What you want to do is to loose as little as possible when converting color — that's the purpose behind intent. Choose one of the Intents listed below depending on the content of your image. You have four options from which to choose that include:

> **Relative Colorimetric.** This option maps white in the source profile to white in the destination profile so the white of the paper is actually the target. The remapping then converts all colors within the printable gamut to the destination profile. The out-of-gamut colors are then clipped. As a result, you loose a little in terms of gradual transitions of color.

> **Perceptual.** This intent converts color in the source image with a visually pleasing rendering in the destination image. The end result is much less noticeable transitions of color.

> **Absolute Colorimetric.** This also maps white in the source profile to white in the destination profile, but the source white may introduce a color to match the target as close as possible. This intent is used primarily when proofing color for press where the objective is to match output on one device to another.

> **Saturation.** As the name implies, the color remapping is primarily concerned with matching saturated colors and it is least concerned with accurate color mapping. This intent might be used in charts and diagrams where solid colors are used. In Figure 2-12, you can see the same image converted using the four different intents.

You won't be able to see any obvious differences using one intent over another when an original image is completely within the gamut of the chosen output profile. The differences are often very subtle.

Relative   Absolute

Perceptual   Saturation

2-12

The image in Figure 2-12 was originally designed for a Duratrans backlit display. The gamut is beyond the ability of CMYK to accurately reproduce the colors, and we can't show you the monitor view. But trust us, the image is a screamer. It shows the differences in color conversion modes and the differences in mapping to the limits of the page you are viewing right now.

5. Use Black Point Compensation. This check box should be selected as a default and left alone. Whites can be remapped to different values according to the intent you use to create smoother transitions. However, any remapping of

black can turn out to be murky grays. To ensure rich blacks appear in the converted profile, the Black Compensation check box is used.

6. Use Dither. Dithering helps smooth out color transitions. This is another default you want left as is; keep the Dither check box selected.

7. Flatten Image. The check box is grayed out unless you are working on a layer or a file containing layers. Selecting this check box flattens the image. If preparing files for layout in Adobe InDesign, you can keep your images as layered files. For importing into other programs, be certain to flatten the layers.

ASSUMING A PROFILE

If a document is *untagged,* meaning that the file does not have an embedded profile and is not color managed, you can assume a profile when opening the document. Because you want to embed profiles for all RGB images, the only time you want to work with assumed profiles is when working with CMYK files.

CMYK files are used for one of two purposes by digital photographers. You may prepare images for graphic artists or lay out your own designs that are intended to be commercially printed on offset or direct-to-press equipment. The other reason you work with CMYK files is when printing to composite color printers that render better output from CMYK files than with RGB files.

If you work with inkjet equipment, film recorders, and digital photo labs, you are almost always involved in an RGB world. If this is the case, you don't need to worry about RGB-to-CMYK conversions, and you don't need to be concerned about CMYK profiling.

To assume a profile when working with CMYK images, you need to make an adjustment in your color settings and make some decisions when you open files. Follow these steps:

1. Open the Color Settings dialog box by choosing Edit ➪ Color Settings.

2. Select the Ask When Opening check box in the Missing Profiles area of the Color Settings dialog box (see Figure 2-13). Click OK and all untagged files will open the Missing Profile dialog box where you can assume a profile.

3. Open an untagged CMYK image. If you want to assume a CMYK profile when the file opens, open a CMYK image. Opening an RGB image provides you options for assuming RGB-only profiles. When you open a CMYK image the Missing Profiles dialog box appears.

4. Assume a profile. The two options for Assigning a profile appear in the Missing Profile dialog box

(see Figure 2-14). The Assign working CMYK radio button defaults to the profile set up in your color settings. If you want to assume this profile, select the radio button and click OK. The Assign profile radio button and drop-down menu offer you options for assuming a profile installed on your computer. Select a menu choice and the third radio button in the Missing Profiles dialog box is selected. Click OK and the untagged file opens assuming the profile you choose in the Missing Profiles dialog box.

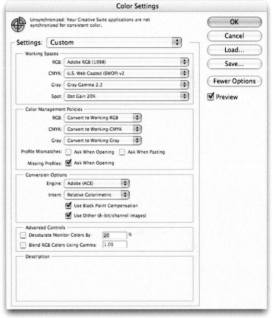

2-13

2-14

The danger you face when using untagged files and within a workgroup is that everyone must be aware of the profile handling and which profile is used when you ultimately print your file. If you work with untagged documents throughout your workflow, the only time the profile is used other than soft-proofing is when printed.

SOFT-PROOFING WITH YOUR OUTPUT PROFILES

After you create profiles and convert color or assume a profile, you want to preview the results on your monitor. Assuming everything is calibrated in your workflow, *soft-proofing,* or previewing on your monitor, should give you a view with a close approximation for how colors will appear on the final print.

OUT-OF-GAMUT COLORS

Out-of-gamut colors are displayed on your monitor from within Photoshop and also within the Camera Raw dialog box. In Photoshop, a gray color appears in all areas outside a printable CMYK gamut. Viewing out-of-gamut colors in Photoshop is used to show you those RGB colors that can't fit within the CMYK color space. If you intend to print to CMYK output devices, look at viewing out-of-gamut colors before you convert to CMYK.

X-REF

For information on out-of-gamut colors in the Camera Raw dialog box, see Chapter 3.

1. Open an RGB image in Photoshop and convert color to your output profile. Choose Edit ➪ Convert to Profile, and select the output profile you want to use for your target printer. You need to convert colors to select your output profile. Using an assumed profile offers you choices for your RGB workspace but not for your destination

source. After converting colors, you can revert to the last-saved version of your file by choosing File ➪ Revert, then convert to a new profile. You might perform these steps if you have some choices for different printers and when the different printers support different color gamuts.

2. Choose View ➪ Gamut Warning. By default, out-of-gamut colors appear with a neutral gray where all the colors are outside the printable color gamut, as shown in Figure 2-15. The color you use to represent out-of-gamut colors is determined in the Transparency & Gamut preferences. If you want to change the gamut warning color, press Command/Ctrl+K and select Transparency & Gamut from the pull-down menu at the top of the Preferences dialog box. In the Gamut Warning area of the Transparency & Gamut preferences, click the gray color swatch to open the Color Picker where you can select a new color for the out-of-gamut display.

The out-of-gamut display is an indicator for some potential editing you may need to perform on your file. Deeply saturated colors may not reproduce on your output devices and may require you to desaturate images or readjust the color. If editing is required, keep the file in the converted color mode and perform your final edits using the defined target profile. In Figure 2-16, you can see the final CMYK image reproduced for the press used to print this book.

CMYK PROOFING

When working on files that need to be converted to CMYK for printing, the standard rule of thumb adopted by many artists is to work in RGB mode and perform the RGB-to-CMYK conversion just before printing. This is not a matter of practice used by all artists. Some people feel that they need to do the RGB-to-CMYK conversion and perform final edits in the CMYK document.

2-15

2-16

2-17

Editing a CMYK image has some disadvantages. File sizes for CMYK images are larger than RGB files, which slows your editing progress. Moreover, your monitor and all your input sources are RGB. At some point, the CMYK files need to be translated to RGB values.

To soft-proof for CMYK without converting the color, you can set your preview in Photoshop to display CMYK color. Choose View ➪ Proof Setup ➪ Working CMYK. Use this choice when your color settings are set to the CMYK output source established in the Working Spaces CMYK drop-down menu.

If you want to use a profile for a device when your color settings are not adjusted for that device, choose View ➪ Proof Setup ➪ Custom. The Custom Proof Condition dialog box appears as shown in Figure 2-17. Select from the Device to Simulate drop-down menu, and you can select from your installed CMYK printer profiles.

PROOFING USING PROFILES

RGB files are easy to proof on-screen without having to be concerned about changing modes for editing purposes. You can convert color or assume a color profile, and if you work in a color-managed workflow, the target printer profile shows you the color in close approximation to what you can expect from your printer. During editing stages in Photoshop, be certain to view your RGB images in the destination work-space by converting the color or assuming a color profile as described earlier. During editing stages in Photoshop, be certain to view your RGB images in the destination workspace using View ➪ Proof Setup, but stay in your RGB working space until all edits are completed.

X-REF

There's much more to soft-proofing images than what we cover here. For a more detailed description of soft-proofing files on your monitor before they are printed, see Chapter 11.

▶ **I have an LCD monitor now. Should I change to a CRT monitor?**

You can get good results using a quality LCD monitor. Working with color correction is an exercise in optimizing all your lighting and viewing conditions. One item left out of the loop won't greatly impact your ability to view color and edit images for color correction. However, a combination of things that you eliminate such as lighting in your workplace, calibrating your monitor, using CRT versus LCD, creating custom color profiles, and so on, collectively can greatly impact your ability to properly handle color correction. What you should strive for is controlling all the variables possible to ensure you create an optimized viewing and printing environment.

You don't have to dump your LCD immediately. Search for bargains on the Web or around town for a second monitor that you can pick up inexpensively. You can add a second monitor to your workplace when you find something that fits your budget.

I use a good-quality desktop printer to print final prints for clients. Should I buy a calibration system to create my printer profiles?

If you have several printers and several computers, it is wise to purchase a calibration system for your equipment. However, for individuals or small studios, you can find less expensive solutions for creating printer profiles.

If you use a vendor for printing oversized prints, photo prints from a digital photo lab, or other printing services, you can ask your vendor if they can create a profile for you. If you do enough business with a vendor, they should be pleased to comply with your request. All you need to do is to print a file it uses with its calibration system and take it back to the vendor. The vendor can create a profile that you can use with your equipment.

Additionally, you may find a vendor who can visit your workplace and calibrate your monitor. Again, if you run a lot of jobs with one vendor, they will want to keep your business and may be willing to comply with your requests.

If you don't have a vendor who can create a custom profile for you, use the Dry Creek Photo service (www.drycreekphoto.com). You can order a custom profile for $50 that will save you much time in trying to fudge a calibration without using any calibrating equipment.

I use a custom photo lab for my output but my vendor doesn't have a color profile for the equipment. How can I get a profile?

Most vendors are always wanting to know how to improve their service. A good number of vendors unknowingly aren't aware of how to perform custom profiling and may be printing output randomly like a shot in the dark. What they need is a little help in becoming aware of cost-effective solutions. Because equipment costs run high at their shops, they may not be interested in investing in professional calibration equipment.

Turn your vendor on to the Dry Creek Photo Web site. Your vendor may not know it exists. You can show your vendor how to search the site for existing profiles matching their equipment. If none exists, a $50 investment is surely within reach. You can encourage your vendor to begin using profiles and they should soon see results and appreciate your guidance.

I use a service to print my files. My photos are converted to CMYK because my vendor uses CMYK inks. My images typically lose a lot of color after converting to CMYK. How can I get prints matching the color I see in my RGB files?

Large-format color printers use CMYK inks, but the inks they use typically have several variations of the CMYK colors and may support six, seven, eight, or more inks to print a larger printable color gamut. These devices, although using CMYK inks, prefer RGB files. Don't convert your RGB images to CMYK before submitting them to your vendor. Almost all commercial large-format printing devices output RGB color. Be certain to check with your vendor for the proper color mode before submitting files, and you should be provided with guidelines to produce the best possible color.

Chapter 3

CAMERA RAW COLOR CORRECTION

"I longed to arrest all beauty that came before me, and at length the longing has been satisfied." — *Julia Margaret Cameron*

Camera Raw is a file format that records the raw sensor data of the camera. Essentially all the data the sensor sees is captured and saved in a special format designed to post process your images. When you open a Camera Raw file in Photoshop, you decide what settings you want to use to process the file.

Camera Raw is not a universal format supported globally by each camera manufacturer. You can find variances in the file attributes according to the camera you purchase. A file, for example, from a Canon camera saves in a Canon.crw format. Minolta saves files in Minolta.mrw, while Nikon saves Nikon.nef files. They're all a version of Camera Raw with the common factor being that they save all the data captured by the camera sensor.

If you purchase a point-and-shoot digital camera, you may not have a version of Camera Raw supported by your camera. The raw format is generally available with higher-end consumer-grade and professional cameras. If your camera dumps JPEG-only files to your media card, you won't be able to use the Camera Raw plug-in supported by Photoshop and Adobe Bridge.

For better quality images and more control over brightness and color correction, Camera Raw provides you much more data to work with than JPEG or TIFF files. Once you copy your files to your hard drive and open the file in either Adobe Bridge or Photoshop, you have a number of choices about how to process your files.

There are several books available dedicated to just using the Camera Raw format. Post-processing images from Camera Raw files is complex with many different options and much to be understood. This chapter covers just some of the essentials of Camera Raw. For a more in-depth description on using Camera Raw, see Rob Sheppard's *Adobe Camera Raw For Digital Photographers Only* (Wiley, 2005).

USING CAMERA RAW

As stated previously, there are a number of books devoted entirely to explaining the Camera Raw format. There's much to understand about raw beyond the scope of this book. What we hope to accomplish in this chapter is a brief overview of Camera Raw, and some important points you want to understand when opening files in Photoshop from the Camera Raw format. We leave the minute detail of technical analysis of Camera Raw to other authors.

NOTE

Raw is not an acronym that stands for anything. It's simply the name used to describe a format in a variety of different flavors from many different camera manufacturers. You may see the term appear as *RAW, Raw,* or *Camera Raw.* In this book, we limit usage to *Camera Raw* or simply *raw.*

UNDERSTANDING CAMERA RAW

The fact that Camera Raw contains more raw data in the saved image does not eliminate the need to control lighting and all other analog conditions that make up shooting a quality image. There is much discussion among photographers about Camera Raw and how it resolves many lighting and color problems. We wish it was that easy, but the fact remains that you need to take as much care in digitally photographing any scene as you do when using film. Figure 3-1 shows an image opened in Photoshop using default settings in the Camera Raw plug-in. In Figure 3-2, the edited Photoshop image is about the best we can make it. No matter what settings we use for processing the file, insufficient lighting makes it impossible to render a quality image.

3-1

3-2

The Camera Raw conversion tool offers methods for defining temperature, white balance, brightness, and so on, before the file is opened in Photoshop. Using the Camera Raw conversion tool processes the image in a way that is similar to running film through chemicals, where you can increase or decrease development times to compensate for under- or overexposures.

The tool you use to convert Camera Raw to an editable image in Photoshop is the Camera Raw plug-in supplied when you install Photoshop. In Photoshop CS2, you have one conversion tool supported by two different programs. You can set the attributes for converting Camera Raw files using Photoshop or using Adobe Bridge.

PRO TIP

The raw file is created from a camera sensor that has a finite range from black to white. Usually it can be said that the better the quality the sensor the greater the range. However, if your shot is outside the range of the sensor, you can't get detail in the highlights and shadows, and the image suffers from a lack of a complete tonal range. You can improve the capture by shooting in controlled lighting environments and shooting for under- or overexposures that can be merged together using Photoshop's Merge to HDR command. For more on Merge to HDR, see Chapter 1.

RAW VERSUS JPEG

There is much debate among photographers as to which format you should save your files when shooting digital. Most cameras that support raw format also offer you the option of saving files in JPEG format. If the option is available with your camera, you typically find a third option to save in both formats.

Using one format over the other has its advantages and disadvantages. Advantages of shooting raw images are:

> **Higher bit depth.** Raw supports 16-bit images. You have more data to work with when making tonal corrections on 16-bit images with more control over shadow and highlight adjustments. JPEG files are 8-bit and you're limited to 256 levels of gray thereby limiting your tonal correction adjustments. JPEG files often clip highlights and shadows that can't be fixed in an 8-bit image. With raw, you can often make adjustments to add detail in the clipped areas that JPEG loses. The results of editing 16-bit images versus 8-bit images are often self-evident in the image histogram. In Figure 3-3, you can see the results of editing an 8-bit image. The gaps in the tone curve ultimately produce some posterization. In Figure 3-4, you can see the histogram in the Levels dialog box after editing an image in 16-bit then converting the mode to 8-bit. The tone curve displays a smooth transition of tones. Slight adjustments in 8-bit images often destroy precious data. Conversely, you can often make wild tonal corrections to 16-bit images without destroying the data.

X-REF

For more information on 16-bit and 8-bit images, see Chapter 1.

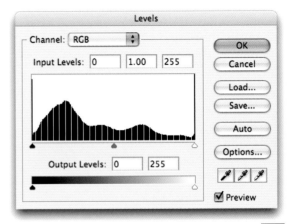

3-3

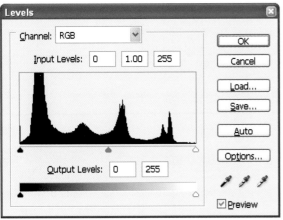

3-4

> **Uncontrolled lighting.** If shooting in an environment where you can't control lighting or lighting changes frequently, you can use raw to capture a wider range of highlight/shadow detail. In variable lighting conditions, raw provides you many options for post-processing your images using different white balance adjustments and exposure settings. With JPEG, you rely on the camera to make these choices for you, and brightness corrections are much more limited once the file is opened in Photoshop.

> **Extracting detail.** With raw and the ability to capture 16-bit images you can extract more detail in highlights and shadows where JPEG often clips detail in these areas.

> **Smooth tonal transitions.** The 8-bit JPEG images can appear with tonal banding after editing due to the limit of 256 levels of gray. Remapping pixels can create noticeable banding as shown in Figure 3-5. Raw images shot at 16-bit have 65,000 levels of gray whereby banding problems are much less apparent. When making tonal adjustments you don't have the same risk of losing smooth transitions between gray tones (see Figure 3-6).

PRO TIP

There remains some debate among professional photographers and Photoshop gurus that in some cases JPEG files can produce images of the same quality as raw files. Moreover, some people make the claim that a good photo saved as JPEG displays less noise than a raw file. In our opinion, these statements are not completely true. We believe that raw is the best at hand and we find no noticeable noise problems in raw over JPEG. We'll let you make the choice for what you want to believe in this regard, hopefully keeping in mind that what you find works in your workflow is something you want to stick with.

3-5

3-6

> **Custom calibration.** You can create your own personal custom calibration profiles for raw images and convert the color when processing the image. JPEG files are fixed at sRGB or Adobe RGB (1998) and conversion is made to your current workspace without having options for adjusting brightness and color during the conversion.

> **Multiple processing options.** Raw provides you the option for processing images using choices you make for white balance, exposures, tints, lighting options, and so on. You can make choices for processing the file and then return to the original raw image and make other choices for processing another file. This capability lets you produce the same image with cooler and warmer tones that may be suited for different purposes. With JPEG, you're stuck with a processed image where you can't change exposure values.

PRO TIP

Viewing and screen refreshes in Adobe Bridge are very slow. When you open a folder of Camera Raw files, the thumbnail views take a long time to render. The raw files also open more slowly than JPEG files. For serious photographic work, you can speed up your workflow by working on a newer computer that offers you more processing speed and adds several gigabytes of RAM. In addition, you can use certain automation features in Adobe Bridge for processing multiple raw files where you can walk away from your computer while it applies settings in a batch mode.

> **Absence of haloing.** Even when you shoot perfectly captured images that have a dynamic range matched to the JPEG processing software, and the white balance is exact for the exposure, JPEG images can appear with halos around the high-contrast edges created from the camera sharpening algorithm (when you can't disable sharpening

on a point-and-shoot camera). Raw files can be processed without sharpening in the raw plug-in, and you can control the sharpening amount in Photoshop.

When shooting JPEG, some advantages include:

> **Smaller file sizes.** JPEG files hold less data and therefore are smaller files. Smaller files mean that the pictures you take are recorded to your memory device faster when shooting photos and they open faster in Photoshop when you want to edit them. Raw files take longer to record to a memory device and much longer to open in Photoshop. If you want to cut the time for recording images and editing them, then JPEG works much faster.

> **Web and screen display.** If your output is for screen and Web, the faster editing for JPEG files makes more sense. If you have a large collection of images, you'll spend much less time working with JPEG images that will suit all your screen display needs.

> **Shooting in controlled lighting conditions.** If your lighting is optimum for shooting, JPEG can often render satisfactory images. Where you don't need to remap tonal ranges for showing detail in highlights and shadows, JPEG can meet your photo needs in certain photo shoots such as shooting 200 prom night pictures or where lighting conditions don't continually change. Modern cameras that capture JPEG images often produce good tonal ranges in good lighting situations. Figures 3-7 and 3-8 show a comparison between JPEG and raw formats where the JPEG file is not so noticeably different than the raw file. In the raw file in Figure 3-8, the warm reds, yellows, and blues are oversaturated, which may not be as apparent as you see in the printed versions of this book.

3-7

3-8

> **Mini-lab compatibility.** If you want to shoot pictures and have them quickly processed at a digital mini-lab, JPEG files offer you a fast solution. You can shoot your pictures, take your memory card to the lab, and get your prints an hour later. This is particularly helpful if you want to run some tests on a photo shoot before shooting the final images. If you shoot raw, you need to process all the images on your computer and then copy the processed images to a media card or external storage disk before taking the images to your lab.

PRO TIP

Inasmuch as you can open raw images, edit them, and save them back to a media card, your work will move more quickly if you first copy your images to your hard drive. Edit your images on your hard drive and copy them back to a media card when delivering them to a photo lab. Doing so also minimizes risk in losing your images if a media card gets corrupted.

> **Archiving files.** If you archive files in original raw formats, you can run the risk of facing obsolescence. Raw is not a universal format, and the camera manufacturers haven't settled on common ground for developing a standard. Each camera's raw format is unique to the specifications of the camera manufacturer. It's like the early stages of the Sony Beta versus VHS wars. JPEG is an ISO standard that has been around for some time and is likely to have a longer life than any current raw format.

PRO TIP

JPEG is a lossy compression scheme, which means that the file you save in JPEG format loses data each time it is saved. When you open a JPEG image, be certain to save your edited file in a format that doesn't lose data. File formats such as TIFF and Photoshop's native PSD format are best.

The third option you have with most digital cameras supporting both formats is to save files in both raw and JPEG. The upside for saving in both formats is that you always have a choice for importing the best image to work with in Photoshop. If the JPEG file loses too much data in the shadows, you can open the raw file and often get better results.

The downside for saving in both formats is that your storage requirements are much greater and the image captures are slower. We think this trade-off is a minor nuisance considering the advantages you have with more editing choices by using both formats. Some cameras offer you an option for shooting in JPEG format and switching to raw on the fly when you press the shutter button halfway. At times this feature may be worthwhile, but if you make a mistake and shoot raw when a JPEG file would have worked, you'll never know it. If you don't mind the burden of more disk space to accommodate both formats and you don't find the slower capture rate to be a problem, choose both formats as your default.

DNG

Digital Negative (DNG) is a format developed by Adobe Systems. This format is an effort by Adobe to try to bring the wide range of discrepancies of Camera Raw between the camera manufacturers to a common ground by accepting an Adobe-developed standard.

Unfortunately, camera manufacturers travel their own way down the digital highway and want to maintain proprietary attributes of their respective Camera Raw formats. For the consumer this is a great disadvantage because a given format by a camera manufacturer may disappear in favor of a newer format resulting in potential problems in recognizing the format in later versions of Photoshop. In some cases, camera manufacturers introduce new camera formats with the introduction of newer cameras, thereby producing two different lines of cameras that save files with different raw formats.

At this point, your only option against obsolescence is to open your raw files and save them in a raw format that is likely to be around for some time. When it comes to software development, Adobe Systems is the professional while the camera manufacturers are more amateurish with much less experience. Adobe has a track record of supporting legacy file formats when introducing new products and you can be confident that your chances of opening a DNG file later down the road are much greater than opening a proprietary raw format from a camera manufacturer.

If you open a raw file in Adobe Photoshop, save the file and toss the original raw file, you lose the raw attributes and the ability to again post-process the file. If you want to convert a Camera Raw file to a DNG file, you can convert the file without opening it in either Adobe Photoshop or Adobe Bridge. A DNG file remains in raw format and you can always return to it to process the files in the Camera Raw dialog box.

To convert a raw file to DNG, take a look at the following steps:

1. In Adobe Bridge, select an image in the Bridge window and double-click it to open the file in the Camera Raw plug-in window. The plug-in window offers options for opening the image in Photoshop by clicking the Open button and saving the raw file by clicking Save. When you click Save, the file is not opened in Photoshop and hence is not yet processed.

2. Click Save. The Save Options dialog box appears (see Figure 3-9). Click Select Folder. The Select Destination Folder dialog box appears where you can navigate your hard drive and identify a folder for your saved image. Select the folder you want to use for your saved file and click Select. You are then returned to the Save Options dialog box.

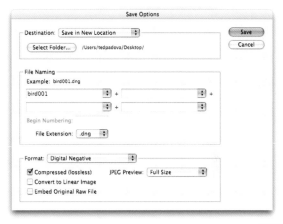

3-9

3. In the File Naming area of the Save Options dialog box, type a name for your saved file. If saving only a single image, type a name in the first text box for the name you want to provide for your new file. The Save Options dialog box also offers you an option to automate your conversion to DNG format. You can open multiple images in the Camera Raw plug-in by selecting multiple images in the plug-in window and double-click any selected image. Along the left side of the plug-in window you see thumbnail previews for all the opened images (see Figure 3-10). Click a thumbnail and press Command/Ctrl+A to select all the image previews. The Save button changes to reflect the number of images selected. For example, in Figure 3-10 the Save button changes to Save 10 Images indicating that 10 images are currently selected. When you click the button the Save Options dialog box opens.

Canon EOS 20D: IMG_1411.CR2 (ISO 100, 1/60, f/5.0, 18-125@26 mm)

3-10

Camera Raw Color Correction

3

If you elect to save more than one option, the File Naming area provides choices for creating unique names for the saved images. Open the first drop-down menu and you can choose from different root name options such as document names or dates. The second text box to the right offers another menu with similar options so the name could include something like a document name derived from the current file name and a date combined together for the root name. The Begin Numbering text box determines the unique name added to the root. You might add 001 to the Begin Numbering text box and the names appear as *root name* + 001, *root name* + 002, *root name* + 003, and so on.

Below the Begin Numbering text box is the File Extension field. By default, .dng is selected for you indicating the file is saved as an Adobe Digital Negative. Leave the menu option at the default when converting files to DNG.

4. Also by default, Digital Negative is selected for the Format. You have options for other file formats; however, to preserve the raw data, leave this item at the default.

5. Be sure the Compressed (lossless) check box below the Format drop-down menu is selected before proceeding. The compression doesn't lose any data in the image but results in a smaller compressed file.

6. Select the Convert to Linear Image option to store image data in an *interpolated demosaiced* format. DNG files can store data in mosaic (CFA) or demosaiced (CAAR) form. Typically, a mosaiced file is preferred because it represents original data captured by the camera's sensor. The demosaiced format is interpolated and results in a larger file size. As a default, leave the check box deselected. Demosaiced form has an advantage when you need to improve compatibility if the camera sensor contains any unusual mosaic patterns that the conversion doesn't support.

7. Select the Embed Original Raw Data option to preserve the maximum acquired from the original file. The resultant file is larger, but your original Camera Raw data is embedded in the DNG file.

8. Select a JPEG Preview. You can choose None, Medium, or Full Size. Choosing Medium or Full Size embeds a JPEG preview that can be seen by other applications without parsing the Camera Raw data.

9. Click Save. Your file (or multiple files) is saved as DNG.

USING ADOBE BRIDGE WITH CAMERA RAW

If you're new to Adobe Photoshop CS2, the first thing you notice is that a File Browser no longer appears within Photoshop. The File Browser has been removed and replaced with a separate program called Adobe Bridge. This separate executable application has all the features of the previous File Browser and has many new features for automating processing of Camera Raw photos.

SETTING BRIDGE PREFERENCES

Before you begin to use Adobe Bridge, it's a good idea to run through the application Preferences and set the preference choices for your workflow. To open the Bridge Preferences press Command/Ctrl+K (alternately

on the Mac choose Adobe Bridge ⇨ Preferences; on Windows choose Edit ⇨ Preferences).

Some of the Preference items you'll want to adjust include the following:

1. Click General in the left pane in the Preferences panel shown in Figure 3-11. Among the available options is Show Tooltips. Tooltips are handy little pop-up notes in the Bridge window that appear when the cursor hovers over a thumbnail image. Sometimes the tooltips can be annoying and prevent you from seeing a good part of the thumbnail preview. Deselect the check box if you don't want to display tooltips.

3-11

Below Additional Lines of Thumbnail Metadata are three drop-down menus where you can select what information is displayed below each thumbnail. If you want the information displayed, check the boxes. If you want to see more thumbnails in the Bridge window, deselect the check boxes to conserve space.

In the Favorite Items section, select the items you want to appear in your Favorites list.

2. Click Metadata in the left pane to see the Metadata options. One of the important Metadata options for digital photos is Camera Data (Exif) that you find by scrolling through the Metadata window (see Figure 3-12).

By default, however, this set of data is hidden from view. You can also add the same information to the IPTC Core. IPTC Core is a newer specification, and you should use it for all data you add to current documents. The IPTC (IIK legacy) data appears from legacy files created before October 2004.

3-12

3-13

Exchangeable image file (Exif) data is written when files are saved from digital cameras. Specific attributes related to your camera settings are included in the Exif data such as shutter speed, flash firing, aperture settings, and so on. The information is recorded by the camera and not editable in Adobe Bridge. Checking the boxes just determines whether the information is displayed in the Metadata pane in the Bridge window. If you don't see certain Metadata in the Metadata pane, look at this preference item to be certain the respective boxes are checked.

Scroll through the Metadata list and you find two other items for Metadata storage respective to your digital camera images. The first item is ITPC (IIM, legacy) shown in Figure 3-13. This data is editable in the Metadata pane. You can add information here for things like copyright information, captions, document title, author, keywords, and location.

IPTC Core is similar to IPTC (IIM, legacy) where all the data here is editable (see Figure 3-14). As a new specification developed by the International Press Telecommunications Council (IPTC) in October 2004, you should use it with all your current documents. The same field data is available in the IPTC Core fields where you find identifying information as described previously with IPTC (IIM, legacy).

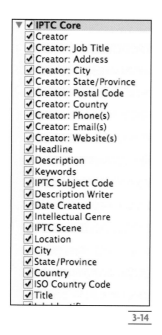

3-14

3. Click Advanced in the Preferences dialog box and you have some settings for options that affect memory and performance of Adobe Bridge (see Figure 3-15). The first item relates to processing image thumbnails. The default is 200MB where a thumbnail is not created for files larger than 200MB. If you want to speed up the Bridge performance, you can decrease this value to a much smaller size. Doing so means you won't see thumbnail previews while working in the Bridge window. However, you can work back and forth in the Preferences dialog box to change the setting when you want to see thumbnails.

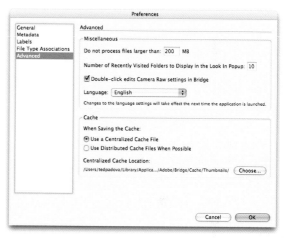

3-15

PRO TIP

Metadata are searchable in Adobe Bridge. Both the fixed data supplied by your camera and data you edit in the ITPC Core text boxes are searchable. As you begin to accumulate many different digital camera images, take a few minutes to add information that can help you find images quickly.

The Double-click edits Camera Raw settings in Bridge check box is used for making a choice for opening the Camera Raw plug-in within Adobe Bridge or within Photoshop. If the check box is selected, the Camera Raw settings are applied in Adobe Bridge. Not all files you open in the Camera Raw plug-in are always opened in Photoshop. You may perform some adjustments and want to apply settings to a collection of files without opening them. In this case, working in Adobe Bridge is a better option for you as you can quickly select image thumbnails for file settings you want to change. As a matter of default, it's a good idea to leave this check box selected.

The Cache section options relate to files that store image previews in a memory cache. Bridge takes some time to generate thumbnail previews of images contained in folders. Once the previews are created, the cache file maintains the previews resulting in much faster displays when you return to the folder. There are two options from which to choose: Use a Centralized Cache File and Use Distributed Cache Files When Possible.

Use a Centralized Cache File places two cache files in a centralized folder. A centralized cache is generally easier to use than a distributed cache, especially when you want to delete a cache file. You don't need to search your hard drive for the cache folder when removing it from your hard drive. All cache files are contained in a single folder in the directory path displayed in the Preferences dialog box. By default, Bridge creates the cache folder for you. You can change the folder and directory path by clicking Choose in the Preferences dialog box.

Use Distributed Cache Files When Possible places the two cache files created for each folder in the same folder containing the respective images. This option is a great benefit when writing files to CDs and DVDs. The cache files can be copied to the media, and viewing thumbnails from CD/DVDs is much faster when saving the cache files to the same folders containing the image files.

SETTING CAMERA RAW PREFERENCES

The Camera Raw Preferences dialog box offers you a few options for file handling in Adobe Bridge. These preference settings are in a different dialog box than the application preferences, and you access the dialog box by choosing Bridge ➪ Camera Raw Preferences (Mac) or Edit ➪ Camera Raw Preferences (Windows). Select the command, and the dialog box shown in Figure 3-16 opens.

The first choice you have in the dialog box is where you want to save settings adjustments made to raw files. The two options include:

> **Sidecar ".xmp" files.** This is the best for collaborative workflow environments and for archiving images. The settings you apply to an image are saved in an XMP file in the same folder where the image resides. The filename uses the same base name as your image file with an .xmp extension. The XMP files can store IPTC metadata and other metadata associated with the file. In Bridge, XMP sidecar files are hidden by default, but they are visible in the Macintosh Finder or Windows Explorer. When you copy, move, and delete Camera Raw images in Adobe Bridge, the XMP sidecar files move along with their corresponding images. You can make the XMP sidecar files visible in Adobe Bridge by choosing View ➪ Show Hidden Files in the Bridge window. Be certain to copy these files when you store Camera Raw files on CDs and other kinds of external media.

> **Camera Raw Database.** If you choose this option from the Save images in drop-down menu, the settings are stored in a Camera Raw database file on your hard drive. On the Mac, the files are stored in the user's Preferences folder located at `Users/user name//Library/Preferences`. Windows machines store the files in the user's Application Data folder located at `Documents and Settings/user name/Application Data/Adobe/CameraRaw`. The filename where the preferences are stored is Adobe Camera Raw Database. The database file is indexed by file content. Therefore, if you move or rename Camera Raw files, the settings in the Camera Raw database stay connected with the images. The greatest disadvantage for using this method is if your hard drive fails and it is not backed up. You lose the sidecar files. With the sidecar files that you copy to CD\DVDs, you preserve your settings on the individual media sources.

In the Apply sharpening to field, you can sharpen images using the Camera Raw plug-in or you can defer sharpening until after you edit images in Adobe Photoshop. The choices are obvious in the drop-down menu. As a matter of default, choose the option for sharpening images in Photoshop when you need to edit files. You have much more control over the sharpening amounts and methods in Photoshop.

The Camera Raw Cache section has settings that enable you to establish a maximum size for the cache file and an option to delete the cache. The default size of 1GB enables you to process about 200 images. If you work on significantly more images you can type a higher number in the Maximum Size field to increase the cache size. The maximum size you can allocate to the cache is 50GB.

If you need to purge the cache because you are low on disk space, click Purge Cache. If you purge the cache, all your images need to be processed again.

In addition to setting Camera Raw preferences, you'll also want to establish defaults for your Camera Raw files for various processing settings. Establishing default settings for your Camera Raw files eliminates a need to deselect check boxes, and step through a number of various options choices each time you open a file. Some kind of adjustment is likely to be needed for just about any file you open, but by disabling many default preferences, you won't need to repeatedly make the same adjustments. To set defaults for your Camera Raw files, follow these steps:

1. Open a Camera Raw file in the Camera Raw dialog box, and deselect all the Auto check boxes in the settings pane (see Figure 3-17).

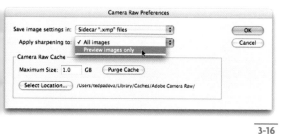

3-16

3-17

2. In the lower-left corner you have several adjustments to make. Select the color space in which you want to open your files. If you want to work with files that have a larger color gamut, choose Adobe RGB (1998) over sRGB.

3. By default, Camera Raw files open in 16-bit mode. You can choose to open your files in 8-bit mode; however, when correcting images for brightness and color, be certain to keep the images in 16-bit mode. You sacrifice some speed when performing edits, but just about all your corrections applied to images are much better when working on 16-bit images.

4. Select the size for your most common output from the Size drop-down menu.

PRO TIP

The Size menu reports image sizes in pixels. If you want to know the equivalent sizes in another unit of measure, create a new document in Photoshop and type the same units in pixels for your new file dimensions. Choose Image ⇨ Image Size and change the pixels to your desired unit of measure. You can determine what size in pixels is needed for your output by entering different values in the Image Size dialog box.

5. Type a value for the resolution in the Resolution text box. By default, Camera Raw images are opened at 240 ppi. If your resolution requirements are different, type the resolution you use most frequently in the text box.

6. Select a White Balance. You may use the White Balance adjustment frequently and change the temperature according to the photos and lighting conditions you shoot. As a matter of default, select As Shot as your default and later individually change the white balance if needed when you open the camera raw images.

7. Click the Detail tab. Rather than use the sharpening settings in the Detail tab, set the sliders to zero and apply all sharpening in Photoshop. Apply sharpening last in your editing process and while working in 16-bit mode before you convert your files to 8-bit images.

8. Save your new settings as a default. From the fly-out menu adjacent to the Settings drop-down menu, select Save New Camera Raw Defaults, as shown in Figure 3-18. After you save your settings as a new default, each time you open a file in the Camera Raw dialog box these settings take effect.

3-18

X-REF

For more information on sharpening images, see Chapters 5 and 6.

UNDERSTANDING THE CAMERA RAW HISTOGRAM

Double-click an image in the Bridge window, and it opens in the Camera Raw dialog box from within Bridge (assuming you have selected Double-click edits Camera Raw settings in Bridge preference option in the Advanced Preferences pane). In the Camera Raw dialog box, you have a number of different settings to adjust that hopefully reduce your editing time in Photoshop and help you get the best image quality out of your photo.

Before you move sliders and select menu commands, take a moment to evaluate your image and try to understand as much as possible about the image attributes. You don't need to travel far because all of what you need appears in the histogram when the Camera Raw dialog box opens (see Figure 3-19).

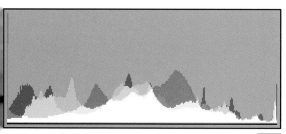

3-19

The histogram is your single source of the most important information feedback related to the current settings in the Camera Raw dialog box. A seasoned pro can just about describe what's going on in the image by examining the histogram without looking at the image preview in the center of the dialog box.

To get up to speed in evaluating your images, you need to understand what those little colored diagrams mean in the Camera Raw dialog box's histogram. There are seven different colors within the histogram, and you should be aware of what these colors mean in terms of defining highlight, shadow, and midtone values:

> **White.** White in the histogram informs you of pixels contained in all three RGB channels.

> **RGB.** The red informs you of pixels that appear only in the Red channel. Green represents pixels only in the Green channel and blue informs you of pixels in the Blue channel.

> **Cyan.** Cyan indicates an absence of pixels in the Red channel. Cyan shows a combination of pixels in the Green and Blue channels.

> **Magenta.** Magenta indicates an absence of pixels in the Green channel. Magenta shows a combination of pixels in the Red and Blue channels.

> **Yellow.** Yellow indicates an absence of pixels in the Blue channel. Yellow shows you a combination of pixels in the Red and Green channels.

As you view the histogram in the Camera Raw dialog box, you often see spikes in many images. If you see spikes at the ends of the histogram, the spikes on the left side indicate clipping of shadow detail. Spikes on the right side indicate clipping in the highlights. If you see spikes at both ends, the exposure is likely to have exceeded the dynamic range of the camera's sensor, where both highlights and shadows are clipped.

A white spike at either end of the histogram indicates that clipping occurs in all three channels. Any other color appearing as a spike on either end of the histogram indicates clipping occurs respective to one or two channels according to the color definitions reported in the previous list.

The histogram informs you at a glance as to what data is lost in processing the image and what data might be resurrected. If you see spikes at both ends of the histogram, the dynamic range is outside the camera's sensor's capabilities and you can't avoid some clipping. If you see spikes on only one end of the histogram, you might be able to remap the pixels to pick up more shadow or highlight detail (depending on which end shows some clipping).

Histograms in and of themselves are confusing to many photographers as well as Photoshop artists. Add to the general confusion of a single color graph all the different colors you see in the Camera Raw dialog box, and the confusion jumps seven-fold. Because

the histogram is such an important item for you to understand, we'll break it down a little and try to explain what a histogram view has to do with an image. For this breakdown, we confine our discussion to looking at histograms opened in Photoshop in the Levels dialog box. Hopefully, after you understand a little more about histograms, you'll be able to apply that knowledge to what you see in the Camera Raw dialog box.

In Figure 3-20, the white rose image is lit to dramatically separate the blossoms from a dark background. The flowers themselves are primarily tones brighter than middle gray with small hints of pure white.

3-20

When we open the Levels dialog box and look at the histogram (see Figure 3-21), we see exactly what is reflected in the image. More data is shoved toward the left indicating a darker image. There exist no absolute whites as we see on the right side of the histogram where no data is represented. The light-gray tones show a wide variation with a peak at light gray.

Now look at Figure 3-22. This jewelry insurance photo was shot on a white background and, as you might expect, the histogram should be weighted on the right side where white is represented.

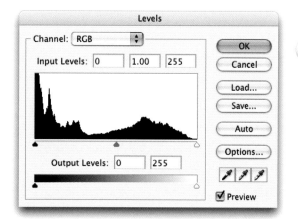

3-21

3-22

When you open the Levels dialog box (see Figure 3-23), you see most of the image tones are very close to white, which is reflected by the huge hill toward the right side of the histogram. The jewelry consists of a full range of tones, but statistically comprises a very small part of the total image information, so it's averaged across the histogram. The black rope is the largest part of the dark tones of the image, and it creates the tall spike near black on the left side of the histogram.

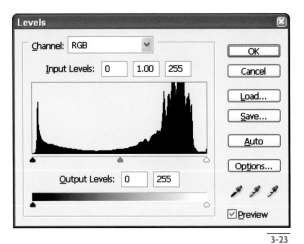

3-23

The aerial photo shown in Figure 3-24 was created for an irrigation advertisement. The art direction required a low-key image (mostly dark tones) with enhanced color saturation for visual impact.

The resulting histogram (see Figure 3-25) shows that most of the tones are darker than middle gray, and the histogram hill is plied high to the left toward black. You also notice the two spikes on both the left and right side. This type of image is a special case. It actually contains almost no full black or white tones.

The RGB histogram shown in Figure 3-25 is a composite of the individual Red, Green, and Blue channels. By default, this is the view you see when you

open the Levels dialog box and the view of histograms in the Camera Raw dialog box. What you see is the result of an image containing some fully saturated colors. By definition, a fully saturated color is one that is comprised of only one or two primary colors, such as red plus blue, red plus green (yellow), or any other combination of the three basic RGB primaries.

The bright yellow water highlights are fully saturated, so the Red channel values go all the way to level 255, and the Green channel is near that value. To see this more clearly, view the individual histogram channels. Click the Channel drop-down menu to see the individual channels. Alternately you can press Command/Ctrl+1, Command/Ctrl+2, or Command/Ctrl+3 to see the respective RGB channels. To get back to the composite RGB view, press Command/Ctrl+~ (tilde). When you select Red in the Levels dialog box, the Red channel histogram appears (see Figure 3-26).

The highlight side of the Red channel is clipped because of the full saturation in the yellow highlights.

A fully saturated RGB mode color isn't necessarily bright and vivid. The dark cyan green tones near the bottom of the image are almost fully saturated, yet are very dark tones. The red values are almost zero, and this shows up in the Red channel histogram. Notice that there are far more pixels piled up in the full black area of the histogram compared to the Blue and Green channel.

Some of the Green channel pixels are also clipped to level 255 (see Figure 3-27) because the water highlights are bright and pure yellow. In order to convey this information in a digital form, only the Blue channel carries any information in the bright yellow highlights.

Fully saturated yellow highlight.

R 255
G 253
B 168

R 002
G 018
B 015

Almost fully saturated
shadow tones...cyan-green

3-24

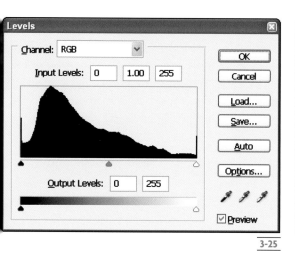

3-25

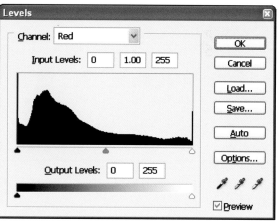

3-26

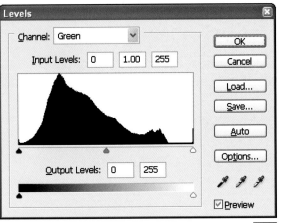

3-27

The lesson to be learned here is this: When examining the full RGB histogram of a highly saturated image, check all the channels separately to see how much tonal information might be available in the highlights and shadows.

After desaturating the image (see Figure 3-29) by 50 percent, the resulting histograms (see Figure 3-30) show far less tone clipping. The image is easier to manipulate for tonal changes. When working with heavily saturated images, keep image saturation controlled during the initial editing steps — especially for all your levels and curves adjustments. If high saturation is desired in the final image, leave the Hue/Saturation adjustments for the final step.

As seen here, the Blue channel (see Figure 3-28) is not clipped. In other words, there's no "blue" in the brightest yellow highlights (fully saturated), so the histogram shows no blue pixels in the highlight side of the histogram.

To bring this back to the Camera Raw dialog box, follow the same principle. Leave your saturation adjustment alone when converting the raw image. You can always add or decrease saturation in Photoshop, and most often using this adjustment in Camera Raw adversely affects your ability to correctly adjust brightness and contrast.

The snapshot in Figure 3-31 shows the result of exceeding the dynamic range of the capture chip in the camera. This type of shot is common when you do average metering with your camera. The exposure is not set properly for either the foreground shade or the background sunlight. As a result, the image consists of just dark and light tones, and almost no middle tones, so the histogram shows a valley in the center (see Figure 3-32). Both shadow and highlight values are severely clipped, making the image difficult to edit for a quality result.

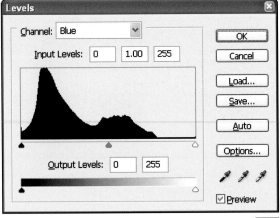

3-28

R 234
G 228
B 183

Reducing image saturation
increased highlight tonal data.

More shadow data
when saturation is
decreased.

R 016
G 028
B 025

3-29

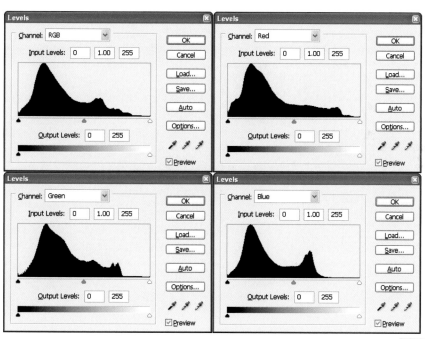

3-30

3-31

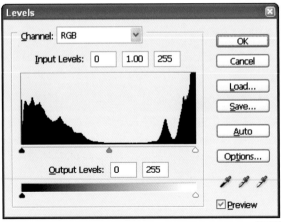

3-32

This type of histogram is very helpful when shooting with DSLR cameras because you can make a quick fix. Professional photographers shoot a Polaroid print before shooting the final photo. They want to study the composition of the scene and the lighting. With a digital camera you have the benefit of getting a pre-view without shooting a Polaroid and waiting for the development time. But that tiny LCD on the back of your camera won't tell you much because you can't see enough fine detail in the preview. Quite often what looks good on a small LCD screen can look pretty bad when opened in Photoshop.

Many DSLR cameras offer you an option to see an image preview on the LCD screen or a histogram. You can toggle back and forth and examine the image composition and see what's going on in the image by viewing the histogram. If you see a histogram like the one shown in Figure 3-32, you might just change your angle for your shot or try metering the scene for the foreground or background. Shoot another shot and take a quick look at the histogram again. As you become more familiar with the histogram and how it relates to the image tones, you can quickly ascertain whether you can successfully edit an image in Photoshop.

In Figure 3-33, you see another image that's easy to determine whether you can successfully edit the file or not. The image preview gives you a clue, but the his-togram tells you more.

3-33

This histogram (see Figure 3-34) shows the result of severe underexposure. The image is obviously very dark, and the histogram reflects that almost all the image tones are near black. A few bright specular highlights from the camera flash leave a trace of data in the highlight portion of the histogram.

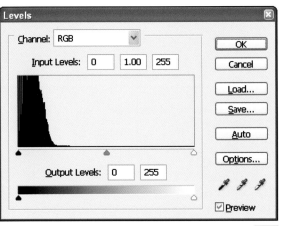

3-34

By now you should have an idea for what might be shown in a histogram of an image the opposite of Figure 3-33, where all the picture appears light from an overexposure. As you might guess, the histogram appears weighted on the right side of the tone curve and appears like the histogram in Figure 3-34 flopped over. Severe underexposure or overexposure is beyond the editing capabilities in Photoshop. If you see histograms like these on your camera, you definitely know you need to change lighting conditions.

Whether you view histograms on your camera in Camera Raw or in the Levels dialog box, the more you know about histograms, the more efficient and faster you'll become in shooting pictures, processing them in the Camera Raw dialog box, and editing them for tonal adjustments in Photoshop.

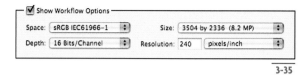
USING CAMERA RAW SETTINGS

Perhaps the single most important dialog box, wizard, or window to become familiar with when shooting Camera Raw is the Camera Raw window. Image processing for Camera Raw images is like processing analog images. You need to exercise care in choosing the right temperature and development time when processing film. Likewise, you want to choose the best settings to process your digital Camera Raw images. A big difference between digital and analog photography is that the digital raw file can be reprocessed a thousand times using different settings. With film, you only have one shot at getting the processing right.

As a routine part of your workflow when shooting images in Camera Raw, you need to process the images in Camera Raw before opening them in Photoshop. The following steps are typically what you do each time you open your raw files.

1. Select the Show Workflow Options check box in the lower-left corner of the Camera Raw window that opens when you double-click an image preview in the Bridge window. You can choose from among color space, bit depth, size, and resolution (see Figure 3-35).

Click the color Space drop-down menu to select sRGB or Adobe RGB (1998). If you output your images at digital photo labs, sRGB may be the choice preferred by your vendor. If you work with graphic artists and prepare photos for offset press or print your files to a desktop color printer, Adobe RGB (1998) is likely to be your best choice. Adjust the Depth, Size, and Resolution settings according to the image attributes for files used in your workflow.

2. Analyze the image. At the top of the Camera Raw window are three check boxes. Select the Preview check box to show the image preview in the window. Select the Shadows and Highlights check boxes and use the Zoom tool in the Tools palette on the top-left side of the window to examine detail where you find clipping problems (see Figure 3-36). If you have several images where

3-36

you used different exposure values, you can compare photos to ones that present fewer editing problems capturing highlight and shadow detail.

3. Adjust the white balance. Select a white balance option from the choices in the White Balance drop-down menu (see Figure 3-37). If the overall appearance of the image is best set between the White Balance menu choices, you can click and drag the Temperature slider left and right to fine-tune the adjustment.

PRO TIP

In the Camera Raw dialog box you can use the same keyboard shortcuts you use in Photoshop to zoom in and out of the image preview. Press Command/Ctrl + (plus) to zoom in, Command/Ctrl - (minus) to zoom out, and press Command/Ctrl+0 (zero) to fit in window.

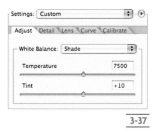

3-37

4. Adjust the white point. Move the Exposure slider to adjust the white in the image. In Figure 3-37, the exposure adjustment helps compensate for the loss of some detail in the image.

PRO TIP

Press Option/Alt as you move the Exposure slider, and you can see the clipping that occurs as the adjustment is made.

5. Adjust the black point. Be certain that the blacks don't appear flat and there is an absence of rich black in the image. You can adjust the black point by moving the Shadows slider.

6. Adjust the midtones. Midtone adjustments can be made by moving the Brightness and Contrast sliders, and you can refine the adjustments using the Curve palette as shown in Figure 3-38.

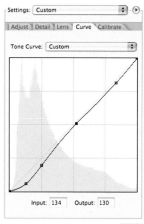

3-38

7. Adjust the Saturation slider to push up the color and give it a boost. Use care if you change the saturation value. You can easily oversaturate your image with the slightest adjustment. As a matter of practice, apply saturation adjustments as one of the last edits you make in Photoshop just before you sharpen images. Unless you have some specific reason for adjusting saturation in the Camera Raw dialog box, keep the saturation adjustment off when converting the raw image and opening it in Photoshop.

8. Click the Detail tab and move the Sharpness and Noise sliders to eliminate sharpening and reduce noise in the photo.

9. Click Lens and make adjustments for chromatic aberrations and add a vignette effect to darken the image border (see Figure 3-39).

10. Open the file. Click Open and not Done. If you click Done, your settings are saved in a sidecar file.

PRO TIP

You can clear settings for a Camera Raw image by opening the Settings drop-down menu and selecting Camera Raw Defaults. This option lets you process an image with multiple settings. You can apply settings, open an image, then return to defaults and apply new settings for a second file you open in Photoshop.

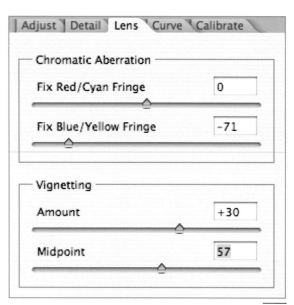

3-39

3

Camera Raw Color Correction

OPENING CAMERA RAW IN ADOBE PHOTOSHOP CS2

The Camera Raw plug-in is loaded and made available within two separate applications. When in Adobe Bridge, the Camera Raw plug-in opens the Camera Raw dialog box within the Bridge workspace. If you open a Camera Raw file in Adobe Photoshop, Photoshop uses the plug-in to open the Camera Raw dialog box. Using either application opens the same dialog box where the same settings and processing options appear. If you're opening a single file, it doesn't really matter which application you use to open a raw image. However, if you want to adjust settings without opening files, manage and organize your photos, add metadata, search for images, and so on, using Adobe Bridge is your best choice.

USING THE ADOBE OPEN DIALOG BOX

If you use Photoshop to open raw images, you can choose which Open dialog box you want to use. With the introduction of the CS2 applications, Adobe developed a new Open dialog box and provides a choice for using your operating system's default Open dialog box or the new Adobe Open dialog box.

Choose File ➪ Open in Photoshop, and click Use Adobe Dialog. The dialog box changes to a different Open dialog box, offering you some different viewing options than your OS dialog box. Click the View button in the top-right corner to open a drop-down menu of different available view options (see Figure 3-40).

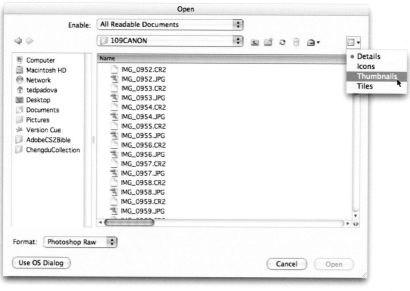

3-40

If you want to see image thumbnail previews, select Thumbnails from the menu choices, and the image previews change (see Figure 3-41). Notice that when viewing files such as JPEGs, you see image previews much like you do in Adobe Bridge. However, the thumbnails for Camera Raw files don't appear with an image preview when using the Adobe Open dialog box. Using your OS dialog box, you can see all image previews for JPEG and Camera Raw files.

If you shoot JPEG and raw together, you'll see a preview for the JPEG files. You can easily locate a raw equivalent adjacent to a JPEG if searching for a photo you want to open in the Camera Raw dialog box. If no JPEG equivalents are present, then you won't have a clue as to what file to open unless you recognize the file name or switch back to the OS dialog box. In Figure 3-42, you can see a folder of Camera Raw files appearing in the Adobe Open dialog box on Windows.

NOTE

If you convert files to DNG and save the DNG files with a JPEG image embedded in the file, you won't see thumbnail previews of raw images in the Adobe Open dialog box.

Regardless of whether you use Photoshop or Adobe Bridge, the file you open appears in the same dialog box where the image settings are applied. In Figure 3-43, you have the same options in the Camera Raw dialog box when the file is opened in Photoshop as you do when opening in Adobe Bridge.

PRO TIP

The Adobe dialog box is also used when you select Import, Export, Place, Save, and Save As from within Adobe Photoshop.

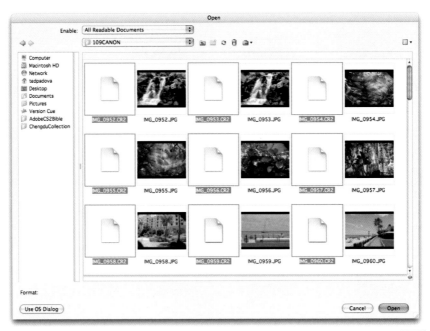

3-41

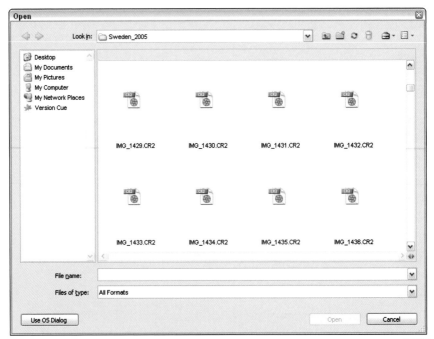

3-42

3-43

AUTO LAUNCHING BRIDGE

Because using Bridge is such an asset when working with Camera Raw files, as well as all other files you edit in Photoshop, you'll want to keep Bridge active in the background at all times. You can instruct Photoshop to launch Bridge when Photoshop is launched without having to launch the programs separately.

Open the Preferences dialog box by pressing Command/Ctrl+K. By default, the General Preferences pane opens. Select the Automatically Launch Bridge check box as shown in Figure 3-44. Click OK, and the next time you launch Photoshop, Adobe Bridge also launches.

If Bridge is not launched while you are in Photoshop, choose File ➪ Browse. The Browse menu command in all the CS2 applications automatically launches Adobe Bridge.

3-44

CAMERA RAW COLOR CALIBRATION

Raw conversion in Adobe Bridge and Photoshop CS2 offers an editing option called Calibration. This feature can be very useful for improving digital camera color output to a higher degree of accuracy under very controlled conditions. Calibration settings vary with changes in shooting conditions, but overall changes to preferred memory colors (such as flesh tones, skies, earth tones, and so on) can be modified to your own personal preferences if you aren't happy with the default results in the raw converter.

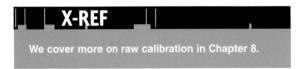

X-REF

We cover more on raw calibration in Chapter 8.

Memory colors are a matter of preference in many cases —especially flesh tones. Professional analog photographers tended to choose color films based on memory color rendering way back in the old days — like 1995 and earlier. Portrait films were usually judged on their flesh-tone quality when balanced for accurate rendering of neutral tones, such as a bride's white dress or a gray card.

The purpose here is to demonstrate a little eyeball calibration to sweeten your favorite memory colors. As an example, we modify the flesh tones in a standard file to our own personal preferences. You might prefer something different, but this process shows you how to get the results you want.

The important point to remember is that the modified calibration settings need to be performed on a file with a known neutral reference in the capture and an accurate setting of white balance. If the reference file has a global (overall) color balance error, the settings are only valid for that particular file. In other words, you can't set up a calibration that works effectively with all your images.

Keep in mind also that the lighting type has to be in the ballpark with the reference file you use for eyeball calibration. For this exercise, we use daylight with daylight-balanced strobe-light fill. The resulting settings are reasonably valid for photos captured at a similar color temperature — around 5000K. Most digital cameras we use give a much different result when using tungsten balance; you're mileage may vary.

For a standard gray reference in the file, a gray card, GretagMacbeth chart with gray scale, a Kodak gray scale, or similar target will work just fine to set white balance without guesswork. Take at least one sample image with the gray card using the exposure and ISO settings you intend to use on the final image. When you change exposures or lighting, shoot another image with your gray card.

A QPcard 101 (see Figure 3-45) is a reference card targeted for professional photographers. It has three patches with white, gray, and black colors with a self-adhesive back. You can purchase a pack of cards for $15.99 at Calumet Photo (www.calumetphoto.com).

The reference capture should also use ISO and exposure settings that reflect your standard working technique.

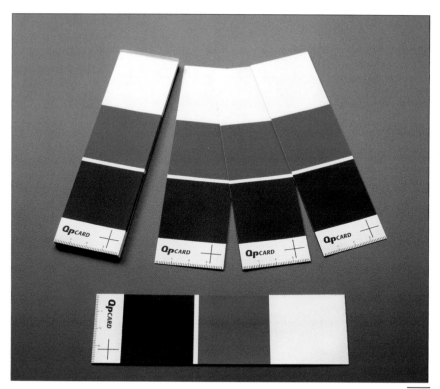

3-45

How does it work? The calibration color controls seem a little strange in the changes they make the first time you try them. They give results somewhat like the selective color command in Photoshop. True neutrals are not affected at all by the adjustments.

For a demonstration on how to use the Calibrate tab and make a calibration adjustment in Camera Raw, the following steps describe how to sweeten memory colors that can be applied to images having similar tonal ranges and hue values.

1. Open the Camera Raw dialog box and click the Calibrate tab. Drag the Red Hue slider to the left; the reds and yellows change to magenta-blue (see Figure 3-46).

2. Drag the Red Hue slider to the right and the image shifts to a yellow-green, as shown in Figure 3-47.

3. Slide the Green Hue slider to the left. It has the least effect overall. Sliding left adds a yellow-green bias (see Figure 3-48), and sliding to the right creates a magenta-red (see Figure 3-49).

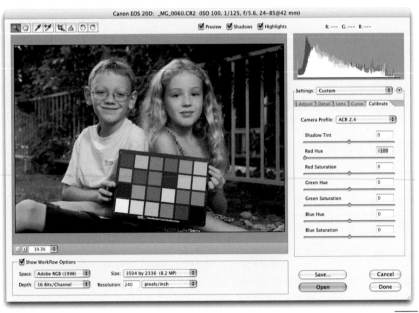

3-46

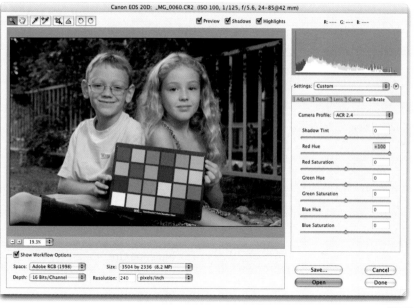

3-47

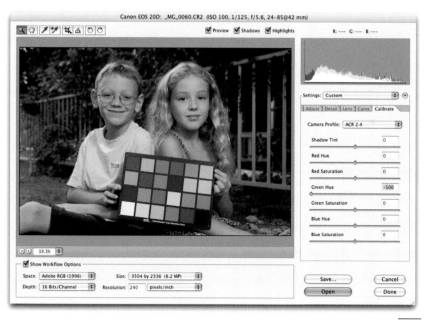

3-48

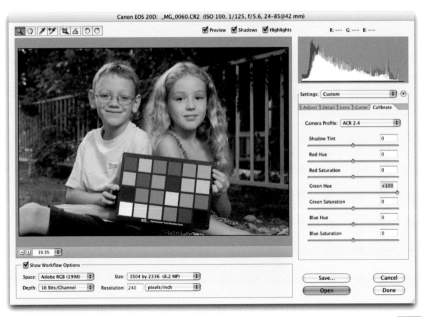

Canon EOS 20D: _MG_0060.CR2 (ISO 100, 1/125, f/5.6, 24-85@42 mm)

3-49

4. Move the Blue Hue slider to the left. This results in an obvious red shift (see Figure 3-50). Move it to the right to create a green color bias (see Figure 3-51).

Of course, the selected primary (red, green, or blue) shows the greatest change from their respective color slider. The selected primary adjustment is very broad and affects all the colors somewhat. Play with the sliders until you are familiar with the results and understand them thoroughly. When you make adjustments to images you typically only move the sliders slightly to add or subtract one primary or another.

5. Before beginning the color adjustments, adjust your reference file until overall contrast and brightness are in the range you prefer; double-check the white balance by clicking the White Balance eyedropper on your neutral reference target. If using a grayscale, click on the light-gray step next to the white patch (see Figure 3-52). If using a gray card, click the neutral gray on the card.

Check the info numbers in the upper-right corner of the Camera Raw dialog box to be certain you have a perfect white balance.

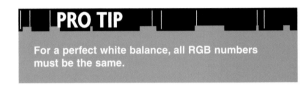

PRO TIP

For a perfect white balance, all RGB numbers must be the same.

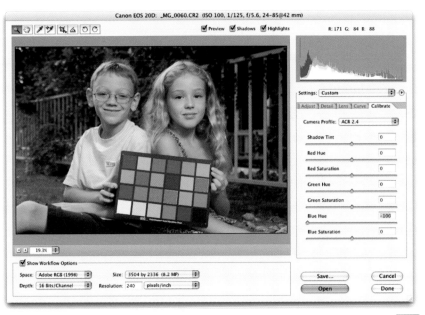

3-50

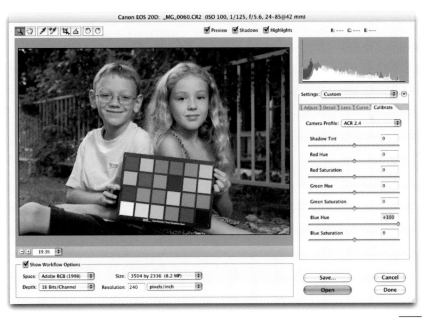

3-51

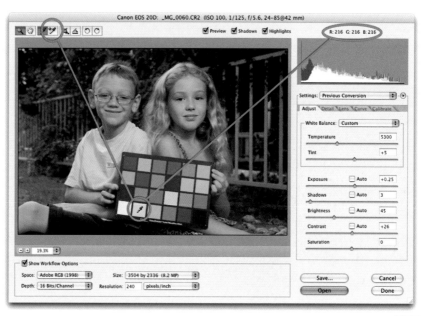

3-52

Once you're satisfied with your tonal adjustment, click the Calibration tab. By default, all the sliders are set at 0. With this file open in the raw converter, we want to warm up the flesh tones to simulate a Vericolor 3 portrait film flesh tones similar to what was used when shooting film.

6. In Figure 3-53, you can see the Green Hue slider moved left to add a little yellow to the flesh tones, and the Blue slider moved left to add a little red. The result of both moves gave the flesh rendering we wanted, while the neutral tones remain neutral. Adjusting the Red slider didn't seem to help, so it was left in the 0 default position.

We made the settings adjustments in Figure 3-53 by just playing around with the sliders until we created the desired appearance. Unfortunately, one of the essential attributes you need for digital color correction is a good color eye. One thing you can't expect from the Camera Raw converter or Photoshop is a universal set of formulas to work on every image.

7. This setting works fairly well for any similar lighting situation and color temperature. When we

saved the Camera Raw defaults earlier in this chapter, we saved a parent set of preferences as our Camera Raw defaults. The Camera Raw dialog box provides an option for saving a child set of preferences known as a *subset.* By saving the calibration settings as a subset, you can open new Camera Raw images using your default settings and then apply the subset to images needing a similar kind of color correction.

To save a subset, make your adjustments in the Calibration tab and open the fly-out menu adjacent to the Settings pull-down menu the same as when you save your Camera Raw defaults. From the menu choices, select Save Settings Subset. The Save Settings Subset dialog box opens (see Figure 3-54). If you are saving just the changes made in the Calibration tab, deselect all check boxes except Calibration. Click Save and the Save Raw Conversion Settings dialog box appears. Provide a name for your settings and click Save. For this example, we saved our subset VPS-3 flesh, so we can easily identify the settings and know at a glance what the settings are used for.

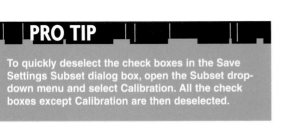

3-53

Settings (see Figure 3-55). The default directory where all your settings files are saved is the target location for loading settings. Just select the settings file you need and the adjustments are automatically applied in the Camera Raw dialog box.

3-54

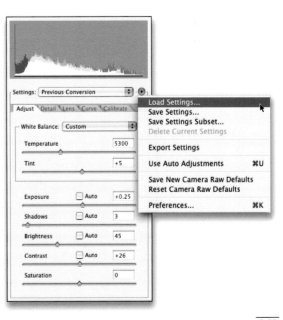

PRO TIP

To quickly deselect the check boxes in the Save Settings Subset dialog box, open the Subset drop-down menu and select Calibration. All the check boxes except Calibration are then deselected.

8. When you open another image that has a similar appearance as the file you corrected, you can load your saved settings. From the fly-out menu adjacent to the Settings pull-down menu, select Load

3-55

BATCH PROCESSING CAMERA RAW SETTINGS

If you have a collection of images shot in the same lighting conditions, you can automate your workflow using Bridge to apply the same settings made for one image to other files. Follow these steps:

1. Open an image in Adobe Bridge. Make adjustments for all the settings as described earlier in this chapter.

2. Click Done when finished making your settings adjustments in the Camera Raw dialog box. You don't need to open the image in Photoshop to preserve the settings.

3. Open a context menu on the image where you applied the settings—Ctrl-click (Mac) or right-click (Windows). A context menu opens as shown in Figure 3-56. Select Copy Camera Raw Settings and release the mouse button. Just like copying image data, the copied information is added to the clipboard and becomes available for pasting the data.

4. Select the images to which you want to apply the copied settings in the Bridge window. Open a context menu and select Paste Camera Raw Settings, as shown in Figure 3-57.

3-56

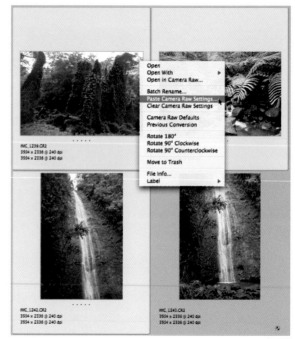

3-57

Camera Raw Color Correction

3

5. When you select Paste Camera Raw Settings, the Paste Camera Raw Settings dialog box appears (see Figure 3-58). Select the check boxes for the settings you want to apply. If you want only the White Balance setting to be applied, you can remove the checkmarks from all other options and select White Balance only. In this manner you apply a single setting with the idea that other fine-tune adjustments are made uniquely to each image.

3-58

The pull-down menu (see Figure 3-59) in the Paste Camera Raw Settings dialog box provides the same choices as the check boxes, but they are organized a little differently. The Settings menu commands select all the options from White Balance down to Saturation and deselects the marks for the remaining options. The Details menu command selects Sharpness, Luminance

Smoothing, Color Noise Reduction, and so on. These commands just make it easier to select settings in groups as well as some individual items that deselect the options not included in the command. You can use the commands or the checkmarks and click OK. The selected settings are then applied to the selected image thumbnails.

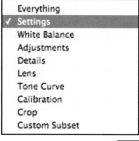

3-59

PRO TIP

All the options for copying Camera Raw settings, pasting them, and clearing them that you have available in a context menu are also available by choosing Edit ⇨ Apply Camera Raw Settings. From the Apply Camera Raw Settings submenu you make choices for handling settings options.

CHANGING CAMERA RAW SETTINGS

One of the very nice features you have with Camera Raw is that the default raw file is always available to you no matter what changes you make to settings. As an example, if you select a White Balance setting and save that setting in the raw file, you can eliminate the setting and return to raw defaults. Processing images from Camera Raw is a temporary solution and never changes the fact that the original raw data is accessible to you when you want it.

To remove Camera Raw settings, follow these steps:

1. Select one or more images where settings have been applied.

2. Open a context menu and select Clear Camera Raw Settings (see Figure 3-60). The settings are immediately eliminated from the raw files after making the menu selection.

Open
Open With ▶
Open in Camera Raw...

Batch Rename...
Paste Camera Raw Settings...
Clear Camera Raw Settings

Camera Raw Defaults
Previous Conversion

Rotate 180°
Rotate 90° Clockwise
Rotate 90° Counterclockwise

Move to Trash

File Info...
Label ▶

IMG.
3504 x 2336 @ 240 dpi
3504 x 2336 @ 240 dpi

3-60

An additional menu command is also available in both a context menu and the Edit ➪ Apply Camera Raw Settings submenu as well as the Camera Raw dialog box that works like a copy/paste operation. When you select Previous Conversion from any one of the three menus, the last settings adjustments you made to a raw file are applied to selected images in the Bridge window or a file you have open in the Camera Raw dialog box.

You can use the Previous Conversion and copy/paste method of changing settings independent of each other. For example, you can choose a White Balance adjustment and apply the setting to an image. You can make a second adjustment for something like exposure on a second image. Your second adjustment is the last setting made and will be used when you choose Previous Conversion. However, you can copy the White Balance setting and when selecting a new image you can paste the setting that changes the white point, or use Previous Conversion that changes the exposure. In this manner you can have two different settings adjustments that can be applied to images quickly by selecting either the paste or conversion method.

PRO TIP

Notice that you also have a menu choice for Camera Raw Defaults in the context menu opened from a selected image in the Bridge window. Making this menu choice performs essentially the same task as when selecting Clear Camera Raw Settings. The Camera Raw Defaults menu command actually just mimics the same menu choice you have in the Camera Raw dialog box in the Settings pull-down menu. The option for returning to defaults is provided to you in both the Bridge window and the Camera Raw dialog box.

Q&A

If I set my defaults for Camera Raw in Adobe Bridge, do I need to set my defaults when opening files in Adobe Photoshop?

Whatever settings you apply to opening images in Adobe Bridge are also applied to the Camera Raw dialog box when you open files in Adobe Photoshop and vice versa. All settings are identical, and you can freely work back and forth between Adobe Bridge and Photoshop without duplicating settings adjustments.

Why do I turn off sharpening in the Camera Raw dialog box.

Sharpening in Camera Raw applies a sharpen algorithm to the entire image at the size you open the file. For best results, it's a good idea to sharpen images after applying all your edits, especially when resizing images. You may find that sharpening might be best applied to a specific area of a photo while other areas would appear best without sharpening, such as when shooting images with a narrow depth of field.

When you resample images you'll want to apply different sharpening amounts to different-sized images. A photo designed for Web use, for example, requires less sharpening than a photo designed for a large print or commercial press. As a matter of default, try to keep the sharpening task to Photoshop as one of the last edits you make in your images.

What if I have my raw calibration set to maximize tonal corrections for skin tones and another set for another lighting situation, and I open a file containing content for both? Which calibration do I use?

As a matter of practice you'll want to correct for the most recognizable content in a photo. Skin tones are much more recognizable than any other image content because we know how skin tones should appear. We don't necessarily know how other image content should appear without being present at a scene.

The first step you should perform is loading your corrections for skin tones. If the background image area shifts noticeably, then open the image without the calibration settings. In Photoshop, you can mask areas and apply corrections to separate areas of an image.

Is there a danger that DNG files will become obsolete?

It's impossible to predetermine the direction of any developer and know precisely what the future holds for recognizing new formats to be later developed and how legacy files will work with newer products and product revisions. History tells us that a developer such as Adobe has an excellent track record in supporting legacy files with new product revisions. As a software developer, Adobe expends great effort and resources on supporting older file formats when introducing new products and product revisions.

Camera manufacturers are relatively new to the software market when it comes to saving digital files. As yet, it's not known how much support these vendors will provide as they introduce new cameras that use different formats. It's somewhat of a gamble now; however, the wisest choice is to follow the vendor with the most experience. Based on this notion, DNG is in all probability going to be supported for quite some time. We can't necessarily say the same for other raw camera formats.

What if I save my settings to a Camera Raw Database file and I later want to have sidecar files copied to a CD/DVD?

In the Camera Raw Preferences dialog box you make a selection for where your settings are saved. If you have Camera Raw Database selected and you make settings adjustments to your images, the settings are recorded in the Camera Raw Database. When you open the Camera Raw Preferences dialog box and select Sidecar ".xmp" files, XMP files are immediately created from data stored in the Camera Raw Database. Just make this preference choice and when you copy a folder of images to a CD/DVD, all the sidecar files will be copied to your media.

If I shoot JPEG images and I want to get my 8-bit images into a 16-bit mode, can I truly create a 16-bit image from an 8-bit file?

We explain more about how to do this in Chapter 4. For a quick overview now, you can convert 8-bit to 16-bit and have more grays to edit by finessing a few commands in Photoshop. First, convert the 8-bit image to 16-bit by choosing Image ➪ Image Mode ➪ 16 Bits/Channel in Photoshop. After the mode conversion, choose Image ➪ Image Size, and resample the image down 71 percent using the Bicubic method. You end up with a rich histogram with more than 4000 levels of gray that permits you to edit Levels and Curves without destroying much data the same as when opening 16-bit images from the raw converter.

IMAGE CORRECTIONS

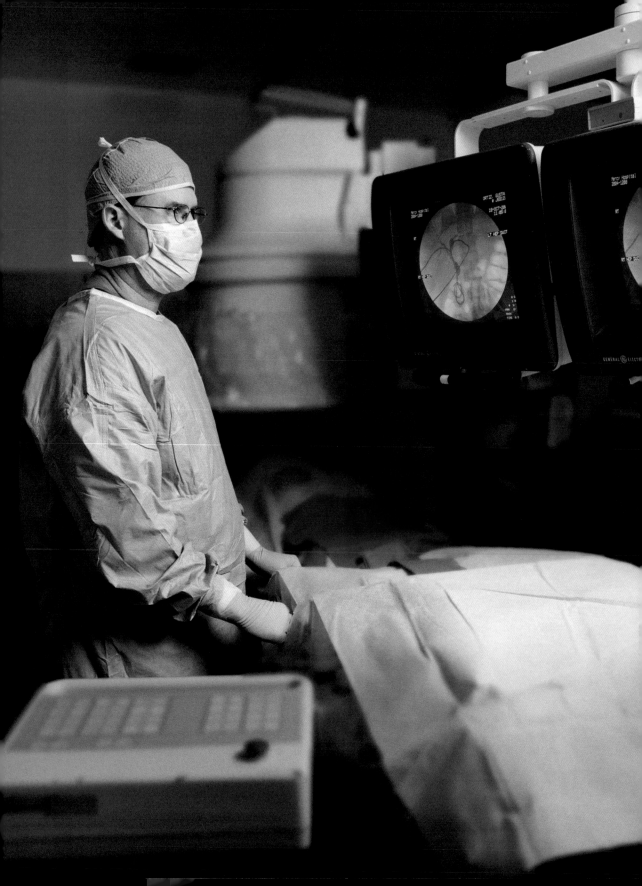

Chapter 4

TONE AND BRIGHTNESS CORRECTIONS

"The camera is a remarkable instrument. Saturate yourself with your subject, and the camera will all but take you by the hand and point the way." — Margaret Bourke White

In Chapter 3, we discuss using the Camera Raw dialog box for making a few tonal adjustments before opening a file in Photoshop. Many of the tonal settings you have in the Camera Raw dialog box are also available to you in Photoshop. The question then becomes, "Which tool do I use to make my tonal adjustments?"

Figure 4-1 shows an example of a photo that had tonal adjustments made in the Camera Raw dialog box and that used no further adjustments in Photoshop. Figure 4-2 shows a file opened using default settings in the Camera Raw dialog box that had tonal adjustments made in Photoshop. As you can see, for many images, you can achieve good results using either the adjustments in the Camera Raw dialog box or adjustments made in Photoshop. However, in most cases, you are best served by making a few settings adjustments in Camera Raw and later fine-tuning your tonal adjustments in Photoshop.

4-2

Regardless of where you make your tonal corrections, your first step is to analyze an image and try to get an understanding for what adjustments need to be made. The Camera Raw dialog box helps you in making your initial examination. From that point, you decide what are the most practical settings to apply in the Camera Raw dialog box and then leave the rest to Photoshop. Unfortunately, there is no magic formula to guide you in where to make one correction over another. More important is for you to try to be consistent and apply similar methods for all your image editing.

EXAMINE AN IMAGE

Whether your images are Camera Raw or JPEG, you first need to examine your image and know where you want to go before editing brightness or tonal ranges. First, look at the highlights and shadows, then look over the midtones. Among the most important things you look for are white and black in the image. Much like you would examine prints in a darkroom, you're looking for a solid white point and a rich black. In many cases, if the lighting is not optimum for shooting your photos, the black in your images is muddy or the black is so apparent there is no detail in the shadow areas.

4-1

The quick at-a-glance evaluation is easy to make when looking at the histograms. In Figure 4-3, the histogram in the Camera Raw dialog box shows the tonal values. In this example, the highlights and shadows are clipped (indicated by the spikes at either end of the histogram) although the midtone area has a smooth transition of tones.

4-3

Compare the histogram in Figure 4-3 with the one in Figure 4-4, which shows the full range of tones from white to black. The histogram in Figure 4-4 tells us that this image should produce good detail in the highlights, shadows, and throughout the midtone ranges. In this file, there is little to adjust in the Camera Raw dialog box and you can rely on Photoshop to tweak the image.

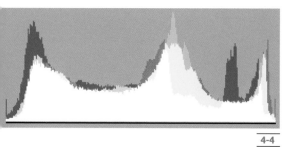

4-4

X-REF

Although we suggest a few color correction opportunities in this chapter while talking about brightness controls, you'll find more specific information on correcting color in Chapter 5.

ADJUSTING BRIGHTNESS VALUES

The Camera Raw dialog box provides a great deal of control to maximize the captured dynamic range and get image tonalities close to the values you want in the final converted file. Therefore, you should perform your initial tonal corrections first in the Camera Raw dialog box and then use Photoshop to perform your final edits.

In the Camera Raw dialog box, several controls are equal to controls you have in Photoshop.

> **Exposure.** This slider in the Camera Raw dialog box (see Figure 4-5) is the same as the Levels White Point slider in Photoshop (see Figure 4-6). Use this control carefully to avoid highlight clipping. Adding exposure shifts the histogram to the right and remaps tones toward the highlight limit. In Figure 4-7, the Exposure slider is moved to the right and the histogram shows clipping of the highlights on the right evident by the spikes on the right side of the histogram. The image preview equally shows a complete washout of the highlights.

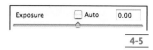

4-5

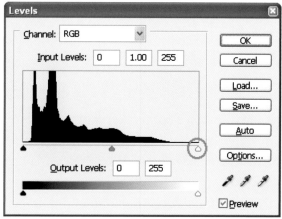

4-6

One certain way to help you avoid clipping when adjusting Exposure or any of the other brightness controls is to press and hold Option/Alt as you move the slider. The image preview dynamically shows you clipping, as shown in Figure 4-8.

> **Shadows.** This slider in the Camera Raw dialog box (see Figure 4-5) is exactly the same as the Black Point slider in the Photoshop Levels dialog box. In Figure 4-9, you see some clipping on the left side of the histogram indicating a lack of a

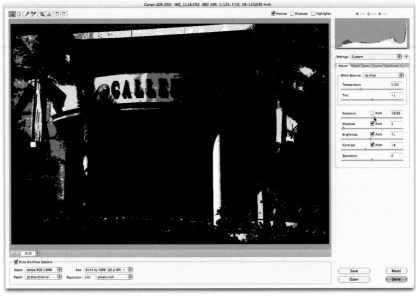

rich black in this image. Moving the Shadows slider remaps the black in the image just like moving the Black Point slider in the Levels dialog box.

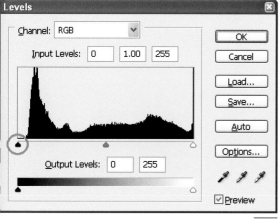

4-9

> **Brightness.** This slider in the Camera Raw dialog box is really the Gamma adjustment you find in the Levels dialog box (see Figure 4-10). Use this slider to remap the midtones.

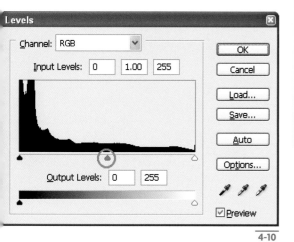

4-10

> **Contrast.** This control applies changes to the tonal curve shape to change relative contrast in the midtones. This control, as well as the Raw Brightness control, is very different from the same controls in Photoshop. In the Camera Raw dialog box, these controls are nonlinear and won't arbitrarily clip the black and white tones unless used to extremes.

You use the Camera Raw dialog box to adjust your settings to capture a full dynamic range where you can see data in the highlights, shadows, and throughout the midtones. Therefore, after capturing the full dynamic range of an image, leave the rest of your color-correction editing to tools in Photoshop. Ideally, use a gray target reference, such as an 18 percent gray chart or the GretagMacbeth chart (see Figure 4-11) in your photos. Using a color or gray chart in an image helps your color correction steps flow more quickly.

PRO TIP

When you shoot scenes, use one photo capturing a gray or color chart as your reference image. Go back and, under the same lighting conditions, eliminate the chart from the scene. At this point you should have two identical images save the chart appearing in one photo. You can then assess the white point on the chart in your test photo and note the white point setting. Open your final image and apply the same setting in the Camera Raw dialog box. If you work with JPEG images, you can open both images in Photoshop and sample the chart in one image while the Levels dialog box is active from the final image.

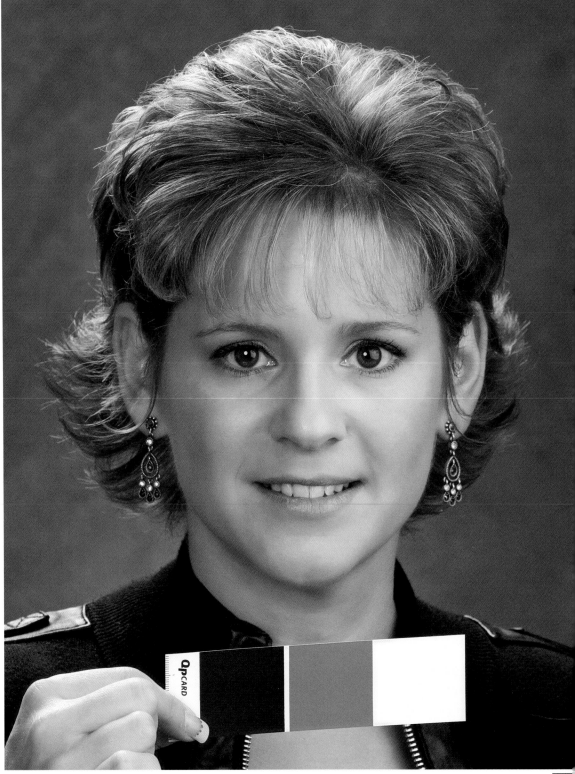

SETTING WHITE AND BLACK POINTS

Figure 4-12 shows an image opened in Photoshop. The image is lit with a large overhead soft box, and white fill cards are used to open the shadows. When the file is opened in the Camera Raw dialog box, the Shadows slider is set to zero and the Exposure slider is set conservatively to insure all highlight data is preserved. These settings result in capturing as much of the dynamic range as possible, yet notice in the photo the absence of a true black and white. Take a look at the black glass background; it looks muddy without a true black. The tennis ball has a white stripe, but it looks more grayish than white.

4-12

In Figure 4-13, on the left side of the histogram the data doesn't touch the black point, which indicates the image lacks a true black. On the right side, the data doesn't touch the white point, which indicates the image doesn't have a true white. The line across the bottom of the right side of the histogram merely shows a little noise in the file. The result of the photo as it opens in Photoshop after making the Camera Raw adjustments is a flat, lifeless photo that lacks snap and good contrast.

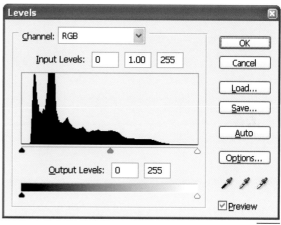

4-13

To add some contrast to the photo, you need to remap the black and white points. If you use Levels exclusively on this photo to set the black and white points, you see an apparent increase in contrast with most deep tones being forced to black. However, we want to avoid the yellow highlights from being devoid of any tonal separations, and we don't want to lose detail in the shadows and highlights. Figure 4-14 shows the result of adjusting levels alone and how the shadow below the tennis ball completely loses detail as well as areas of the white stripe, which are completely devoid of any detail. Pushing the Levels sliders in to remap the histogram prohibits recovery of detail in these areas. The solution is to first use the Levels dialog box to set the white and black points without clipping too much data, then use the Curves dialog box to adjust the tonal range.

4-14

The first adjustment is to change the defaults for the Auto Levels. With the image open, press Command/Ctrl+L to open the Levels dialog box. Click Options and the Auto Color Correction Options dialog box opens. Select the Enhance Monochromatic Contrast option, and change the clipping amounts in the Target Colors & Clipping area to 0.01 (see Figure 4-15). Select the "Save as defaults" check box, and you can use these settings as a default when adjusting levels in all your images that have similar contrast problems.

4-15

An easy way to make a Levels adjustment is to use the Auto Levels option in the Levels dialog box. However, the default amount applied when you click Auto Levels is 0.10 percent. If you click Auto Levels and clip the image at the default amount, you clip too much and destroy data. The default Auto Levels option resets each channel individually, which can really mess up images that lack neutral blacks and white tones.

Click OK in the Auto Color Correction Options dialog box, and the new settings are saved as a default. Photoshop applies the new settings to your image. If you examine the separate RGB channels, you can see the results in Figures 4-16, 4-17, and 4-18.

PRO TIP

You can always add more clipping later; but if you clip too much with your first adjustment, you can't bring the data back.

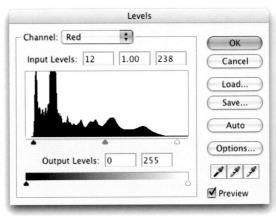

4-16

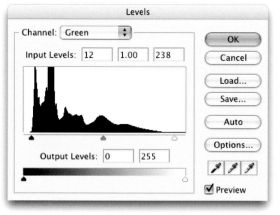

4-17

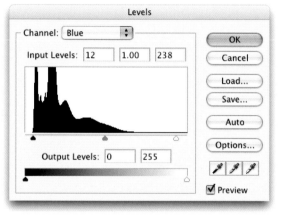

4-18

4-19

At this point, you have an image with improved contrast, but you're not home free quite yet. Further adjustments are needed to show a nice crisp black, a true white, and ensure your tonal range provides a smooth transition of tones to capture detail throughout the image. For these adjustments, perform corrections in the Curves dialog box.

CREATING SMOOTH TONAL CURVES

Experienced Photoshop users typically use the Levels dialog box exclusively to adjust brightness and contrast in images. Although the Levels dialog box is a great tool for remapping the black and white points in photos, it offers three adjustment tools to handle all the 256 levels of gray. When you move one slider, the grays are remapped from either 255 or 0 to the mid-tone position — all gray values between are recalculated by Photoshop.

Notice that each channel receives the same amount of clipping. If you take a look at the composite RGB channel, you don't see too much clipping. The adjustment is slight but you can take care of the rest of the adjustments needed to be applied to this image in the Curves dialog box and be assured now that you haven't clipped too much data. At this point, the image still appears devoid of a true black (see Figure 4-19), but a slight amount of contrast has been added after the black and white points we remapped.

When you use the Curves dialog box, you can adjust any one of the 256 gray tones, which provides much greater control over the tonal range and specifically where you want to remap the values. The Curves dialog box is really another graph that shows you, by default, a linear path from the 255 gray to 0 gray. When you open the dialog box, it appears in reverse to what you see in the Levels dialog box. The white point is in the lower-left corner and the diagonal line progresses up to the black point in the upper-right corner (see Figure 4-20). To keep your dialog boxes consistent, you can switch the black and white points easily in the Curves dialog box. Just click one of the arrows at the middle of the horizontal gradient below the graph and you can reverse the gradient so it progresses from black to white, just like the Levels dialog box.

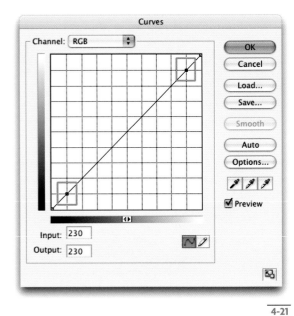

4-20

After making the Levels adjustment in Figure 4-19, increase contrast with smooth tonal transitions. To accomplish that task, you create a basic S curve in the Curves dialog box. Follow these steps:

1. Click the cursor to plot a point on the diagonal line at the first quadrant in the lower-left corner. Click again on the line at the top-right corner to plot a second point (see Figure 4-21).

4-21

2. Move the tone level by dragging the first point plotted in the lower-left corner down 10 tone levels (see Figure 4-22). You can easily accomplish this by pressing Shift and pressing the down arrow once. Without the Shift key depressed, striking the arrow key moves the point one tone level. Alternately, you can also type **15** in the Output level text box.

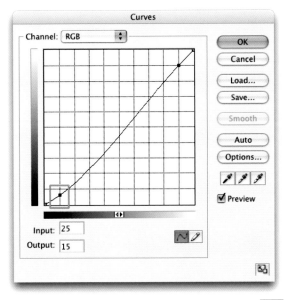

3. Move the top-right tone point up 10 tone levels. Likewise, you can press Shift and press the arrow key once to move the point 10 tone levels (see Figure 4-23). Notice the Output level text box shows 240.

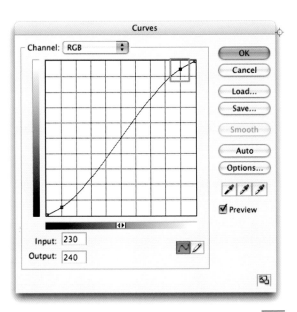

PRO TIP

You can adjust tone points by typing values in the Input and Output text boxes. Lowering the value in the Input level text box moves the tone point to the left, which lightens the image. Conversely, typing higher values moves the tone point right, resulting in a darkened image. Adding lower values in the Output level text box moves the tone point down, darkening the image. Typing higher values in the Output level text box moves the tone point up and lightens the image.

4. Click OK in the Curves dialog box, and the curve adjustments are applied. As you can see in Figure 4-24, the resulting image has increased contrast with smooth tonal transitions and no tonal clipping. The final image has a true black and the highlight areas show good detail.

One problem you find frequently with contrast adjustments: Adding or subtracting contrast also changes saturation of color. You can flatten color or wind up with an obviously oversaturated image. This isn't a problem with Figure 4-24 because it needs a little more pop in the color. The saturation change improves the image, as you can see in the bright yellow tennis ball.

Figure 4-25 is an image that appears properly saturated, but it needs a little decrease in contrast. When making tonal adjustments to this image, we want to lower the contrast without changing saturation. The skin tones appear correct, and we don't want to mess with them.

You can increase or decrease saturation in the Hue/Saturation dialog box. However, it's a bit of a pain to toggle back and forth between the dialog boxes considering we can handle all our tonal adjustments in the Curves dialog box.

4-24

In Figure 4-25, the photo can use a little more fill light, and there's a little too much light on the bottom where you see the reflection off the chessboard edge. Also, just a bit more detail is needed in the highlights on the hand and white cuff. The objective here is to lower the contrast without affecting the saturation.

To change brightness and contrast without changing color, you can convert your RGB image to Lab color and adjust brightness and contrast by applying curves adjustments to only the Lightness channel. You can use this method, but we don't recommend it if you have another viable alternative. One reason that makes

this choice less desirable than others is that you convert color to another color gamut when changing the mode from RGB to Lab. The difference can be very subtle and hardly noticeable in some images, but it can be more apparent in other images. Furthermore, if you change to Lab mode to perform your edits and then change back to RGB, you're spending time going back and forth between color modes to edit the contrast. This can all be avoided by simply using an adjustment layer while you have the image in RGB mode. Here's how:

4-25

1. Assuming you need to adjust only a slight bit of contrast in an image like Figure 4-25, create a new adjustment layer by choosing Layer ⇨ New Adjustment Layer. The New Layer dialog box opens. From the Mode drop-down menu, select Luminosity (see Figure 4-26). Selecting Luminosity applies your curve adjustments to the brightness in the image without changing color just like you would make edits in the Lightness channel in a Lab color image. Click OK and the Curves dialog box opens.

4-26

2. Plot two points — one in the lower-left quadrant and the other in the top-right quadrant. In this image, you need to lower the contrast slightly. To do so, click the lower-left tone plot and press Shift. Press the up-arrow key to move the point up 10 tone levels. Click the top-left point and press Shift, and press the down-arrow key to move the point down 10 tone points as shown in Figure 4-27. The overall effect is that the contrast is reduced because the curve line for the midtones flattens out. White and black are maintained because those anchor points are not moved horizontally during the curve adjustment.

3. If you try to apply the same curves adjustment using the Normal blend mode, the image appears as seen in Figure 4-28. Notice that the image is flat and a bit diluted in color.

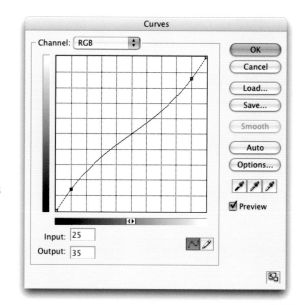

4-27

4-28

Using the adjustment layer and adjusting curves in the Luminosity blend mode, you see a different image (see Figure 4-29) where the contrast is lowered, but the image retains snap and crispness.

When you open the Levels dialog box or you choose Window ⇨ Histogram, you get an idea for the kind of tonal adjustments you need to make. While viewing the histogram only, you make some assumptions about how to approach the Brightness/Contrast adjustments. Take the histogram in Figure 4-30 as an example.

4-29

4-30

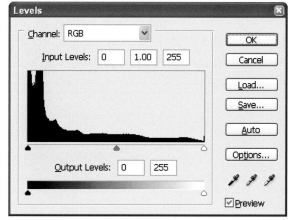

4-32

At first glance, the histogram appears to demonstrate an image with severely clipped highlights. However, when you look at the photo where this histogram is generated, you see a high key image with a lot of near-white tones. The image as it appears in Figure 4-31 requires no brightness adjustments even though the histogram suggests otherwise.

The tennis still-life photo shown in Figure 4-24 is a low-key image. When you open the Levels dialog box on the final edited image (see Figure 4-32), the histogram is skewed left indicating by examination of the histogram that the image is dark. However, when viewing the final photo, you can see the histogram is normal for an image with many black tonal transitions.

4-31

One important lesson when making tonal adjustments is that you cannot rely completely on the Photoshop tools to give an accurate representation for how your final images need to appear before printing. Equally important to assessing an image for tonal balance in histograms is to examine the image itself. Through examination of the image appearing on a calibrated monitor in an appropriately lighted studio and careful assessment of the histograms, you can begin to understand what edits need to be made to your image. Try to develop a road map for what edits you need to make before moving tone points in the Curves dialog box.

THE SIX BASIC CURVE SHAPES

With all the options available to you in handling tonal corrections, it's easy to get confused. Even though you may assess image tonality properly, you might get stuck on what adjustments you need to make. To help simplify a process for tonal corrections, we find that most images fall into one of six categories, and there's a simple solution — or at least a common starting point — for each of the six common image types.

The six basic curve types are as follows:

> **Basic Curve #1: Lighten.** This is a very simple curve used for lightening an image without changing contrast. Create a new adjustment layer (choose Layer ⇨ New Adjustment Layer). Select Curves for the layer and select Luminosity for the blend mode. Click OK and the Curves dialog box opens. Click at the center point on the line and move it up to adjust brightness (see Figure 4-33).

PRO TIP

Be certain your tonal curve appears from black to white as shown in Figure 4-33. If the curve is flip-flopped, you need to move the center point down.

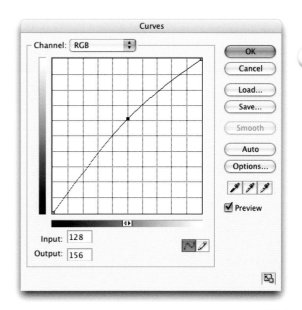

4-33

The amount you move the point determines how much lightness you want to apply to the image. Use the arrow keys to nudge the point up or press Shift+up arrow to move 10 tone points. In Figure 4-34, you can see the results of lightening the tennis image.

4-34

> **Basic Curve #2: Lighten with more contrast.** Use this curve when you need to both lighten an image and add more contrast. To begin with, open the Curves dialog box and plot two points — one point in the lower-left quadrant and one in the upper-right quadrant. Set the lower anchor point first to maintain the deep shadow tones. This point remains fixed, and you don't move it. Setting it as shown in Figure 4-35 usually works best. Move the upper-right point straight up to lighten the image.

4-36

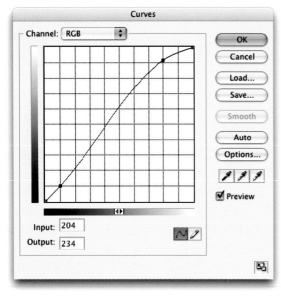

4-35

The image gains contrast while lightening because the shadows are anchored in place and the midtones gain contrast. Notice the graph line is steeper in the midtones. In addition, the image gains some saturation because the mode is Normal. In Figure 4-36, you can see the results of the curve adjustment.

If you create an adjustment layer and apply the same curve settings using the Luminosity blend mode, the image is lightened but the saturation is not affected. Compare Figure 4-37 with Figure 4-36, and you can easily see that Figure 4-37 appears flatter with less contrast and saturation.

4-37

4-38

> **Basic Curve #3: Lighten with less contrast.** This curve is just the opposite of the previous curve adjustment. The highlight values are anchored in place, and tone lightening occurs most in the shadow part of the curve. The midtone slope is less, so contrast decreases.

Like the previous curve, plot two anchor points in the same positions. This time keep the top-right point fixed and move the lower-left point up to lighten the image. The curves adjustment appears in Figure 4-38.

Although not appropriate for the tennis shot, we use the effects of this curve on the tennis image to provide a comparison you can see in Figure 4-39. Notice that this adjustment lowers the saturation.

4-39

To preserve the saturation, use an adjustment layer and apply the same curves adjustment to the same image using the Luminosity blend mode. The results are shown in Figure 4-40. Keep in mind that the mode change to Luminosity is very apparent with contrast decreasing curves.

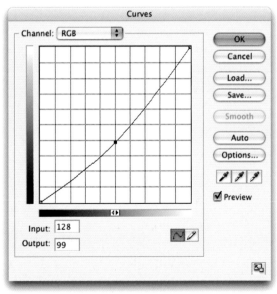

4-41

4-40

> **Basic Curve #4: Darken.** This is the opposite of the Lighten curve setting. Click the center of the tone curve to plot a point, and move the point in the opposite direction (down) as shown in Figure 4-41.

As you can see in Figure 4-42, the image is obviously darkened. Although this is not the right adjustment for this image, you can clearly see what happens when you move the midpoint down to darken the photo.

4-42

> **Basic Curve #5: Darken with more contrast.** This can also be referred to as the drama curve. This curve is one you'll use frequently — it really puts the punch in an appropriate image. The adjustment darkens the shadow tones and ramps up midtone contrast while maintaining the light highlight values. Shadow tones lose saturation unless the luminosity mode is used. Saturation loss in shadows can be a plus with some types of images.

Start by plotting two points in the same position as the other curve settings. The black point in the lower-left corner is moved horizontally to the right to darken the image (Figure 4-43).

4-44

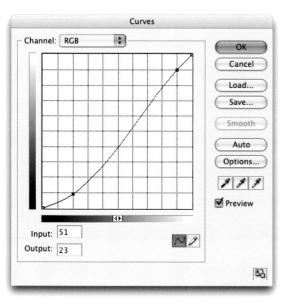

4-43

This adjustment adds a lot more punch to the image as you can see in Figure 4-44. If you use an adjustment layer and apply the same settings to the Luminosity blend mode, the image doesn't quite snap to the same saturation level (see Figure 4-45).

4-45

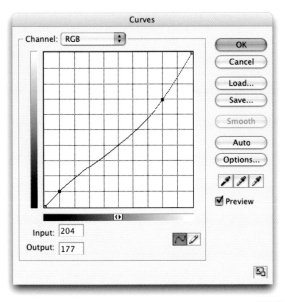

4-46

As with the other curve adjustments, first plot the same two points. The lower-left point remains fixed. Move the top-right point straight down to darken the image. The tone curve moves down, as you can see in Figure 4-46.

The results of the curve adjustment are shown in Figure 4-47, where you see an overall darkening effect and the saturation is lowered. This image obviously lacks some punch and appears flat.

> **Basic Curve #6: Darken with less contrast.** This curve can be a big help when trying to maintain shadow detail while darkening. It requires less use of other shadow recovery methods later, such as the Shadow Highlight filter. It is also useful if an image needs darkening when it is too contrasty to begin with. A little levels tweak in the shadows is useful sometimes after using this curve to insure the appearance of a few full-black pixels.

4-47

If you create an adjustment layer and set the blend mode to Luminosity, applying the same curve adjustment keeps the saturation preserved while darkening the image (see Figure 4-48).

4-48

These six basic curve adjustments are not set in stone but are a good starting place. Fiddle around with both set point adjustments to really fine-tune the results. Don't try to duplicate the point settings exactly, but try to keep in mind what direction you need to move a point to produce a result. Like all tonal corrections, you need to look carefully at an image, study it, and know exactly what you want to do. Ask yourself, "Do I need to lighten and increase contrast or just lighten the image?" Questions like this help you develop a plan for the direction you want to go. Once you're clear about what to do, it's a matter of fiddling around with the tone points to apply more or less adjustment.

TONAL CORRECTIONS WITH JPEG IMAGES

Many of the steps you take in correcting Camera Raw images are equally applied to JPEG images. However, your starting point when correcting image contrast with JPEG images requires one initial step. Rather than begin editing the default 8-bit image, you need to first push it up to 16-bit.

The examples discussed thus far in this chapter start out as Camera Raw files opened in 16-bit image mode. When you change the brightness and contrast settings on a high-bit image, the edits are much more forgiving than when editing 8-bit images. A slight adjustment on an 8-bit image can destroy some precious data and put some obvious holes in your tone curve. The holes, so to speak, appear as gaps in the histogram. Look at Figure 4-49, and you see gaps in the tone curve. Each of those white spaces in the graph represents grays that are missing along the tonal range.

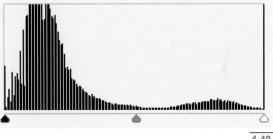

4-49

What happens ultimately is that Photoshop uses the same pixel values as neighboring pixels to fill in the gaps. The result is an image that appears posterized. The more gaps and the wider those gaps appear in the histogram, the more obviously you can see the posterization on some printing devices.

Figure 4-49 is a histogram from an image where a slight bit of adjustment was made to remap the white point. Compare that histogram with Figure 4-50. In Figure 4-50, the Levels sliders in a 16-bit photo are moved significantly more to remap both the black and the white in the image. Upon returning to the Levels dialog box after the adjustment, the new tonal curve shows no gaps at any of the gray levels. As a matter of practice, you find 16-bit images much more forgiving when making tonal adjustments. Because there are so many more grays in a 16-bit image, tossing quite a few away doesn't affect the tonal range the same way as you find when working with 8-bit images where only 256 grays are present.

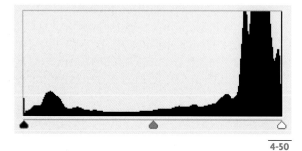

4-50

When you begin with 8-bit JPEG images, you'll want to convert the images to 16-bit to make your brightness/contrast adjustments. To convert an 8-bit file to 16-bit, follow these steps:

1. Open a JPEG image in Photoshop, and choose Image Mode ⇨ 16 Bits/Channel.

2. Choose Image ⇨ Image Size to open the Image Size dialog box. In the Document Size area of the Image Size dialog box, open the Width drop-down menu and select Percent. Type **71** in the Width text box to reduce the file size 71 percent as shown in Figure 4-51. Select the Resample Image check box and select Bicubic for the resample method.

PRO TIP

Changing your image from 8-bit to 16-bit mode alone won't give you the data you need to edit your file in 16 Bits/Channel mode. If you apply tonal corrections after converting the mode you end up with the same tonal curve as when you edit an 8-bit image. At this point you need to resample the entire image to remap the pixels to produce an authentic 16-bit image. By downsampling a file 71 percent, you are reducing the pixels by 50 percent (100 x 100 pixels = 10,000; 71 x 71 pixels = 5041 — almost precisely one half the number of pixels).

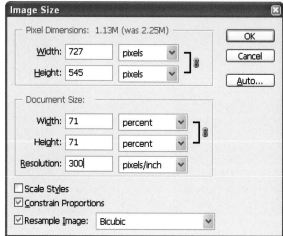

4-51

3. Click OK in the Image Size dialog box and the file is resampled providing you with a 16-bit image with more gray levels than working with a standard 8-bit image. The tonal adjustments you make now are applied the same as with 16-bit images. In Figure 4-52 you can see an 8-bit image edited using the Levels and Curves dialog boxes — notice the visible banding due to gaps produced in the tone curve when the brightness/contrast adjustments were made. In Figure 4-53, the image is converted to 16-bit and resampled; it was edited using Levels and Curves. In comparing the two images, the result is much better using the 16-bit image.

4-52

4-53

ADJUSTING SHADOW/HIGHLIGHTS

Photoshop CS introduced the Shadow/Highlight command to provide photographers with a quick adjustment for bringing out detail in shadows and highlights. When you open the Shadow/Highlight dialog box by choosing Image ⇨ Adjustments ⇨ Shadow/Highlight, you find a number of options that enable you to make tonal adjustments to specific areas of an image such as the shadows, highlights, color correction, and midtone contrast.

At first glance, the Shadow/Highlight command appears to be just the solution for correcting exposure problems. The command looks at your image and determines what areas are contained in shadows and what areas of the image are in the highlights. You then adjust sliders in the Shadow/Highlight dialog box to tweak your image by applying more or less brightness for lightening and darkening the image.

The Shadow/Highlight command works well as a quick, easy method for adjusting shadows and highlights in photos. However, if you are skilled at using other tonal adjustment tools in Photoshop, you can equally and often make better corrections without the Shadow/Highlight dialog box. As you peruse this section of the chapter, be aware that other tonal correction methods, such as using the Curves dialog box, are a better choice.

For an example of an image that needs Shadow/Highlight adjustment, look at Figure 4-54.

PRO TIP

You can use the Shadow/Highlight command with 16-bit images. Be sure to keep all your Camera Raw images in 16-bit mode while making your tonal adjustments and brightness settings before reducing the file to 8-bit mode.

4-54

In Figure 4-55, brightness adjustments are made using the Shadow/Highlight dialog box. The Shadow/Highlight settings produce the following flaws compared to using a Curves adjustment:

> The far right-hand wall by the window has a strange masking artifact on the highlighted portion of the wall. It looks similar to a bad burn-in job from an old-fashioned darkroom print.

> The left-side window reflection on the floor has the same burned-in effect.

> The photo is heavily oversaturated in the dark blue tones throughout the image.

> The highlight correction on the vertical window columns looks flat with no brilliance.

Brightness adjustments are made in Figure 4-56 using Curves.

The first curve we use is a modified contrast-reduction curve with a hard bend near the white point anchor, which brings in as much near-white highlight contrast as possible. Anchor points are set to keep the curve under control near the highlight point. A steep upslope on the low quartertones is used to open the shadows.

The second Curve layer is used to open the shadows. More anchor points are used to fine-tune the amount of lighting in the midtones — just a little is added. The highlight tones are anchored in place. As you can see in Figure 4-56, we do a bit better on tonal corrections in the Curves dialog box.

4-55

4-56

Shadow/Highlight has its place, however, when you're not preparing images for high-end production work. Where this particular Photoshop feature is helpful is when editing a variety of images needing shadows and highlights adjustments that you need to turn around quickly. If your photos are destined for screen viewing or Web hosting, this Photoshop feature can save you a lot of time particularly when you have many different images that cannot be automated using the same settings.

To use the Shadow/Highlight dialog box, choose Image ⇨ Adjustments ⇨ Shadow/Highlights. The Shadow/Highlight dialog box shown in Figure 4-57 opens. The first two areas in the dialog box contain the same adjustment sliders for making brightness adjustments, first in shadows, and second in the highlights. Below the Highlight adjustment sliders are sliders for Color Correction and Midtone Contrast.

Shadow/Highlight ✕

Shadows
Amount: `50` %
Tonal Width: `50` %
Radius: `45` px

Highlights
Amount: `0` %
Tonal Width: `50` %
Radius: `30` px

Adjustments
Color Correction: `+20`
Midtone Contrast: `0`
Black Clip: `0.01` % White Clip: `0.01` %

Reset Defaults
☑ Show More Options

[OK] [Cancel] [Load...] [Save...] ☑ Preview

4-57

The sliders work like this:

> **Amount.** As the name suggests, this slider is used to specify the degree to which the shadows (or highlights) are lightened (or darkened). Pushing the slider to the far right results in the most change in an image. As is the case when using the Levels and Curves dialog boxes, be careful not to push the sliders to extremes. Doing so results in image posterization. The default Shadows slider is placed at 50 percent, which is a good starting point when you first open the dialog box. From this point, move the slider left to lighten the shadows and to the right to darken them.

For the Highlights Amount slider the default is 0 percent. As you move the slider to the right, you lighten the shadows, which results in more detail in the darker areas of the image. Just like the Shadows slider, be careful to not push the slider too far to the right. Fortunately, when the Preview check box is enabled, you can dynamically view the results of your adjustments. If you see some image posterization begin to appear, be certain to back off the adjustment. In Figure 4-58, the sliders are moved to extremes resulting in an absence of smooth tonal transitions.

> **Tonal Width.** This adjustment handles the range of pixels in the shadows represented by lighter pixels and the shadows represented by darker pixels. Think of the radius adjusting the gray levels in these areas that are going to be affected by the Amount adjustment. As you move the Highlights slider toward the right, the range of pixels that is ultimately darkened increases. Conversely, moving the Shadows slider toward the left means more pixels are identified for lightening the image.

The default for both the Shadows and Highlights Tonal Width sliders is 50 percent. If you find the amount of lightening an image to be too much, decrease the Shadows Tonal Width slider.

> **Radius.** This adjustment assesses neighboring pixels to the pixels being adjusted. If any stray pixels are found in neighboring areas, they are grabbed according to the Radius adjustment so the Amount and Tonal Width adjustments are applied to these offending pixels in noncontiguous areas. As you move the slider to the right, more neighboring pixels are included in the evaluation and ultimately are affected by the Shadow/Highlight adjustments.

4-58

The default value for the Radius is 30 pixels for both Shadows and Highlights. Exercise care when moving this slider back and forth. If you increase the Radius, less change is applied to the image. The more you move the slider to the left and decrease the Radius, the more contrast you lose in the image.

> **Color Correction.** Below the Highlights area you find another slider used for making color corrections after you make the shadow highlight

adjustments. This slider pumps up the saturation in your image that may have been lost by making adjustments to the shadows and highlights.

The more you lower the Color Correction amount by moving the slider to the left, the more it desaturates the image. If you push the slider to the far left, the shadow areas appear in grayscale (see Figure 4-59). As with other adjustments in this dialog box, exercise care in moving the color correction slider so as not to over- or undersaturate your image.

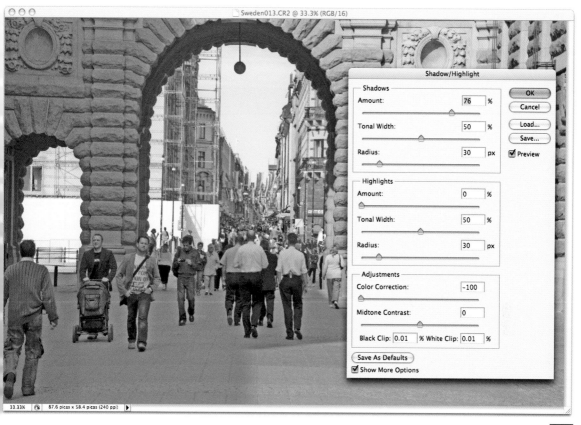

4-59

> **Midtone Contrast.** This slider permits you to adjust contrast in the midtone areas. As you adjust the Shadows/Highlights sliders, the image tends to flatten out and loses some contrast. You can use this slider to pump up the contrast a little. However, you have many more options for adjusting image contrast more precisely after leaving the Shadow/Highlight dialog box and using Levels and Curves.

> **Black Clip/White Clip.** These adjustments are similar to the clipping amounts you find in Auto Levels in the Levels dialog box. You can set the amount of clipping for the white point and the black point by typing values in the text boxes. As a general rule, be sure you set the default to .01 for each text box just like you do when using Auto Levels.

SHARPENING IMAGES

All photos shot with digital cameras require some degree of sharpening. The amount of sharpening needed depends on many factors including your lens, camera sensor, and some variables you want to consider in your workflow.

You can apply some sharpening in the Camera Raw dialog box when processing images, but this option is really best left for Photoshop. Whereas the Camera Raw dialog box offers some sharpening adjustments, it really doesn't match the more sophisticated tools you have available in Photoshop. Moreover, you'll want to sharpen your images after making all your brightness and color corrections as the last step before applying any noise to replicate film grain and printing the file.

The task of sharpening by many digital photographers is usually to open the Unsharp Mask filter, throw in some numbers in the Unsharp Mask dialog box, take a look at the results on screen, and when it looks good, click OK. Although part of these steps is what you do when sharpening images, a little more thought needs to be devoted to the process. As a workflow standard you should consider:

> **Input.** Consider the type of film (when using scanned images), ISO speed, type of digital camera, camera lens, and also your subject matter. Landscapes and aerials, for example, might have more sharpening applied to the images than portraits.

> **Sharpening techniques.** Consider what tool you might use to sharpen your images. You can use one of Photoshop's filters and select one of the methods discussed here to apply sharpening, or you can use a third-party plug-in such as Pixelgenius Photokit Sharpener (www.pixel genius.com).

> **Output.** Consider the type of output you intend to use. If outputting to film or plates for prepress and printing, your sharpening amounts vary with slightly more sharpening than when outputting to inkjet printers. Preparing files for the Web requires different sharpening amounts than files prepared for any kind of print.

There is no magic number that can be applied to all images and some experimentation is required on your part to come up with the formulas that work best for your camera, methods, and output sources. What we can hope for at best is to provide a starting point and from there, you need to test your own files and generate your own output. Observe the results and take some notes on what works best.

The one thing you always want to be concerned about is oversharpening. Too much sharpening is visibly noticeable in your output. In Figure 4-60, you can see the obvious results on contrasting edge pixels where too much sharpening is applied.

In Figure 4-61, you can see the original image opened in Photoshop without sharpening on the left and after sharpening on the right.

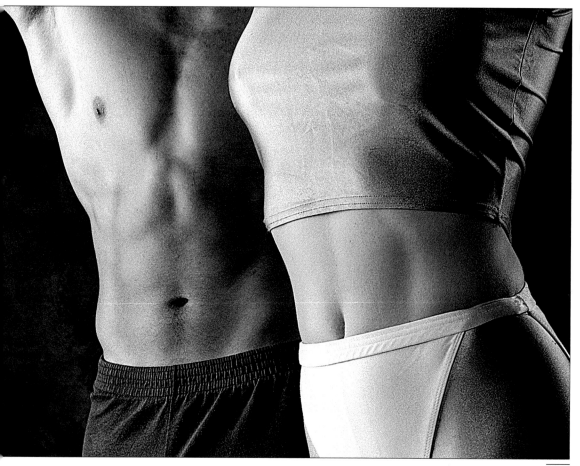

4-60

4-61

USING THE UNSHARP MASK FILTER

The most common method of sharpening is using the Unsharp Mask filter (Filter ⇨ Sharpen ⇨ Unsharp Mask). The other sharpen filters appear in the Filter ⇨ Sharpen submenu. The Sharpen and Sharpen More filters apply sharpening by increasing contrast on the selected area in the photo. The Sharpen Edges filter applies sharpening only to the edges. The Unsharp Mask filter sharpens only edges or the selected area in the image according to attributes you assign in the Unsharp Mask dialog box.

When you select Filter ⇨ Sharpen ⇨ Unsharp Mask the Unsharp Mask dialog box opens (see Figure 4-62). You have three sliders to control the amount of sharpening:

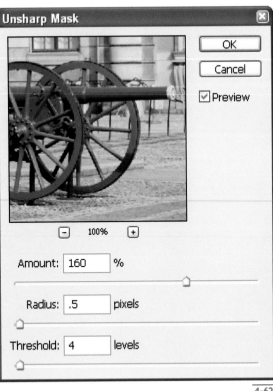

4-62

> **Amount.** This slider applies the strength of the sharpening to the image. The farther right you move the slider (or the higher the number in the text box), the more sharpening you add to the image. This item is one of the most confusing for digital photographers. Just how much do you push the Amount slider to the right is ambiguous for any kind of photo. Most people move the slider while the Preview check box is selected and observe the results on-screen. But what you need is a target to begin with, and from that point adjust the slider left or right to apply less or more sharpening while considering the variables for your original photo, the content, and the output.

As a general rule, start with a calculated formula. Take the resolution of your image and divide it by 1.5. For example, a 300 ppi image requires an Amount of 200 ppi (300 ÷ 1.5 = 200). A Web graphic at 72 ppi requires an Amount of 48.

The calculated value is not necessarily the final amount you want to apply. Your output might be prepress and commercial printing, and for sharpening these images you might add between 20 and 40 percent to the Amount. For composite color output, you might take the calculated Amount and decrease it 40 to 80 percent. This is where your testing comes in. You need to run some tests for certain output sources and see what final formula best suits your particular device.

Image content is also a consideration. You may need to consider not only the amount of sharpening to apply to your image, but also what area in the image needs to be sharpened. In this case, you might need to create a selection mask and sharpen only part of the image. For example, a narrow depth of field where the background is diffused might best be left as shot with your camera while the foreground subject needs some sharpening. In Figure 4-63, the foreground subject is sharpened while leaving the background unedited from the original shot.

ISO speed is also a consideration. The higher you push the ISO value, the more noise you introduce in the image. Noise always presents a problem when sharpening images. The sharpening accentuates the noise problem and becomes counterproductive. You need to find the fine line between adding some sharpening without creating a greater visual problem by exaggerating noise in the image. In Figure 4-64, you can see an image shot at a high ISO speed where no sharpening is applied. In Figure 4-65, you can see the results of sharpening the image and the problem the noise creates in the final result.

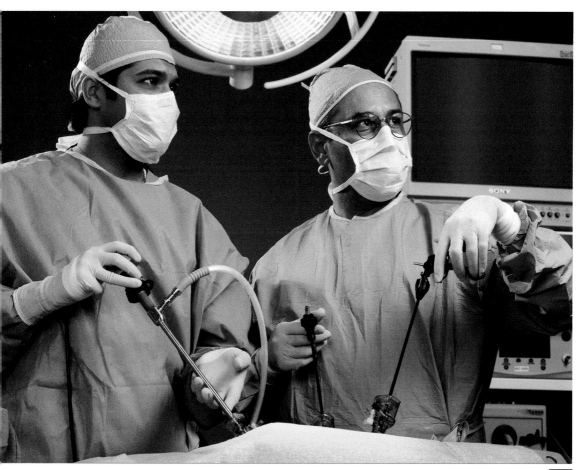

4-63

4-64

4-65

> **Radius.** This slider is used to determine the width of the sharpened edges. Moving the slider too much can cause halos at the light and dark edges. You've seen photos no doubt where the edge contrast is obvious and appears with these halo effects. In Figure 4-66, the Radius slider is pushed too much and the halos at the contrast edges are quite visible.

Calculating Radius is easy. Just take the image resolution and divide it by 200. The 200 value is a constant and applies to all Radius settings regardless of your output. For a 300 ppi image, the Radius is 1.5 (300 ÷ 200 = 1.5). For a Web graphic, the radius is .3 or .4 (72 ppi ÷ 200 = .36).

> **Threshold.** This setting evaluates the tonal values of neighboring pixels. If you use a Threshold setting of 4, then the pixels that have a difference in tonal values of 4 are ignored for the sharpening effect. As you move the slider to the right toward the 255 maximum, more pixels are ignored. If you set the Threshold to the maximum it actually produces no sharpening regardless of what settings you use for Amount and Radius because all pixels are ignored.

4-66

As a general rule setting the Threshold to a value of 4 is good for many image scenes. When preparing images for the Web, use a higher value of 5 or 6. When shooting portraits where you don't want to accentuate wrinkles, blemishes, and skin pores, push the Threshold slider up to about 8. In Figure 4-67, the tonal selection is exaggerated by setting the Threshold to 1 on a portrait image where the sharpening exaggerates lines in the face. Compare the results of setting the Threshold to 8 in Figure 4-68, and it gives you an idea for what the Threshold setting does when sharpening images. In this example, the lower sharpening amount keeps lines and facial pores less visible.

4-67

4-68

SMART SHARPENING

The magic of the Unsharp Mask filter is helpful for some of the images you shoot with your digital camera. However, there are many photos that can benefit from another method that more closely simulates the original unsharp masking technique used by traditional analog plate makers before the digital revolution.

When working with black-and-white photography and photocopying and restoration, you may find the film grain accentuated and becomes a problem when using the Unsharp Mask filter. Radical changes in image tones can be problematic, and another method for sharpening is something you may want to consider.

X-REF

For more information on black-and-white photography, see Chapter 9. For more information on photocopying and restoration, see Chapter 8.

For example, look at Figure 4-69. The original image on the left appears soft and in need of sharpening. You may have a number of photos you want to restore that present similar problems. The image on the right is the result after applying the Unsharp Mask filter where the film grain becomes quite noticeable.

To help reduce the film gain appearance, use an edge-sharpening method that applies the Unsharp Mask to a mask created from the edge pixels. Accentuating just the edge pixels produces a sharpening effect without disturbing any of the remaining tones in the image.

PRO TIP

All the steps in this method can be used with 16-bit images.

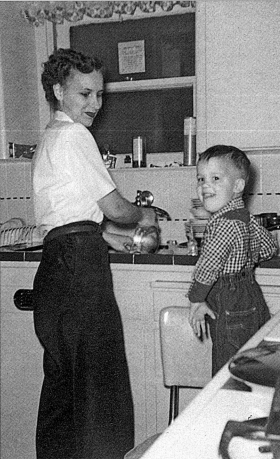

4-69

4

Tone and Brightness Corrections

1. Duplicate a channel to create a working channel. If you use a grayscale image, you have a single channel. Duplicate the Black channel by dragging the channel to the Create new channel icon in the Channels palette (see Figure 4-70). If you have an RGB image, choose Image ➪ Mode ➪ Lab Color to convert the RGB color to Lab color. After converting to Lab color, select the Channels palette and drag the Lightness channel to the Create new channel icon in the Channels palette.

4-70

2. Use the Find Edges filter. Choose Filter ⇨ Stylize ⇨ Find Edges. This filter examines all the contrast edges and creates an outline where edge contrast is detected (see Figure 4-71).

3. Invert the image. Choose Image ⇨ Adjustments ⇨ Invert or press Command/Ctrl+I to invert the image from a positive to a negative. Make sure that you have the duplicated channel selected and invert only that channel.

4-71

4. Select the Maximum filter. The edges are defined in the image at narrow widths; the next step is to widen the edge pixels. This is easily accomplished by choosing Filter ⇨ Other ⇨ Maximum. When the Maximum dialog box opens (see Figure 4-72) adjust the Radius to a value between 2 and 5. A lot depends on your image and the amount of sharpening you want to apply. Start out with a value of 3 or 4 and test the results. You can oversharpen the image if you use too much Radius here and in the remaining steps. If the final result looks oversharpened, you can use the History palette and go back to this step and apply a lesser amount for the Radius as well as the following steps.

5. Select the Median filter. The Median filter reduces noise in the image by blending the brightness of pixels. Some pixels are discarded that differ too much from adjacent pixels. The center pixel is replaced with a median brightness value creating a bit more smooth tones on the edges.

Choose Filter ⇨ Noise ⇨ Median. For the Radius amount, use the same value as when you used the Maximum filter in step 4.

4-72

6. Blur the image. The two filters thus applied to the image create more harsh tonal transitions that need to be smoothed out. For this step choose Filter ⇨ Blur ⇨ Gaussian Blur. Use the same Radius as used with the other two filters in steps 4 and 5.

7. Create a selection outline. Click the Black channel if working on a grayscale image or the composite channel if working on a Lab image. To create a selection from the working channel, Command/Ctrl-click on the working channel in the Channels palette and a selection appears as shown in Figure 4-73.

4-73

8. Sharpen the selection mask. Now is the time to sharpen the image, but only the selected area is sharpened when you apply the Unsharp Mask filter. Choose Filter ➪ Sharpen ➪ Unsharp Mask. For the Amount, move the slider or type in the text box an exaggerated amount of sharpening. In some cases the maximum 500 pixels can be used. Somewhere between 300 and 500 is where you want to be. An Amount of 400 is used for this example. Again, test the results and make sure the Amount you use doesn't oversharpen the image. For the Radius, use 2.0; set the Threshold to 0.

9. Delete the working channel. Drag the working channel to the Trash icon in the Channels palette. The final result appears in Figure 4-74 on the right. On the left side of the figure you can see the appearance of film grain when using the Unsharp Mask filter; on the right, by following the previous steps, the image is sharper with less appearance of noise.

4-74

ELIMINATING ARTIFACTS

One of the byproducts of sharpening images is the appearance of *artifacts*. Regardless of the settings you use in the Unsharp Mask filter, artifacts can make your image appear oversharpened. If you reduce the sharpening to eliminate all artifacts, the end result can appear too soft and almost as though you applied no sharpening. The objective is to eliminate artifacts while sharpening the image that ultimately produces a photo that has a more neutral appearance along the contrasting edges.

This following method of eliminating artifacts is described by many Photoshop experts as being one of the best ways to sharpen digital camera photos. You might try some comparisons between using this method and using the Unsharp Mask filter to see what works best for your kind of photography.

1. Duplicate the Background layer. If you have multiple layers, flatten the image. Drag the Background layer to the Create new layer icon in the Layers palette.

2. Add a High Pass filter. Choose Filter ➪ Other ➪ High Pass. In the High Pass filter dialog box (see Figure 4-75) move the slider to bring out the edges in the image. Keep the Preview check box selected so you can see the results of the High Pass filter as you move the Radius slider. Generally, you want to stay within 3 to 6 pixels for the Radius amount. Again, be careful to not oversharpen the image. Although artifacts aren't as apparent using this method, oversharpening can create an artificial and unnatural look to the photo.

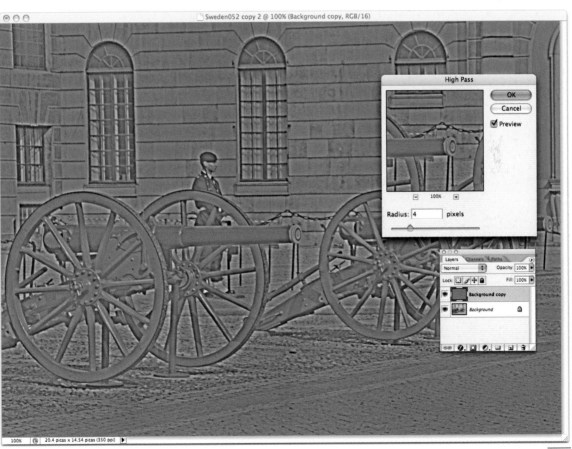

4-75

3. Change the Blend mode. In the Layers palette, select Overlay, Soft Light, or Hard Light to eliminate the gray and return to the tones captured in the original photo. Overlay keeps the contrast about the same as when you first opened the file. Soft Light decreases the contrast slightly and Hard Light shows a noticeable increase in contrast.

4. Adjust Opacity. Using this method makes one great option available that you don't have with other sharpening methods. In the Layers palette, move the Opacity slider to adjust the amount of sharpening. In Figure 4-76, you can see a digital camera image sharpened using the Unsharp Mask filter on the left and using this method on the right.

4-76

Q&A

When I deselect the auto adjustments in the Camera Raw dialog box and open my photos, they appear with less contrast and brightness than if I use the auto settings. Why should I turn these settings off before converting the Camera Raw image?

The Camera Raw dialog box provides you with some settings that you can use to adjust exposure and brightness by remapping pixels in the image. Once those pixels are remapped, your adjustment opportunities are more limited in Photoshop. Photoshop provides you with a similar slider in the Levels dialog box for remapping pixels, but you also have much control over individual gray levels when using the Curves dialog box. In many cases, you find yourself making a minor adjustment in Levels where the real work for adjusting brightness and contrast is handled in the Curves dialog box.

The adjustments you want to make in Camera Raw are to obtain as much tonal range as possible without clipping data. After that, you leave the brightness controls to Photoshop.

Regardless of what you do in the Camera Raw dialog box as far as brightness controls go, you can accomplish the same tasks in Photoshop. One of the more important things to consider is setting the white point in your image in the Camera Raw dialog box. From there, the other controls can successfully be applied in Photoshop.

Keep in mind that if you make a mistake or want to start over, you can always return to the raw image and open it again in the Camera Raw dialog box applying different settings. The best solution is to find the workflow that best suits your photography and use the methods that satisfy you.

Why can't I use Levels for all my brightness and contrast adjustments?

Levels is a good starting point for adjusting brightness and contrast. However, because the Levels dialog box essentially provides you with three control items for adjusting the range of 256 tones, you don't have the discreet options for adjusting individual tonal values along the tone curve. In many cases, you need to edit tone values between the white point and midpoint adjustments, or the black point and midpoint adjustments. You can make these discreet tonal adjustments in the Curves dialog box, which offers you editing options for each individual tone level across the 256 grays in your image.

If I convert an 8-bit image to a 16-bit image, can I leave the image at full size without reducing it?

If you change an 8-bit image to 16-bit and edit Levels and/or Curves, you run into the same problem with destroying data as when the image was originally in 8-bit mode. Resampling the image size down 71 percent is an optimum choice for converting 8-bit to 16-bit without destroying data in your image.

If you find that your original JPEG image requires an image size close to the original size, you can use a lesser amount. At some point the image needs to be resampled to take on the attributes of a 16-bit image. You can resample the image 99 percent (just 1 percent lower than the original size) and your tonal corrections are much better than when adjusting tone curves in 8-bit images.

How do I know when I have applied the right amount of sharpening to an image?

If you prepare images for screen and Web use, you know when the right amount of sharpening is applied to your image by viewing the file on your computer monitor. Unfortunately, images designed for print can't be judged on your computer monitor. You need to see the printed image and carefully view it for any sharp contrasting problems creating by your sharpening method.

With composite color prints that are output to desktop printers, oversized inkjets, and mini-photo labs you can get some test prints and observe the results. When printing CMYK process color on press, you can't completely judge the output from proofs obtained on inkjets. The good news is that if you don't see oversharpening problems on proof prints, you most likely won't see a problem on offset prints. The bad news is that the offset prints may appear a bit softer and could have been sharpened more due to the fact that the CMYK images tolerate a little more sharpening than composite proof prints.

If you prepare files for press, you can always obtain a Match Print or some kind of prepress proof created from film separations. This proof should show you exactly what you can expect on the offset prints.

The most important thing to remember is that using your 72 dpi monitor to proof sharpening for printed output is not a reliable source. You may see some exaggerated sharpening problems, but you may also not see some problems on your monitor that appear on the prints. Running test prints gives you a good idea for how far you can push your sharpening methods.

CATERCISE

Cat Fonda

Feline Fitness

Body Purrfect

"The thing that's important to know is that you never know. You're always sort of feeling your way."
— *Diane Arbus*

Colorcasts can appear in your images as a shift in natural color to another color either globally throughout the image or in isolated areas of an image. If you shoot photos with mixed lighting, such as an indoor shot with artificial light — and if the camera's white balance is not set to compensate for the lighting imbalance — you see a colorcast throughout your photo. For example, standard household incandescent light bulbs produce a yellow/pinkish colorcast in the photo. If you shoot photos in an office building with fluorescent lighting, a cooler white balance is produced resulting in a blue/green light.

These kinds of colorcasts need to be corrected so your subjects don't appear jaundiced or as little green people. Sometimes you can achieve a moderate overall balance for your images and still have a colorcast in some isolated areas of the photo. Skin tones, for example, may need to be corrected while the other foreground/background data may appear within a proper color balance or need a different color correction. In this regard, you need to create selection masks to isolate those areas in a photo and apply correction techniques specific to the areas where you see color problems.

IDENTIFYING COLORCASTS

Color correction is easy. All you have to do is identify the color in excess and remove it. That's a very simple statement. Unfortunately, it's not always so easy to edit. We may be oversimplifying this, but before you can correct a colorcast, you first have to identify the colorcast. You need to first know the excess color that creates your color correction problem, and then you can go about the task of removing it.

Colorcasts are not limited to an overall cast in your photos. You can have some images that look fine in

terms of proper color adjustment in earth tones, sky tones, and other areas, yet other areas such as skin tones can be out of proper color balance. Sometimes, the overall exposure for an image may be properly set to produce a photo with a good exposure, yet because of shadows or uneven lighting, you can find colorcasts in the underexposed or overexposed areas of the image.

When it comes to exposure problems, there are three primary areas you can use to visually assess your images for the appearance of a colorcast:

> **Proper lighting.** Look over your images for proper lighting when the shot was taken. If you adjust white balance in the Camera Raw dialog box and the white balance doesn't take care of the colorcast, you know you need to make some adjustment globally on your photo to correct color. The obvious colorcast problems appear with indoor photos taken in incandescent light and fluorescent light.

> **Underexposures.** Look over your images for not only a photo taken without the proper exposure, but for those images where average metering is used that produces specific areas in the photo that are underexposed. When you view photos with underexposed areas, be certain to carefully view those areas for color problems.

> **Overexposures.** The same visual assessment you use for underexposures should be applied to overexposed images. Be particularly aware of a potential colorcast after you make brightness and contrast adjustments. As you view either underexposures or overexposures after making brightness and contrast adjustments, carefully evaluate the photos for a potential colorcast.

So how do you learn how to identify which color is creating the problem? It all starts with knowing the six basic primary reference colors. Knowing the six primary reference colors is essential when working in

Photoshop, because that's how the Photoshop editing tools are designed to work.

THE BASICS OF PRIMARY COLORS

There's no need for us to engage in offering already overstated color theory here, but you do need to understand how to identify a colorcast in terms of the basic primaries. Red, green, and blue are additive primaries while cyan, magenta, and yellow are sub-tractive primaries. What's essential for you to know is how these colors are mixed to obtain a different color.

Remember your days in kindergarten? Your teacher was probably the first person who demonstrated how to mix colored paints together to make another color. That's the key to color correction — knowing the mix required to obtain a different color. For example, red is equal parts of magenta and yellow; green is equal parts of cyan and yellow; and blue is equal parts of magenta and cyan. This is fairly obvious when you look at the color wheel like the one shown in Figure 5-1 and see where the color boundaries blend together to create the different primaries.

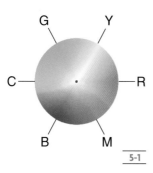
5-1

Notice how these colors really appear on your output or your monitor, and it's important to identify the colors in Photoshop terms and not in Kindergarten terms, or you'll have a heck of a time trying to correct a colorcast. You have to do it the way Photoshop wants to do it.

Look at the wheel again. Most people would call cyan the color blue and blue the color violet. Blame your kindergarten teacher if your interpretation of these colors is as stated here. She showed you that blue and yellow paint make green. It made your painting more fun, but it was actually *cyan* and yellow you mixed to make green. So look carefully and know the difference. In general, the novice eye tends to identify the Photoshop primaries as follows:

> Cyan looks blue

> Blue looks purple

> Yellow looks yellow (an easy one!)

> Green looks yellow green

> Magenta looks deep hot pink

> Red looks red (the other easy one)

PHOTOSHOP'S COLOR-CORRECTION TOOLS

We still get frustrated with Photoshop when working with light greens, because Photoshop insists that the color is more yellow. The point is, you just have to learn to think in Photoshop primaries to make color correction easy. Knowing how the colors mix makes color correction far easier. For example, look at the colorcast in the image in Figure 5-2.

5-2

Your first instinct is to remove green from the image to correct it. However, that doesn't work. Try mixing the paints. It's supposed to be yellow, but looks green, so what color do you mix with yellow to make green? Look at the color wheel again. If you said cyan, that's correct! It's the color in excess! So you have to remove cyan from the image, and the opposite of cyan is red. Therefore, you need to add some red to the image (see Figure 5-3.) There are many ways to do this with Photoshop. Quickly review the basic tools that you can use to correct the cast:

5-3

> **Levels.** Some Photoshop old-timers can do amazing color correction with the Levels command. We don't recommend that, but it can be useful for making a final small color tweak in an image if you happen to be in the Levels dialog box for a final brightness adjustment. The Gamma slider (midtone slider) in the individual color channels works just like placing an anchor point in the center of a Curves color channel. Keep in mind also that the Eyedropper tools' function in Levels is the same as the ones in the Curves dialog box. In fact, a preset in the Curves eyedroppers places the same preset in Levels.

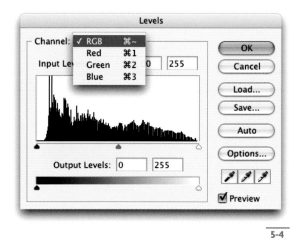

5-4

The Levels dialog box allows you to pick the color channel you want to manipulate. Open the Channel drop-down menu as shown in Figure 5-4 and select the channel to which you want to apply an edit.

After accessing the Red channel Gamma slider and moving it left to Gamma 1.23 (see Figure 5-5), the cyan cast is neutralized and the file is corrected.

> **Color balance.** The Color Balance command (Figure 5-6) gives you more control than Levels, and the sliders are set up with the complementary colors for each primary on opposite sides of the sliders. (Any two complementary colors, when equally mixed, make gray, because they are exact opposites on the color wheel.) The tone balance options allow you to bias the correction to shadows, midtones, or highlights. We don't really recommend this tool, either. The adjustments for different tone levels overlap, making it tricky to use for complex corrections. Furthermore, you can't save correction settings like you can when using Levels and Curves.

If you are a novice, you might find it useful in the beginning to help memorize the primary colors and their compliments; but as you become more skilled, the command is frustrating to use.

5-5

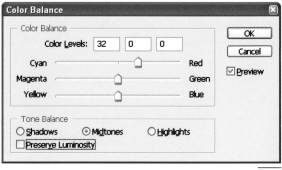

5-6

> **Variations.** This command is a digital imitation of an old-fashioned color ring around from the wet lab days. In the old analog days, a set of proof prints was created in equal correction amounts of the six color primaries to help determine proper color balance of a problem original. The person viewing the ring around clicks on the variation that looks best (see Figure 5-7).

There are two big problems with this tool: It only works with 8-bit files, and it can easily clip color channels when a correction is taken too far. It can be useful for the novice to act as a color-balance guessing guide. If you want to use it that way, open the command, check the corrections that seem best, and then exit the command by clicking Cancel and use a better tool. This old tool is still in Photoshop CS2. Adobe has hung on to this command for the most simplistic edits for the novice user.

> **Curves.** As you might suspect from all the times Curves has been used in previous chapters and throughout the book, it is by far the best tool in Photoshop to use for both tone and color correction. Although it may seem to be the most abstract for color correction, Curves is just an input and output graph, and with just a little bit of use becomes an instinctive and easy tool to use.

Like Levels, Curves has a Channel menu at the top of the dialog box. Clicking the menu gives access to the individual color channels as shown in Figure 5-8.

Using the color channels to add or subtract color is easy. Drag the channel upward to add more of the primary color of the channel. Drag it down to subtract the same color. Because the rose has an excess of cyan the file needs more red — the opposite of cyan. A simple upward drag of the Red channel curve shown in Figure 5-9 balances the file perfectly.

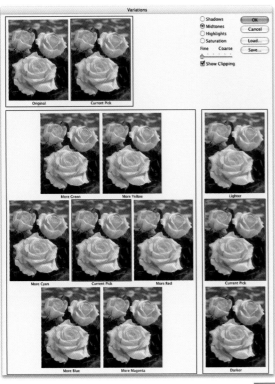

5-7

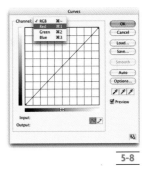

5-8

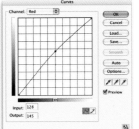

5-9

In many cases, a colorcast can be very simple to identify. An image that contains content that is easy to recognize as a neutral colored object takes on the exact hue of the colorcast. For example, the image of a white rose with a subtle yellow tint (see Figure 5-10) makes it very easy to identify the colorcast. Because the rose has no real hue of its own, it takes on the exact color of the cast. In Figure 5-10, you can see

the various colorcasts compared to the corrected image in the lower-right corner.

When trying to eyeball for true color balance, always look at the neutral or pastel midtones first if the image content contains them. Avoid highly saturated colors to determine overall color balance. Colors with high saturation change little, even with large changes to

Cyan Cast

Red Cast

Green Cast

Magenta Cast

Yellow Cast

Color Corrected Rose

5-10

the overall image color balance. Tones near white or black are very difficult to judge for correct color balance. Notice that the midtone neutral background and the lower shaded rose petals in Figure 5-10 show the colorcast most easily. The bright white highlights and the dark background shadows show very little change.

WHITE BALANCE COLORCASTS

Colorcasts also appear in images where the white balance is not properly adjusted for the lighting conditions. You can have the proper exposure for an image, but if the lighting is out of balance for the film (or camera sensor), a cast appears on your image similar to what you might see if a color filter is placed over the lens during the shot.

In Figure 5-11, you can see an example of an image where the exposure is appropriate for the scene, but the lighting on the scene produces a colorcast. The camera white balance is set for tungsten to match the house lighting, but the ambient light has a much higher color temperature. The capture is far too blue. You make a few Curves adjustments to correct this problem. If you're not sure about exactly where to go to make your adjustments, create a Curves adjustment layer and return to the Curves settings to refine your edits. For this demonstration, you apply the Curves adjustments to the Background layer without creating an adjustment layer just for simplicity. Here's how:

5-11

1. Open the Curves dialog box and select the Blue channel. The excess blue is subtracted by a strong drag downward of the Blue channel curve as shown in Figure 5-12.

2. Open the Red channel in the Curves dialog box by selecting Red from the Channel drop-down menu. The excess cyan in the image is corrected by adding red. Use a smaller upward drag in the Red channel as you can see in Figure 5-13.

Figure 5-14 shows the results of the image after it is corrected for proper color balance in Photoshop. The correction requires subtracting both excess blue and a little excess cyan. In most cases, colorcasts are not completely one primary. Experiment a little to find the right correction mix.

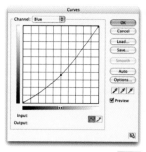

5-12

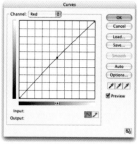

5-13

5-14

UNDEREXPOSURE COLORCASTS

Colorcasts can also appear in underexposed images. The underexposed image in Figure 5-15 has a colorcast. In this example, the image is too dark because of the underexposure, but you also see a color-balance problem.

To correct a problem in such an image, follow these steps:

1. When working with exposure problems, always begin your edits by adjusting for brightness and contrast. Making the brightness and contrast adjustments can solve the colorcast problem or at least get you closer to a proper color balance. If you attempt to adjust images for color correction before adjusting for brightness and contrast, making the latter corrections throws your image off in terms of color balance. It becomes a never-ending battle between brightness/contrast adjustments and color adjustments. In Figure 5-15, start correcting for the colorcast problem after adjusting the brightness and contrast.

5-15

2. The image of the warehouse interior is underexposed because the camera's metering system is set on averaging. The bright lights on the ceiling cause the meter to underexpose the image. The camera's white balance is set to fluorescent, but the mixed mercury-vapor lighting still captures the photo with a greenish cast. In this kind of correction situation, open Curves and lighten the image first by dragging the RGB composite channel downward.

3. With the Curves dialog box still open, make needed color balance adjustments with the individual color curves. We got lucky with this warehouse image. The island office structure in the foreground has neutral paint on the exterior walls. After a curve adjustment to lighten the image, we clicked the gray eyedropper on the bright painted surface (see Figure 5-16) and the image came into color balance.

4. While still in the RGB channel, plot a second anchor point in the shadow area and raise the point to add a bit more shadow detail as shown in Figure 5-17.

5. Click OK. The final correction is shown in Figure 5-18.

X-REF

For more information on adjusting brightness and contrast, see Chapter 4.

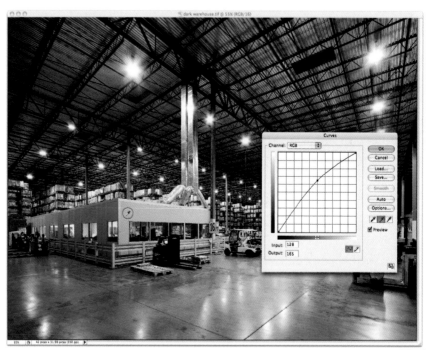

5-16

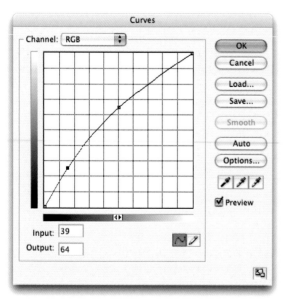

5-17

OVEREXPOSURE COLORCASTS

Overexposures can also produce colorcasts. Overexposures usually result in images that appear with an overall white cast.

Figure 5-19 is just about as bad as a photo can get and still be recoverable. You can see the overall white cast in an image that is overexposed. This file needs more than just a simple curves correction to fix all the problems. The image is captured as a JPEG file, so no adjustments for white balance can be made in the Raw converter. You have to work with the image in Photoshop as you see it shown here. Here's how:

1. Assess the file for where the image data is contained. In Chapter 4, the Levels dialog box is used to look at histograms to analyze data. Another tool you can use to quickly determine where the data falls on the tone curve is to check the Threshold. Choose Image ⇨ Adjustments ⇨ Threshold to open the Threshold dialog box shown in Figure 5-20. The histogram in the Threshold dialog box shows highlight clipping that appears as spikes on the right side, but the main problem is all the tonal compression toward the highlights where you see most of the data falling above the midpoint 128 tone level.

5-18

5-19

The first thing to do with this image is to fix the tonalities, then you can work with the odd color balance. The Multiply command is a bad choice here because it kills off most of the shadow detail. A better choice is to make your tonal adjustments in the Curves dialog box.

2. Open the Create new fill or adjustment layer drop-down menu in the Layers palette and select Curves to create a Curves adjustment layer. You need a special curve shape here. The blown highlights need an extreme contrast boost while you need to maintain all the available shadow detail.

3. Place a shadow anchor point on the lower-left grid intersection to hold the shadow tones in place. Next, place an anchor point at the upper-right grid intersection, and move it to the right with the arrow keys until you see some separation form in the brightest highlight tones. The first Curves adjustment and the document preview are shown in Figure 5-21.

5-20

X-REF

For more information on using Threshold to analyze image data, see Chapter 7.

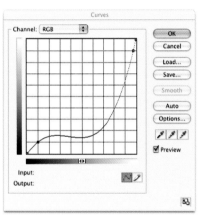

The curve vector seems to have a mind of its own with that first edit move. The next few edits bring the tones into balance.

4. Place a midtone anchor point, and move it down a little from its normal position. Add an additional anchor point to the light quartertone position (see Figure 5-22). As you observe the document window, you should see the image tones coming under control.

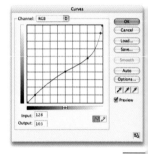

5-22

5. The final Curve adjustment shows where you are going with this tonal edit. A super contrast kick and darkening in the highlights, a moderate darkening of the midtones, and the darkest shadows remain the same with the lowest anchor point. To see how you accomplish this, look at the tone points and how they are positioned on the tone curve shown in Figure 5-23.

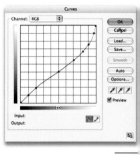

5-23

When making a curve like this to recover an over-exposed original, remember to create a smooth graceful curve and play with the midtone and highlight anchor points to achieve the best tonal balance possible. Don't worry if the image is a little too light or dark overall. You can always add another Curve adjustment layer to fine-tune the result.

Once the image is a more normal tone level, it is easy to see that the file has a colorcast. The building is supposed to be a yellow tan color but it looks green (see Figure 5-24).

6. Cyan plus yellow make green, so the solution is to add some red to the image.

With the Curves dialog box still open, access the Red channel, place an anchor point near the highlight portion of the curve, and raise it a little. (Place the anchor point there because most of the building elevations tones are in the highlight area of the curve.) A second anchor point is placed near the center and moved upward one click to add a bit more red to the midtones as shown in Figure 5-25.

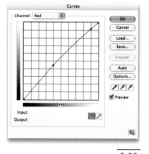

5-25

7. The resulting image has some hue/saturation errors that can't be fixed with Curves (see Figure 5-26). The overexposure also creates a mild color crossover distortion to the image. Notice the shift in sky hue toward primary blue in the darker sky tones.

8. To fix the saturation errors, start with an overall saturation boost of 10 percent to pep up the blue-sky saturation. First, add a new Hue/Saturation adjustment layer by selecting Hue/Saturation in the Create a new fill or adjustment layer drop-down menu in the Layers palette. When the Hue/Saturation dialog box opens, move the Saturation slider to +10 as shown in Figure 5-27. This adjustment is made to the Master channel.

5-24

5-26

5-27

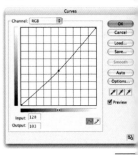

5-29

9. The yellows and greens in this image are oversaturated and the master saturation boost makes it worse. To correct the problem, while still working in the Hue/Saturation dialog box, select Yellows from the Edit drop-down menu to adjust Hue/Saturation in the yellows. While Yellows is selected in the Hue/Saturation dialog box, move the cursor into the document window. The cursor changes to an Eyedropper tool. Click the eyedropper on the building elevation to target the range in the yellows, and then drag the Saturation slider down to -15 percent. Drag the Hue slider toward red (to the left) to -5 to further add red to the building elevation, which ultimately corrects the greenish-looking colorcast (see Figure 5-28). The Hue moves also help desaturate the yellows, as shown in Figure 5-29.

10. The image still seems too bright overall, so you can use a second Curves adjustment layer to darken it some more. Create another Curves adjustment layer. In the composite RGB channel, darken the overall image by dragging the midpoint straight down, as shown in Figure 5-30. The overall brightness in the image is corrected, but the sky has a color shift toward magenta in the darker tones. The Hue/Saturation adjustment can't really make such a close distinction in the subtle color balance error to correct it because the hue values are so close together.

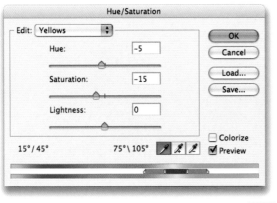

5-28

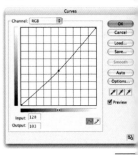

5-30

11. Create a selection for the sky so the correction is isolated and is applied to only the sky area. Choose Select ⇨ Color Range to open the Color Range dialog box to create the selection. Sample colors in the sky by clicking the eyedropper in the far upper-right corner of the sky. With Fuzziness set to 125, obtain a nice tapered selection of the problem color area (see Figure 5-31). Click OK, and the selection appears in the document window.

12. Create a new Curve adjustment layer from the selection to create a layer mask. The dark sky area has a primary bluish cast and needs to match the rest of the sky. Because you need to add more cyan in that area, use the Red channel curve to subtract red, which adds more cyan.

In the Curves dialog box, select the Red channel and drag the midpoint down about the same distance as when you made your composite channel adjustment in Figure 5-30.

13. The dark sky tones now match the lighter sky tones, but the entire sky is still a little too primary blue overall. For a final little color tweak, use a second Hue/Saturation layer.

Select Create new fill or adjustment layer in the Layers palette and chose Hue/Saturation. From the Edit drop-down menu, select Blues and then click the Eyedropper on the center of the sky. The dialog box renames the color Cyans 2 because it falls between the default primaries. A small move of the Hue slider toward cyan (-4) fixes the color-cast nicely. Add just a touch of extra saturation (+5) as shown in Figure 5-32.

To achieve the final results in Figure 5-33, use a number of different adjustment layers. In this example, a simple fix isn't possible, and you need to make several corrections using the same adjustment dialog boxes. Of equal importance in knowing what tool to use for your color correction work is to realize that in many cases a single application of one edit may not be possible. You can toss a number of adjustment layers at your image to fine-tune and finesse your color corrections to get the best possible results.

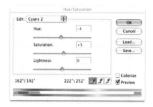

5-32

5-31

5-33

COLOR-CORRECTING SELECTION MASKS

In the previous section, we introduced the Color Range command to isolate a part of an image so you can apply corrections to a selection mask.

You are probably familiar with a number of different tools that you can use to create selections. Throughout this book we are concerned with color and tonal corrections, and we don't have the room to properly address all the methods you have available in Photoshop to create selection masks. However, we want to at least offer one method for creating selections using the Color Range tool so you can understand a little about how to make some quick selections to target different areas of an image that need corrections apart from the entire photo.

In case you haven't mastered the use of the Color Range tool (actually the Color Range command that opens a dialog box as shown in Figure 5-34), it is to your advantage to develop some skill in using Color Range over some of your other preferred choices for creating selections.

Why use the Color Range command? When you create selections using other tools such as the Lasso tool or Pen tool, your selections are surrounding individual pixels. Each pixel can represent several different tones; and if you select a given pixel, you may include some unwanted tones as part of your selection. By using the Color Range command, you can, among other things, select what appears like a graduated selection or for simplicity purposes, a partial pixel selection. This feature provides you with a bit more power when creating accurate selections of target areas you want to isolate to adjust color correction or brightness and contrast.

5-34

CREATING A SELECTION WITH COLOR RANGE

Examine your image and decide what area you want to work with and where you need to make a selection. A good first step is to isolate the offending area with a gross selection using one of the other selection tools. You may have an area that can be easily isolated by using one of the Marquee selection tools, or you may prefer using the Lasso or Pen tool to create your first selection without being precise to select contrasting edges. When you use the Color Range command, the selection you create is confined to the gross selection area in the image while ignoring the nonselected areas.

Without commenting about the color problems in Figure 5-35, start editing by applying corrections to the foreground subject and the background area separately. In order to do this, use the Color Range command here, save the selections you create with the Color Range command, and then in the next section use your channel masks to apply your color corrections.

To help simplify creating a selection with the Color Range command, we'll finesse the color a little on a temporary layer. Our example image contains warm colors in the foreground and cool colors in the background. Before using the color range command, we'll create a duplicate layer and boost the image saturation by +65% in the Hue/Saturation dialog box. This edit makes it much easier to create the foreground selection using the Color Range command.

Follow these steps to create the selections that will be used to correct foreground and background color:

1. First step is to create a Hue/Saturation adjustment layer. In the Hue/Saturation dialog box, push the Master Saturation slider to +65 and push the Master Hue slider to -10 to cool the flesh tone reds a bit and create the greatest possible color separation from foreground to background (see Figure 5-36).

5-35

5-36

As you can see in Figure 5-37, the image looks freakish, but this is only a temporary work layer, so don't worry about what you see in the document window. The huge saturation push creates a big color range difference between foreground and background because the background hues are cool and the foreground is warm.

2. Choose Select ➪ Color Range to open the Color Range dialog box. Move the cursor into the document window (the cursor appears as an Eyedropper) and click in the area you want to select. (Note that you can also click the cursor in the image preview to make your samples with the

5-37

Eyedropper tool). In this example, the face of the foreground subject is clicked. By default, Sampled Colors is selected from the Select drop-down menu. Leave this menu choice at the default for this sample.

3. In this example, the Fuzziness slider is set at 40. This slider behaves similar to the Tolerance setting when using the Magic Wand tool. In Figure 5-38, you see the results of the first sample.

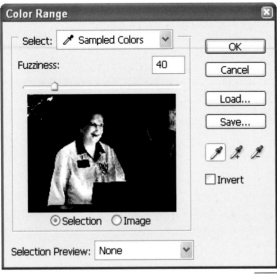

5-38

4. To add to your selection, use one of two methods: Click the eyedropper with the plus symbol in the Color Range dialog box, or press Shift while the default Eyedropper tool is selected. In this example, we pressed Shift and clicked on the red coat (see Figure 5-39).

5. As a final addition to your selection, press Shift and click on the shadow side of the foreground figure's hair. The selection now includes most of the foreground figure nicely isolated and the other foreground subject's face and hair on the right as shown in Figure 5-40. (Note that the selection is the white area in the image preview).

6. Click OK. The active selection appears in the document window. Choose Select ⇨ Save Selection to save your selection in an alpha channel as a channel mask. While in the Save Selection dialog box, name your selection *foreground* so you can easily identify it.

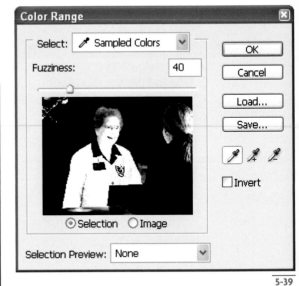

5-39

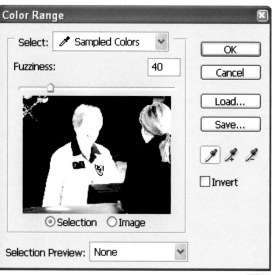

5-40

5-41

7. The selection needs some cleanup. Select the alpha channel and duplicate it by dragging the alpha channel to the Create new channel icon in the Channels palette. Click the name of this channel and edit the name as **foreground painted**. Select the Brush tool and paint white to polish the section for the foreground subjects' faces and black to polish the selection on the background and coat as shown in Figure 5-41.

8. You need another selection for the background to stand alone without including the selection for the name badge, collar on the foreground subject, and other foreground items such as the computer monitor. To add more to the *foreground painted* selection, drag that channel to the Create new channel icon to duplicate it and name this channel **foreground painted again**. It isn't a very descriptive name, but you are going to use only two channels to color-correct your file — *foreground painted* and *foreground painted again*. The *again* file is used as your background.

9. Paint out the foreground areas to isolate the foreground shown in Figure 5-42 for this channel. This background currently appears inversed. You can invert the channel so when you load the selection the selection appears ready to apply your edits. When you move quickly through channel masks, if you forget to invert a channel, you can always choose Select ⇨ Inverse or simply press Command/Ctrl+ Shift +I. We just moved rapidly through the edits and left the channel as you see it in Figure 5-42.

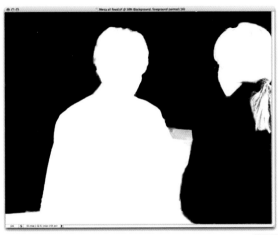

5-42

10. At this point, you can delete any channels not expected for use or leave them alone to finish your edits. Having more channels than you need slows down your computer, but deleting a channel you may later decide you want to use could slow you down more than working with a larger file. We left the original channel in the document just in case you want to return to the original Color Range selection. The file is now ready for you to perform your color corrections.

USING SELECTIVE COLOR

The photo in Figure 5-35 was shot in a hospital lobby area for an in-house marketing magazine. Although we always do our best to create a high-quality capture, this photo has some problems. High traffic flow in the lobby made setting up completely controlled lighting a danger to the hospital clients; and because the woman pictured was actually working, we had to shoot quickly.

The foreground admitting area is lit with halogen incandescent lamps and the background with cool white fluorescent lamps. An umbrella key light was placed just off-camera to the right to light the woman's face with a nice pattern. We used a tungsten light for the key in order to match the color temperature of the foreground lighting. We shot the photo knowing that some heavy Photoshop editing would be required to fix the color problems, but that's how it works out in the real world sometimes.

For the photo in Figure 5-35, use the Curves and Hue/Saturation tools, and we also add some edits using Selective Color to produce the final corrected image.

To combine using correction tools such as Curves, Hue/Saturation, and Selective Color, follow these steps:

1. The file was shot in Camera Raw, so we open the image in the Camera Raw converter where we do our best to adjust the white balance and pump up a little contrast as shown in Figure 5-43.

2. The unedited file is presented to the client art director. We discuss cropping while mentioning that the file is not yet color corrected. The client specifies the crop desired, which you can see in the final image later at the end of this section.

   When we began work on the image, we cropped according to the specifications of the art director, and we added the channel masks we covered in the section "Creating a Selection with Color Range."

3. The colors in this image are a complete mess. The foreground flesh tones are reasonably close, but the background has green and cyan shifts from the ambient lighting, and the poor woman's hair is picking up a green cast from the fluorescent office lighting.

X-REF

For more information on correcting problems with fluorescent lighting, see Chapter 7.

5-43

We begin the edit by setting the black point in the image. We know from shooting the photo that the woman in the foreground is wearing a black coat so the coat is a good place to start. To check for a neutral tone we select the Eyedropper tool and click on the black coat in the photo. From the reading in the Info pallet shown in Figure 5-44, we can see that the coat isn't neutral (equal values in the RGB channels is a neutral tone).

4. The coat is the darkest tone in the image so we open the Levels dialog box without creating an adjustment layer by pressing Command/Ctrl+L with the default background selected in the Layers palette. In the Levels dialog box, we click on the black eyedropper and move around the coat in the document window until we find a neutral color. We find R=8, G=8, B=8, and click on the coat.

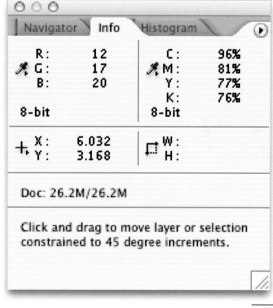

5-44

The info pallet shows the change to a dark neutral gray as shown in Figure 5-45. We don't use the default zero setting of the black eyedropper because we want to maintain a slight bit of tone in the darkest blacks of the image. We can always clip the black later if we want to.

5. Select the white eyedropper, while still in the Levels dialog box, and move around the name tag to check the whites without clicking to set the white point. This shows a slight warm bias in the Info palette. The values R-217, G-215, and B-213 shown in Figure 5-46 translate to a slightly warm white — a little orange to be specific. Leave this setting in place because the mixed lighting is

already creating a slight cyan cast on the left side of the collar. The change isn't really noticeable on screen, but at least the black and white points are as close as we can get. The photo now provides a good starting point to perform color-correction edits.

6. For this kind of problem file, adjustment layers are a safe bet. You might want to tweak your settings as you go, and using adjustment layers provides options for returning to the layers to make changes to your adjustments.

The next step is to again load the *foreground painted* channel mask and create a Curves adjustment layer. While the selection is active, select

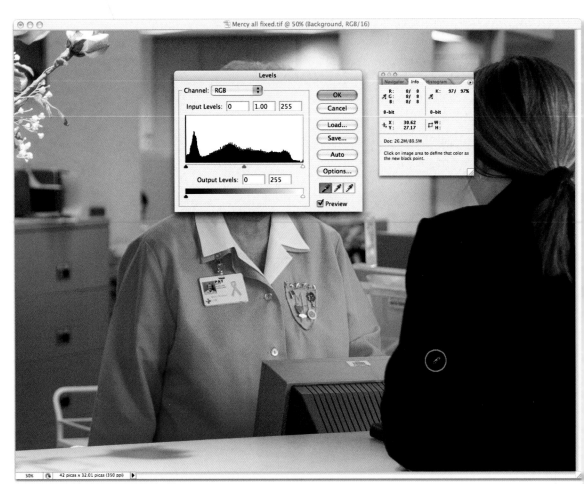

5-45

5-46

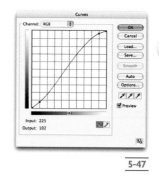

5-47

5-48

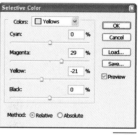

5-49

Create new fill or adjustment layer in the Layers palette and choose Curves from the menu choices. By having the selection active, a layer mask is created where only the selected foreground area is affected by our Curves adjustment.

In the Curves dialog box, a contrast increase curve is created with a bump at the highlights to lighten the foreground and add contrast. The foreground has a lot of lighting mix from the lighting environment. This results in multiple casts on the skin tones that can't be easily fixed with curves. The Curves adjustment is shown in Figure 5-47.

7. Because the skin is a combination of mostly red and yellow tones, you can access those colors using the Selective Color Options dialog box. This edit can get a little tricky. The skin tones show an excess of magenta in the darker tones and too much yellow in the lighter tones. In the Selective Color Options dialog box, magenta is added to the yellows and subtracted from the reds, as shown in Figure 5-48.

Yellow is also reduced by selecting Yellows from the Colors drop-down menu to help reduce overall warmth of the skin a bit more, as shown in Figure 5-49.

Notice that the correction removes the green shift from the top of the hair and renders the lab coat in its natural orange color, as shown in Figure 5-50. The Selective Color channels overlap quite a bit, so you have to play around with the settings to get it just right. Unfortunately, Adobe hasn't upgraded this tool since it was first introduced. However, it still works great if you fiddle with it long enough.

5-50

PRO TIP

The sliders along the spectrum at the bottom of the Hue/Saturation dialog box are moved similar to moving sliders in the Levels dialog box. Moving the sliders expands or compresses the color range selected in the Edit drop down menu.

5-51

8. The next edit is an effort to correct the strange color shift in the hair of the woman facing the camera. You need to select a very narrow range of yellow to make this correction. Again, load the *foreground painted* channel mask and create another Hue/Saturation adjustment layer.

To narrow the yellows, select the Yellow channel and squeeze the color range selector on the bottom of the Hue/Saturation dialog box down to a very narrow range. Click the eyedropper on the very top of the woman's hair to produce the setting shown in Figure 5-51. A small hue move toward red and some desaturation finally fix the strange color shift in her hair.

9. After correcting the subject, you need to work on the background. Load the *foreground painted* channel mask and create another Hue/Saturation adjustment layer. In the Master channel, move the Hue slider down to reduce it 50 percent (-50) to help tone down that awful background color. Yellows is selected and the greenish background hue on the wall in the background is sampled, which reduces the resulting yellow-green saturation an additional 50 percent (-50).

10. For the next edit, reduce the background highlight values and lighten the midtones a little to provide a better mood in the image and make the foreground highlights stand out more. Load the *selection painted again* channel (the third channel mask created in the section "Creating a Selection with Color Range"), inverse the selection, and create a new Curves adjustment layer.

In the Curves dialog box, add a curve adjustment in the composite RGB curve to kill background whites and boost midtones a bit. Notice the lower anchor point to lighten the midtones. The white point anchor is pulled down to kill the white values. The foreground separates much better now. Also add some red and yellow to the background overall color balance by dragging the blue curve down and the red curve up. This is just an eyeball judgment. In Figure 6-52, you can see the composite channel adjustment on the left followed by the Red channel adjustment in the middle and the Blue channel adjustment on the right.

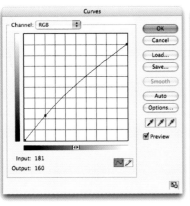
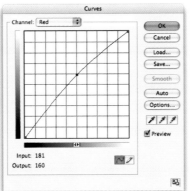
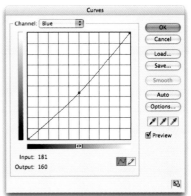

5-52

11. At this point, the background looks too desaturated, so we reduce the opacity of the background Hue/Saturation layer in the Layers palette by 50 percent. This edit seems like the best compromise. Last, add a final overall Curves adjustment layer to tweak a little bit more overall contrast in the image (see Figure 6-55). The final edited image appears in Figure 6-53.

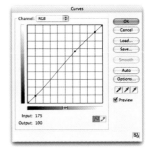

5-53

5-54

THOSE PESKY FLESH TONES

Flesh tones are, without a doubt, the most difficult memory color to work with when editing photos. The development of affordable color technologies in the movie, photography, and print media businesses over the last 50 years has left a visual imprint on society and a visual expectation of what a pleasing flesh tone is supposed to look like.

The popular use of Technicolor movies in the late 1930s left a visual legacy of rich, vibrant skin tones. Pancake makeup became the rage as young women tried their best to achieve the artificially smooth and color consistent faces seen on the silver screen. Humorously, the use of pancake makeup was a necessity under the harsh and intense specular light sources needed to allow color cinematography with the slow films and heavy filtration required for those early Technicolor movies and not intended as a fashion enhancement.

The early Kodachrome and Kodacolor films also delivered color that was over the edge, so to speak. High color saturation meant higher sales volumes, and the look of saturated flesh tones became a kind of cultural norm when viewing color photographs.

As time has passed, color technologies have matured. Modern color reproduction methods can deliver amazing accuracy without the limitations of prior years. Yet countless focus groups and marketing studies have shown that most people prefer a flesh tone in print that is richer in color than flesh tones are in reality.

So what is a perfect flesh tone? The answer is, there's no such thing. But there is a range we can call pleasing flesh tones. Within the range of pleasing, there are some guidelines that define a quality result. First, a skin tone has to fall within a somewhat narrow range of hue. The tonal quality will vary depending on race, sun exposure, and general health. If we are talking specifically in terms of hue, black people and white people (and everyone in between) are almost exactly the same color, they just vary in tone and saturation. Second, saturation is the other parameter that has to fall within a reasonable range for a believable result.

Most of the people images in this book have flesh tones that are richer and a little more saturated than reality, but they look pleasing. (At least we hope you think they do.) As far as the hue goes, that can vary depending on the mood and surrounding colors of the image. It's not always a by-the-numbers issue, but the numbers can be of great help at times. So, look first at editing color by eyeball — or seat of the pants, if you like the term.

Once you complete your tonal edits, you're ready to examine the flesh tones. Keep in mind all the color-balancing tricks to help you along. In many cases, the image contains a known reference color, such as a white shirt, a gray object, or other easily defined neutral target. Try adjusting those known colors first.

Having said all that, here's how to make some nice skin tones:

1. Once you decide to manually adjust flesh tones, the first thing to examine is flesh tone saturation. Oversaturation results in terrible flesh tones, even if the color balance is perfect. In Figure 5-55, you can see normal flesh tones on the left and oversaturated flesh tones on the right.

5-55

A condition appearing even worse than a little oversaturation is a slight red or magenta cast combined with oversaturation, as you see in Figure 5-56.

Look at this wedding snapshot file. The JPEG image in its original form looks like Figure 5-57. The red eye is removed so it doesn't distract from the color-balance issue. Other than that single edit, Figure 5-57 shows the image as it was captured by a point-and-shoot camera. The red cast in this image is common with many point-and-shoot cameras, depending on internal flash for not so well-balanced lighting.

5-56

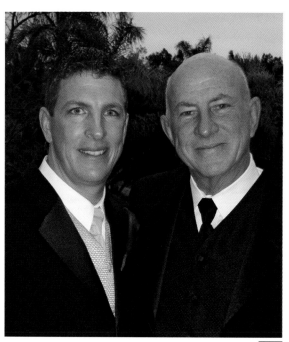

5-57

2. This file has problems — a magenta cast, over-saturation of reds and magentas, and is too dark overall. First, as you do with all color correction, adjust the brightness and contrast. Open the Curves dialog box and lighten the image overall by dragging the RGB channel curve upward. Neutralize the magenta cast by selecting the Green channel with a similar upward pull on the curve. In Figure 5-58, you see the RGB and Green channel curve adjustments.

3. The shadow color cast was really easy to correct because we know the tux coats are pure black. In this file, the darkest tones in the coats should be very near Red-0 Green-0 Blue-0 to obtain neutral black tones. Click the Levels black eyedropper on the bottom left corner of the image to correct the full black tones to neutral values. After the Levels adjustment, the image appears as you see in Figure 5-60.

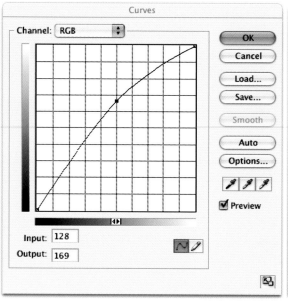

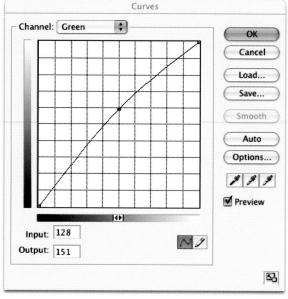

5-58

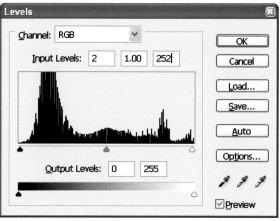

5-59

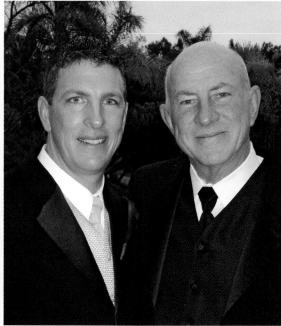

5-60

4. Now comes the hard part. A good overall color balance is obtained in the image, but the evening light mixes with the flash to give the flesh tones an overly cool appearance, and the older fellow's flushed skin is really exaggerated in this lighting. Because the skin is really the only yellow-red colors in the image, correct this problem by using a Hue/Saturation adjustment applied to the overall image.

First, create a narrow range selection of the cool red tones in the man's face on the right. In the Reds edit channel, narrow the Red selection range of the red spectrum by bringing the tolerance sliders closer together, and also narrow the feathering sliders by dragging the Hue slider over to +15, as shown in Figure 5-61.

Once you complete the edits, click the sample eyedropper on the reddest part of the far-right cheek. The slider resets itself slightly to the left of default red.

A large edit move of 15 percent to the yellow trend corrects the red blush on the face, but the skin still looks a little pasty and cool (see Figure 5-62).

5-61

5-62

PRO TIP

To determine the exact range you've selected, drag the Hue slider all the way to one side. In this example, the pixels most affected turn cyan and you can see the cyan color under the slider. This confirms our selection. If the selection is not quite right, try dragging the slider back and forth until you see the exact selection range you want.

Select the yellow Edit channel, leave the sliders in default position, and click the sampler on the left side of the right subject's forehead. The bottom slider jumps left to the warm red position and the yellow channel name changes to *Red 2*. A saturation slider move to add 10 percent more warm red saturation (see Figure 5-63) brings the flesh tones to life (see Figure 5-64).

X-REF

There's more to getting flesh tones color corrected. We cover a section on portraiture in Chapter 6 and introduce a custom flesh tone gradient picker that can help you correct portrait photographs.

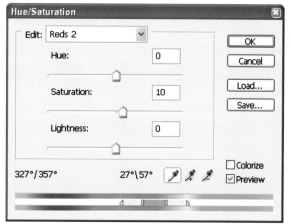

Hue/Saturation

Edit: Reds 2

Hue: 0

Saturation: 10

Lightness: 0

OK
Cancel
Load...
Save...

327°/357°   27°\57°   Colorize
                                     Preview

5-63

5-64

When I create selections I tend to use the Magic Wand tool and with a few clicks I can make accurate selections. Should I abandon this tool in favor of the Color Range command?

In a few words, use the tool that gets the job done the fastest. If you have large areas in a photo that can be selected with a few Magic Wand clicks and you can quickly make a precise selection using the tool, then by all means use the method that works for you.

In many other cases, however, you will find using a single tool not so easy to make the selections you need for adjusting color or making tonal corrections. We offer a little discussion here for performing selections using Color Range for certain files where we want to target areas for corrections. The Color Range dialog box is not a panacea for making all your selections in Photoshop.

Photoshop offers you a number of tools and methods to make selections. The number of options you have are so vast it's impossible to cover all of them in this book. If you want to learn more abut creating selections and masks, look to some well-crafted books written by such leading authors as Deke McClelland, Katrin Eismann, and Scott Kelby to name a few.

When I look at an image and I'm not sure exactly what the colors of the content should be, how do I know if I have a colorcast?

The best way to determine whether you have a colorcast for unknown image content is to check the neutral color in the photo. Colorcasts are prominent in neutral colors. If you don't have an easily identifible color, it's easy to solve this problem. When you shoot any kind of photo, be certain to shoot a gray card, as we explained in Chapters 3 and 4. Taking a shot of a gray card or a GretagMacbeth color chart assures that you know where neutral gray appears in a photo.

Why is using the Curves dialog box the best tool to use for color correction in Photoshop?

The Curves dialog box provides you an easy and intuitive method for adjusting color in individual channels along a tone curve. The same kinds of edits can be made in the Levels dialog box, but you don't have options for adjusting multiple tone points with a single edit. Both Curves and Levels provide you a means for saving your color correction efforts so you can load the same settings to apply to similar images needing the same color corrections. This advantage is one feature you don't have when you use the Color Balance adjustment. Although Variations provides you an option for saving settings, using the Variations tool is risky because you can easily clip data in your image.

Why don't I spend more time using the Match Color options?

Match Color is used in very limited circumstances. Photoshop makes a guess at matching the color from a source image to the target image that may or may not be the proper color adjustment. Unless you shoot images with very similar lighting conditions and image content, Match Color is likely to deliver a poor correction. If the conditions are so similar, you can perform the same steps by making a Curves adjustment, save your settings, then load the saved settings in files having similar image characteristics.

I do a lot of color correction on portraits. Is there an easy way to determine flesh-tone values for correcting color?

Unfortunately, Photoshop doesn't have a good flesh-tone picker that provides you a range of hues common in skin tones. There is an alternative where you can create your own gradient flesh-tone picker that you can use to map the midtone grays to when correcting for colorcasts. Turn to Chapter 6 and check out the section on color correction for portraits. We provide you an easy method to create your own custom gradient flesh-tone picker you can use when correcting color for all kinds of color problems in skin tones.

EDITING STUDIO AND LOCATION SHOTS

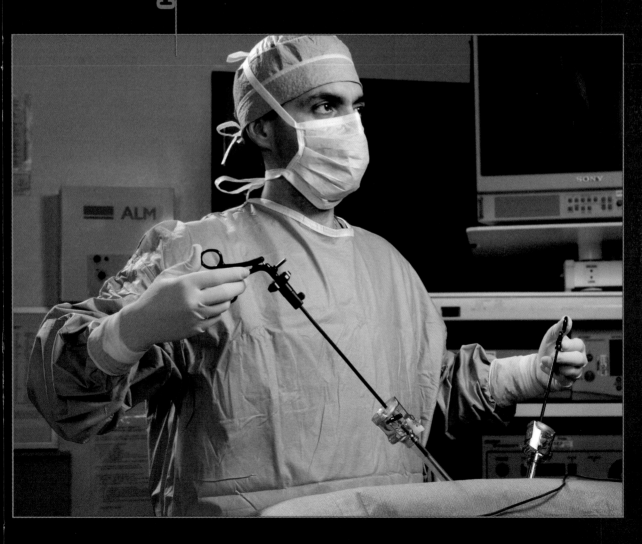

"Once the amateur's naive approach and humble willingness to learn fades away, the creative spirit of good photography dies with it. Every professional should remain always in his heart an amateur."
— Alfred Eisenstaedt

If you're a professional photographer or serious amateur, you probably have a good handle on your lighting and all other aspects of optimizing your conditions before you shoot an image. That is, you exercise the control when you can, and you certainly know the old axiom *garbage in, garbage out* applies well to photography.

Just like when working with film, you still need to spend some darkroom time on your photos to perfect them. Although your darkroom has evolved into a computer monitor, the care you must exercise in producing a quality print remains the same. No matter how much you control the elements, you still need to perform some correction work in Photoshop.

With all the different kinds of photography you can do as a commercial photographer, or even a serious amateur, it stands to reason that different shooting conditions and subject matters require some different treatments. There are many more different specializations than we cover in this chapter, but because our space is limited, we just picked out some conditions for aerial photography, photojournalism, and portraiture to cover a few common problems. You'll find handling problems similar to product photography covered in Chapter 8, other location shooting in Chapters 5 and 7, and architectural photography covered in Chapter 5.

ON LOCATION

We picked out a few areas of specialization in photography and added them here to make some mention of different kinds of edits you may need to perform on your photos and some thoughts on shooting some different kinds of photos. This section is not inclusive, but serves more like an example for how editing images can change from one type of photo to another. The basic formulas for color and tonal corrections apply to almost any kind of photography, but after that you may have additional considerations such as preparing files for different output sources, emphasizing your edits by paying particular attention to one correction or another, or at the least be aware that when you shoot there is some correction you consistently need to make.

AERIAL PHOTOGRAPHY

You may not be an aerial photographer, but some of the problems encountered with atmospheric haze can be experienced with other kinds of photography such as nature, wildlife, and various outdoor scenes. If aerial photography is not something you do, you may find this section helpful when encountering problems similar to what we describe here.

The two biggest problems encountered with aerial photography are image contrast and sharpness. Other problems include atmospheric haze and color balance. An aerial photo can never be too sharp. Aerial photos, by nature of their use, tend to be examined more closely than other types of commercial photography. The client expects good detail in all the tiny objects in the photo!

Image noise used to be a huge problem in the film era. Large format was needed in many situations to eliminate obvious visible film grain. Digital imagery has reduced the noise problem, but you still have to be careful with your editing because big contrast enhancements bring out digital noise.

Consider the following example, which was shot in less-than-ideal conditions. The client needed a land track that was under development photographed for inclusion in a bank financing proposal. The photo needed to illustrate the availability of nearby schools and other recent development in the area. The unedited example in Figure 6-1 is one view of 12 delivered to the client. Because of the tight deadline, the job had to be done on a hazy day. Visibility was rated at 10 miles by the FAA ATC (Air Traffic Control) tower nearby. In this view, the haze is very apparent.

To correct the problems for aerial haze and apply sharpening to this kind of photo, follow the steps below:

1. Open the file in the Raw converter and leave all the auto settings enabled. Set white balance to 5000K (Figure 6-2) for a sunny day, and then begin any other adjustments needed in the tone sliders.

   The auto settings result in a little highlight and shadow clipping. You want the full tonal range for custom editing in Photoshop, so drag the shadow slider to 5, and drag the exposure slider back

to -0.95. The image is a little dark, so drag the brightness slider up to 84 (Figure 6-3).

Click the Detail tab and turn off all sharpening by dragging the Sharpness and Color Noise sliders to zero. Custom sharpen this file in Photoshop. Any Raw converter sharpening at this point will cause haloing problems later.

2. Open the file in Photoshop and open the Levels dialog box to set a clean black point and set a rough neutral color balance for the image. The Raw converter settings are shy of a true black and white, as intended. Long-view aerial photos always tend to have a vertically wedged blue-yellow colorcast with the top of the image blue

6-1

Canon EOS 20D: _MG_0122.CR2 (ISO 400, 1/640, f/11, 24–85@24 mm)

☑ Preview ☑ Shadows ☑ Highlights   R: --- G: --- B: ---

Settings: Custom

Adjust Detail Lens Curve Calibrate

White Balance: As Shot

Temperature   5000
Tint   0

Exposure   ☑ Auto   -0.10
Shadows   ☑ Auto   22
Brightness   ☑ Auto   60
Contrast   ☑ Auto   +50
Saturation   0

☑ Show Workflow Options
Space: Adobe RGB (1998)   Size: 3504 by 2336 (8.2 MP)
Depth: 16 Bits/Channel   Resolution: 240 pixels/inch

Save...   Cancel
Open   Done

6-2

Settings: Image Settings

Adjust Detail Lens Curve Calibrate

White Balance: As Shot

Temperature   5000
Tint   0

Exposure   ☐ Auto   -0.95
Shadows   ☐ Auto   5
Brightness   ☐ Auto   84
Contrast   ☑ Auto   +50
Saturation   0

6-3

and the bottom more yellow. This characteristic is the result of the atmospheric haze. For now, set the color balance for the center and foreground area.

Because aerials almost always tend to have a full color mix, use AutoLevels instead of AutoContrast to set the final white and black point. Use the same Clip amounts of 0.01 described in Chapter 4 for the AutoLevels setting and select the Enhance Per Channel Contrast radio button in the Auto Color Correction Options dialog box that opens after clicking Options in the Levels dialog box. The final black and white points are set very accurately. Because the overall color balance shifts slightly blue, click the gray eyedropper on the asphalt parking lot in the center of the photo.

6

Editing Studio and Location Shots

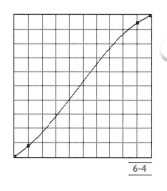

6-4

3. After setting Levels, open the Curves dialog box. Use a basic contrast increase curve to add some more snap to the image as shown in Figure 6-4. Be careful to not overdo the edit at this point.

6-5

X-REF

For more information on creating contrast curves, see Chapter 4.

4. The basic edit is complete, but the haze needs to be corrected as much as possible along with the color wedging in the file. For this correction, a gradated alpha channel and another pass though curves are needed again.

   Start with a duplicate of the Green channel to make it easier to see what you are doing as you make the needed selections. Open the Channels palette and select the Green channel. Drag the channel to the Create a new channel icon to duplicate the channel.

   The hazy portion on the image is the top 25 percent. Create a gradient that is white on the top and goes to full black at about one-fourth of the way down on the alpha channel. This places the first transparency of the mask at the beginning of the objectionable haze. Drag the gradient cursor from the top to about a third of the way down the alpha channel to create a gradient similar to the one shown in Figure 6-5.

5. Load the selection and open the Curves dialog box. Add a modified curve to darken while adding contrast. Place a limiting anchor point near the black point to keep the darkest shadows in the selected area from darkening further to keep a believable look to the edit. At the same time, open the Blue channel in curves and remove the blue wedging from the top of the file by dragging the Blue curve down as shown in Figure 6-6. The haze is corrected about as far as you can go with it, and the overall image tones are much improved.

6. Now, sharpen the image as much as possible. The Anti-alias filter in the camera capture chip makes an unsharpened image appear very soft. You need to sharpen a great deal. The two main limits to sharpening the image to a high level are digital noise and haloing of high-contrast edges. Aerials are exceptions when it comes to sharpening. You get far closer to an oversharpened look than what is normally tolerated with any other type of image.

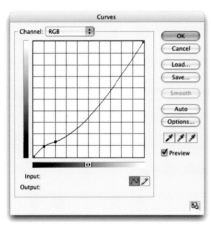
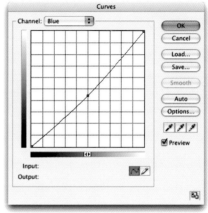

6-6

PRO TIP

Keep in mind also that the 100 percent screen view always looks a little overdone on an aerial. Always consider that the final output will be at least 180 dpi and probably higher than that for press use, so the image must be far smoother looking on output.

For final use as an Epson inkjet output, for example, give the file a final check at 50 percent screen view to get a realistic idea of what the final output will look like. Output to a Fuji Frontier or Noritsu photo printer has similar viewing criteria for aerial photos.

To perform your sharpening edits, start with a modified edge mask. Duplicate the Green channel. Then choose Image ⇨ Adjustments ⇨ Auto Contrast to add a little more contrast to the channel image.

Choose Filter ⇨ Stylize ⇨ Find Edges. Blur the channel using a Gaussian Blur filter set at 1.5 pixels. Choose Image ⇨ Adjustments ⇨ Invert to invert the image. The results of these edits appear in Figure 6-7.

7. Next, visit the Levels dialog box. With the Green channel mask still selected press Command/Ctrl+L to open Levels, and set the white point slider to the start of the histogram hill. This position varies depending on the file being edited. Set the black limit slider to 120, as shown in Figure 6-8, and click OK.

You have created an edge mask that allows 100 percent sharpening on high-contrast edges and 50 percent sharpening on the rest of the image. This minimizes digital noise while maintaining a realistic look to the image after sharpening.

8. You are not yet ready to use the mask. The top area of the image has a huge contrast boost and is now much noisier than the bottom. Also, the top of the image, because of the haze, doesn't have as much recoverable detail. Hold back the Unsharp Mask filter in that area, but don't eliminate it completely.

Remember the haze correction mask (the second duplicated Green channel)? Use that to modify your custom edge mask. Select the Haze

6-7

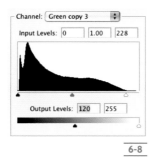

6-8

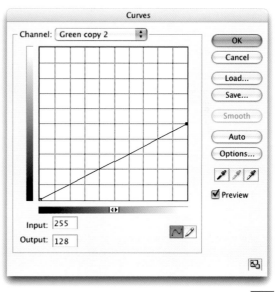

6-9

Correction mask channel, and choose Select ⇨ Load Selection. With the selection loaded, open the Curves dialog box (Command/Ctrl+M) and drag the highlight anchor point down to level 128. It doesn't have to be exact, but get it in the ball-park (see Figure 6-9). At this point, your final channel mask appears in Figure 6-10.

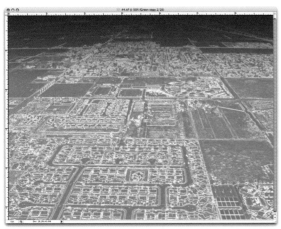

6-10

9. To sharpen the image using the channel mask, apply the sharpening to the Lightness channel in Lab Color mode. Deselect any active selections, and chose Image ➪ Mode ➪ Lab Color. Open the Channels palette and click the Lightness channel. Choose Select ➪ Load Selection; from the Channel drop-down menu load the channel mask created in step 8. To hide the selection, press Command/Ctrl+H.

You're going to use the Unsharp Mask filter twice at a subpixel setting. Choose Filter ➪ Sharpen ➪ Unsharp Mask. In the Unsharp Mask dialog box set the Amount to 500 percent, Radius to 0.25 percent, and Threshold to 0. Click OK.

This sharpening results in a big improvement, but it needs a second pass. Open the Unsharp Mask filter again and set the Amount to 500 percent, Radius to 0.20, and Threshold to 0.

The second pass brings edge sharpening to the maximum possible. The sharpening mask keeps random file noise from overwhelming the image, while the extra density of the mask you added at the top with the gradient channel keeps the sky from becoming noisy, and it will look very natural when you print the file. The final image appears in Figure 6-11.

PRO TIP

When applying the second sharpening pass, leave the Amount at 500 percent, but make small changes to the Radius to reach maximum sharpening without excessive artifacts. Add more Radius in 0.01 increments — such as 0.21, 0.22, and so on. Small changes can have a big effect.

Aerials captured with an 8-megapixel DSLR and sharpened in this manner can easily be enlarged to 16 x 24 inches with a very sharp result. Genuine Fractals Print Pro is a great tool for adding file smoothness through upsampling on aerial files sharpened this way with no loss of visual sharpness on output at sizes up to 24 x 36 inches.

X-REF

For more information on Genuine Fractals Print Pro, see Chapter 1.

PHOTOJOURNALISM

We won't get into the composition of the photojournalistic image. You can find many tips and techniques on the Internet for shooting photos in this category. The one thing in common among the working pros in Photojournalism is that they work in very fast-paced environments while on assignment. If you submit images via a wire service or to a publication Web site, most likely you just upload your images to someone in the art department who performs all the editing tasks while you return back to the action of your assignment. If you work freelance or for a small publication, you may do your own image editing before handing off your work.

Quite often the photojournalistic image is a combination of great skill with a little added luck. You can't art direct an action shot of an event or wartime drama. You pretty much need to take what you can

6-11

get hoping that the right moment comes along. This was the case in Figure 6-12 where Ted got lucky capturing former President Raul Leone of Venezuela. The crowd was amassing around the president, not to mention the military brass prohibiting close contact; by a stroke of luck, a little opening pierced the crowd with the president dawning a great smile at the right moment. A second later and this shot wouldn't have been possible.

Tonal corrections for these kinds of photos aren't much different than the corrections discussed in Chapters 4 and 5 for color images and Chapter 7 for black-and-white images. The one distinctive difference with photojournalism is that your photography is probably going to get printed on press. Unlike the

many other kinds of photos discussed throughout this book where the primary output device is a composite color printer, photojournalist images are most often printed on large web presses.

The rules and guidelines don't change that much when preparing images for press except where you may want to control the output within the Photoshop file — especially for the low-key images. Many photojournalist images can appear dark when shot in shelters, indoors without the right lighting, and the action shot that requires a quick snap of the shutter without setting up the photo for the best possible lighting conditions. If you find yourself in this situation, you can make adjustments to your photo using brightness and contrast tools, but the resultant image when

6-12

printed on a web press may emphasize the darkness of a shot even though the image looks great on your monitor. As ink is printed on newsprint, the ink is absorbed by the paper; and newsprint absorbing ink tends to swell the dots creating what we call *dot gain*. Dot gain can turn your Pulitzer Prize photo into a blob of black ink when printed on heavy absorption papers such as newsprint and uncoated stocks. A couple of ways to control the dot gain is by lowering halftone frequency and adjusting the transfer functions.

If you check the Internet and look over all the ad specifications by publishers and wire services, you see many publishers asking you to not preserve halftone frequency or transfer functions. You also find many publishers telling you that you should preserve halftone frequency and transfer functions. Unfortunately, not too many services provide you guidelines for what to preserve.

X-REF

For more information related to halftone frequency and conditions required for preparing files for press, see Chapter 11.

Controlling halftone frequency in a Photoshop file means you embed the halftone frequency for the file to be printed, and that file overrides the settings the prepress operator controls when printing to an imagesetter or platesetter. This can be handy if your images are high key with most of the data in the tone curve falling toward black. To make sure that the dot gain doesn't plug (show masses of black in the print), you might have some photos you want to print with a lower halftone frequency than other photos; for example, printing at 71 lpi (lines per inch) rather than 85 lpi, or printing at 85 lpi for a press that can handle 100 lpi.

Transfer functions are used to compensate for dot gain or dot loss. Much like you adjust the tone curve in the Curves dialog box for changing tone values, applying adjustments to the Transfer Functions controls how much ink is printed along the tone curve. You might have better results printing your photos on press by remapping the black, midtones, and white in a photo. The one thing you need to be aware of is that whether you select the Preserve Transfer Functions option or not, there is absolutely no effect on your printed file unless you do something to the tone curve. We find it amusing that many publishers ask you to preserve transfer functions but still ask you to save your file as a TIFF or JPEG (two formats that don't support preserving the transfer functions).

PRO TIP

Checking the Preserve Transfer Functions option is actually handled in the EPS Options dialog box, the same place where you find Include Halftone Frequency. Saving as EPS is the only file format that provides you a setting to preserve either halftone frequency or Transfer Functions.

To make this clear and see how it all works, look over the following steps that explain how to work on a grayscale image because most photos in newspapers are black and white. Color photos require additional information setting color frequencies and angles and color conversions to achieve the same results. If you work with color photos, follow the advice of your publisher and the guidelines set forth for submitting photos to the source.

PRO TIP

Setting halftone frequency and transfer functions have nothing to do with continuous-tone devices. Regardless of whether you adjust these settings or not, you won't see any different results on your color printer. These settings apply only to files that are printed on devices that print dots such as imagesetters, platesetters, and laser printers.

1. Open a file in Photoshop where you have made all your tonal corrections. Choose File ⇨ Print with Preview. In the Print with Preview dialog box, select Output from the drop-down menu under the image preview box. Click More Options to expand the dialog box if it's not expanded.

Under the Output menu selection are buttons and check boxes used for setting print options for your file. Click Screen to open the Halftone Screen dialog box.

X-REF

For a complete description for using the Print with Preview dialog box and more understanding of halftone screen, see Chapter 11.

2. Deselect the Use Printer's Default Screen check box. The Frequency text box becomes active. Type a frequency in this text box for the line screen you want to print. In Figure 6-13, 71 is selected to print a 71 lpi halftone screen.

PRO TIP

You also have options for choosing a dot shape from the Shape drop-down menu. If you submit files to a service or publisher who requests embedding halftone frequencies in your Photoshop files, the service will also tell you what dot shape to use. If in doubt, choose Ellipse.

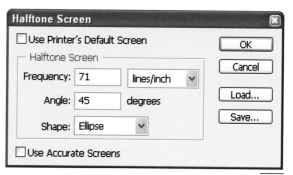

6-13

3. Click OK. You return to the Print with Preview dialog box. Click Transfer.

Before you make adjustments here and also before you add any halftone screen, you need precise guidelines from your publisher. These settings should be the results of tests run in the print shop where the printers have determined what settings work best with their press. Above all, avoid making any arbitrary settings in either the Halftone Frequency dialog box or the Transfer Functions dialog box.

When the Transfer Functions dialog box opens, type the values supplied by your publisher. In Figure 6-14, arbitrary values are used to show how the tone curve is remapped using a custom setting. These settings are not intended to be duplicated. You must get the values from your publisher. Select the Override Printer's Default Functions check box and click OK.

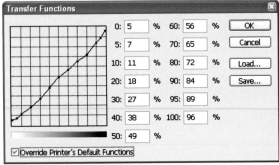

6-14

4. Click Done in the Print with Preview dialog box. Do not click Cancel or you delete all the settings you made.

Now that your frequency and transfer functions have been made, you need to embed them in the Photoshop file. No matter what program prints the file, these values will override any other program defaults. To embed the settings you can only use one file format. The file must be saved as a Photoshop EPS file. Saving as TIFF or JPEG won't preserve your edits.

5. Chose File ⇨ Save As and choose Photoshop EPS for the format. Click Save. The EPS Options dialog box opens (see Figure 6-15). Select the Include Halftone Screen and Include Transfer Functions check boxes. Click OK. Your settings are embedded in the Photoshop EPS file.

6-15

Because this book is printed on press, custom halftone frequencies are added to the files shown in Figure 6-16. The file in the top-left corner is printed at 45 lpi, the top right is 65 lpi, the lower left is 85 lpi, and the lower-right image is printed at 100 lpi. The default frequency for this book is 150 lpi.

PORTRAITURE

Our constant barrage of glamour and movie posters has conditioned us to think that perfect skin is normal and what we should all look like. The unfortunate reality is that there is no such thing as perfect skin — well, that is unless you happen to be Beyoncé. The other unfortunate reality is that we expect to see perfection in photographs, particularly in portraits.

Photographing and enhancing images of children and babies are easy. Father time has yet to do his worst. However, for the rest of us, with the exception of the few Beyoncés of the world, most adults benefit from some digital skin enhancement.

6-16

NHANCING SKIN TONES

any specialty books have been written on
hotoshop digital retouching and how to use the
any Photoshop tools to digitally retouch portraits.
'e don't need to rehash all the great tips and tech-
ques from the many Photoshop masters who have
)cumented how to go about removing wrinkles,
hitening teeth, adding sparkle to eyes, and carving
f a few extra pounds. As a digital photographer, you
obably have a few of these books near your com-
ter, and you don't need another lesson in all the
)ssible retouching techniques. Our task is to show
me methods for reasonably fast aging reduction
d overall enhancement of adult portraits.

The subject for this demo is a PR portrait of a sweet 54-
year-old client named Betty. She was gracious enough
to allow her image to be used for this demonstration.
The untouched portrait is shown in Figure 6-17.

Cameras can be cruel instruments when it comes to
capturing images of faces up close. The high sharpness
and the lingering view of a moment in time tend to
make the viewer zero in on obvious flaws of the subject. No wonder most people hate to have a portrait
sitting. This is especially true of women. Our culture
seems to expect eternal youth as women make their
way through life while men are allowed to age grace-
fully.

6-17

Betty is not the smiling kind and is very uncomfortable on-camera. In a situation like this, keep the conversation light and try to distract your subject as much as possible. Looking over the top of the camera while engaging in conversation is also helpful. Look for a relaxed and warm expression of the eyes and keep shooting until you are sure you have the best capture possible. After viewing all the files, the final picture is opened from the Camera Raw capture. A gray card capture at the start of the sitting is almost essential with portrait shots to set custom white balance. After the cropping and the initial tonal and color balance edit, the image is ready for printing. For this particular image, no diffusion was used on the camera lens. Betty wears light makeup, so there are no obvious color shift problems from a makeup foundation on the face area.

The first step in retouching this image is to remove the facial wrinkles with the Healing Brush tool. For this particular image (see Figure 6-18) we start with the largest neck and facial creases.

As a general rule, we strive to remove 10 years or so off the aging process for middle-aged females. For the purpose of this discussion, we take it a little farther. Betty is a slim woman, with a fairly narrow face and a healthy head of hair. Her face shows an average amount of aging for a 54-year-old woman. Because of her face shape, frontal lupe lighting was used, with a 1 to 2 fill ratio to add width to her face.

X-REF

For more on correcting skin tones, see Chapter 5.

1. Create a new layer by clicking the Create a new layer icon in the Layers palette, or press Command/Ctrl+Shift+N. A new transparent layer added to the document, as shown in Figure 6-19. Photoshop permits you to use a transparent layer to carry the Healing Brush strokes, which is handy because the result is easily erased or modified after the brush strokes are applied.

6-18

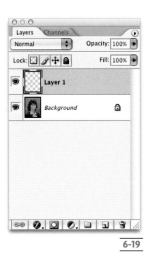

6-19

options, as shown in Figure 6-20. (Alternatively you can press Command/Ctrl+J then press Shift+Command/Ctrl+J to toggle the tools). After selecting the tool, make sure the Mode in the Options Bar is Normal and the Source is Sampled, also shown in Figure 6-20.

3. Zoom in on the photo to at least a 100 percent view or higher by pressing Command/Ctrl++ (plus). In the Options Bar, open the Brush drop-down menu and select a brush size large enough to cover the targeted wrinkle or flaw. A feathered brush usually works best.

Sample a skin area with similar color and texture by placing the cursor on the Background layer. Press Option/Alt and click the mouse once. Place the cursor over the wrinkle and drag on the trans-parent layer. Let Photoshop process a moment and check the result. Figure 6-21 shows a few retouching strokes made on facial wrinkles.

2. Select the Healing Brush from the Tools palette. If either the Patch tool or the Red Eye tool is selected, click on the tool just below the Crop tool in the Tools palette to open a pop-up toolbar. Select the Healing Brush tool from the tool

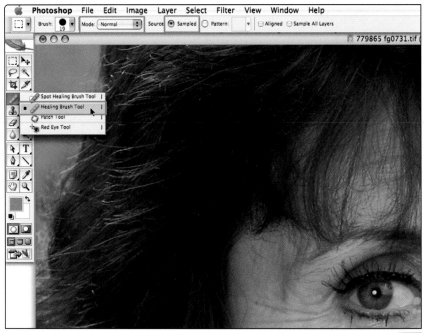

6-20

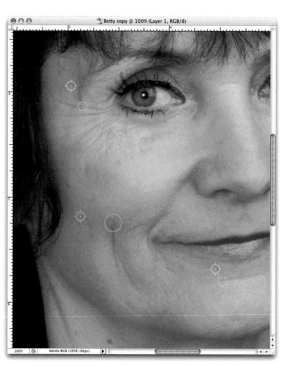

6-21

4. Keep working the wrinkles and blemishes with the Healing Brush tool until the corrections appear reasonable. A little eyeball judgment is needed here. In Figure 6-22, you can see the image after the blemish removal.

6-22

Because the tool is painting a separate layer, any retouch moves that are unsatisfactory can be removed with the Eraser tool. Strokes that are a bit too light or dark can be corrected by making a loose selection around the retouch stroke and then lightening or darkening with Curves. Note that the skin selected for sampling does not have to be right next to the area to be retouched. Anywhere on the face with similar tonalities and color is fine. The tool simulates target placement texture automatically. Vary the brush size to match the area to be corrected as you work.

PRO TIP

To quickly size the brush tip press [(left bracket) to make the tip smaller; press] (right bracket) to make the tip larger.

5. Betty has a problem with shiny skin under the eye area, and the area also shows a slight magenta shift. A subtle smoothing and correction of the color can be done with a transparent Brush tool. Flatten the image, and then create a duplicate layer. This allows an easy undo or feathering of the correction with the Eraser tool if needed.

Change the screen view to 50 percent by zooming out in the document window. You want to have a good overall reference of the subtle paint retouching.

Go to the Tools pallet and click the Set foreground color tool. When the Color Picker opens, move the sampling cursor to an average sample area of the facial flesh tones, as you see in Figure 6-23. The center cheek area looks good on this photo. Sometimes you have to try more than once for a good sample. After you select the required flesh tone, click OK in the Color Picker and the color appears in the Foreground color swatch in the Tools palette.

PRO TIP

Setting the Eyedropper options for a 5 x 5 sampling area can make the job of sampling much easier. To make the adjustments for sample size for the Eyedropper tool, click the tool in the Tools palette and open the Sample Size drop-down menu in the Options Bar. To set the size to a 5 x 5 sample, select 5 by 5 Average from the menu options.

6. Select an appropriately sized Brush, and set hardness to zero and Opacity to 10 percent in the Options Bar. You want a brush tip large enough to paint a fairly wide area, as shown in Figure 6-24. The transparency of the Brush allows the skin texture to show through. You aren't too worried about masking the texture somewhat, because the next step softens all the skin texture.

In Figure 6-25, you can see the edits after painting in the area around the eyes.

7. Next, smooth and soften the overall facial skin. This method reduces the amount of after-softening cleanup and preserves sharpness in the rest of the image. Start by creating a Hide Edges mask that you use later.

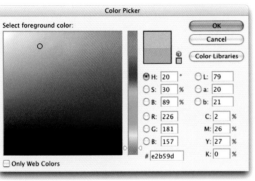

Color Picker

Select foreground color:

OK

Cancel

Color Libraries

H: 20 °   L: 79
S: 30 %   a: 20
B: 89 %   b: 21

R: 226   C: 2 %
G: 181   M: 26 %
B: 157   Y: 27 %
e2b59d   K: 0 %

Only Web Colors

Betty2 copy @ 50% (Layer 6, RGB/8)

50%   Adobe RGB (1998) (8bpc)

6-23

6-24

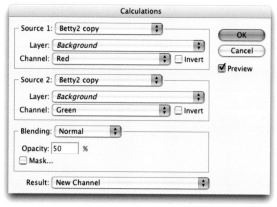

6-26

6-25

Flatten the image in the Layers palette, and choose Image ⇨ Calculations to open the Calculations dialog box. Set the Source 1 Channel to Red, set the Source 2 Channel to Green, set the Blending mode to Normal, and set Opacity to 50 percent. Leave the Result set to New Channel, and click OK (see Figure 6-26).

8. Your screen view turns to black and white. Your color image is still there. Photoshop is showing the new alpha channel you just created. At this point, add some contrast to the image. Use the Auto Contrast adjustment to accomplish this, and leave the view set to the newly created alpha channel. Choose Image ⇨ Adjust ⇨ Auto Contrast, and the Auto Contrast command adds a little more contrast in the image shown in the alpha channel (see Figure 6-27).

9. At this point, create a mask you later use as your skin-softening mask. Keep in mind that you're still working in the alpha channel. To create the mask, use edge pixels and spread the range of pixels to create enough area to soften the edges a bit. Choose Filter ⇨ Stylize ⇨ Find Edges. The image should look like Figure 6-28.

10. After finding edges, soften the edge appearance. Use the Gaussian Blur filter. Choose Filter ⇨ Blur ⇨ Gaussian Blur, and move the Radius slider to 4 pixels. This amount can vary depending on the sharpness of the original image. For most portrait images similar to what you see in this example, 4 pixels work well. After blurring the alpha channel, the image appears as shown in Figure 6-29.

6-27

6-29

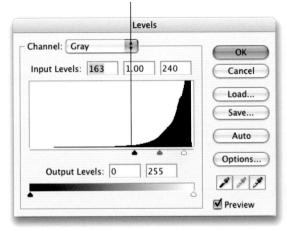

6-28

11. Now, maximize and spread the blacks in the mask using Levels. Files can vary, so eyeball the histogram and the mask. Open the Levels dialog box and drag the black slider to the second cliff on the histogram. Drag the white slider left to clean up the skin area (see Figure 6-30).

Second cliff

Levels

Channel: Gray

Input Levels: 163 1.00 240

OK
Cancel
Load...
Save...
Auto
Options...

Output Levels: 0 255

☑ Preview

6-30

Click OK, and the image appears as you see in Figure 6-31. It completes the Hide Edges mask that you use as you adjust color in the image.

6-32

6-31

12. Duplicate the Background layer, and with the new layer selected, choose Image ⇨ Adjust ⇨ Hue/Saturation. In the Hue/Saturation dialog box, add 50 percent overall saturation by moving the Saturation slider to +50. The image appears overly saturated (see Figure 6-32), and you know the skin tones are way off the mark. But don't worry, this layer is a temporary work layer that you toss later.

13. Choose Select ⇨ Color Range to open the Color Range dialog box.

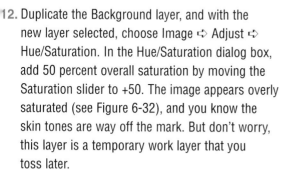

When the dialog box opens, use the default Sampled Colors and move the Fuzziness slider to around 150. Move the cursor into the document window and click the eyedropper on a medium-toned area of the oversaturated flesh tone. Try clicking around to find the best overall selection of just the flesh tone area. White represents a 100 percent selection, and black a 0 percent selection. The idea is to get the brightest selection you can of just the flesh tones similar to Figure 6-33. Keep the Color Range dialog box open as you move to the next step.

14. Now click the + eyedropper, and click on a darker area of flesh tone. See if you can open the selection without selecting non-flesh-tone areas. A perfect selection is not needed because this selection is used for a blurring layer, but get it as close as you can — something like the result shown in Figure 6-33.

PRO TIP

You can use a single Eyedropper tool in the Color Range dialog box and toggle between the + (plus) eyedropper to add to a selection and the − (minus) eyedropper to subtract from a selection using keyboard modifiers. Press Shift with the Eyedropper selected and click additional sample areas to add to the selection. Press Option/Alt and click to remove tones from the selection.

6-33

A second click with the + eyedropper on the cheek area opens the selection considerably. All the important flesh area is now selected. Click OK in the Color Range dialog box and the selection appears in the document window. Choose Select ⇨ Save Selection to open the Save Selection dialog box. Add a descriptive name for your selection in the Name text box. This example is named Flesh. Click OK and the selection is saved to an alpha channel. You have two alpha channels. One channel is the mask and the other the current selection.

15. At this point you have exhausted the use of your temporary layer and no longer need it. Drag the topmost layer to the Trash icon in the Layers palette to delete it.

PRO TIP

If you want to delete layers in the Layers palette without an annoying dialog box opening to confirm your action, press Alt/Option and click the Trash icon while the layer to be deleted is selected. The layer is deleted without an annoying confirmation dialog box opening.

16. In the last series of steps you worked on preparing your masks for the actual correction work that lies ahead. With the masks saved in alpha channels you are ready to create the skin-softening mask. Choose Select ⇨ Load Selection to open the Load Selection dialog box. From the Channel drop-down menu, select the skin selection. In your example the skin selection is named Flesh.

With the selection active in the document window, create a layer from the selected pixels. Choose Layer ⇨ New ⇨ Layer via Copy or press Ctrl/Command+J. The new layer is comprised of only the selected data.

17. Again choose Select ⇨ Load Selection, and select Alpha 1 from the Channel drop-down menu to load the other selection that is the edge mask. Press Ctrl/Command+H to hide the selection.

18. You now have the current layer created from the selection mask for the flesh tones and an active selection created from the edge mask. Make sure you remain on the new layer and select Filter ⇨ Blur ⇨ Gaussian Blur. In the Gaussian Blur dialog box move the Radius slider to 8 pixels.

Press Command/Ctrl+D to remove the edges selection. As you look at the image you notice the blurring applied with the Gaussian Blur filter is much too soft and creates an artificial appearance, as you can see in Figure 6-34.

6-34

19. Use a little eyeball judgment to bring this image to a natural enhanced appearance. Select the skin layer and reduce the opacity until the result conforms to your personal preference. Reproduction size is also a factor. A file for huge enlargement needs more softening than a small enlargement. For this image, decrease the Opacity to 40 percent.

For a much younger subject, 20 percent would probably be just fine.

Once you determine the Opacity amount, use the Eraser tool with a soft-edge brush around the eyes and perhaps the lip area to bring back full sharpness. This is all a subjective judgment and you again need to make adjustments according to your visual preference. When you're satisfied, flatten the image. The final result should look something like Figure 6-35.

The steps in this section at first view must seem tedious and extensive. If you repeat the process three to five times and you can commit to memory each step in the process, you can expect to perform all steps within five minutes. It may seem like a long shot at this point, but we guarantee that you can swiftly move through the steps in a relatively short time.

6-35

USING A FLESH TONE GRADIENT PICKER

Sometimes, you just have to do the color balancing the hard way, identifying a colorcast using just the flesh tones as your guide. After some experience, it's not all that difficult assuming you have reasonably good color vision. With time, flesh tone colorcasts are easy to recognize.

Here is a basic little flesh tone ring around shown in Figure 6-36. In this close-up of Don's little friend and her pet chicken named Honey, there aren't any easy reference colors except for the flesh tones. Even the chicken isn't much help. Her feathers are very close to a flesh tone, too. Observe the six different primary color errors in the ring around and compare them to the corrected image in Figure 6-37. The saturation is normal and the color error in each example isn't that great. The curve box for the red ring around example shows just how small of an edit can result in a flesh tone error in color.

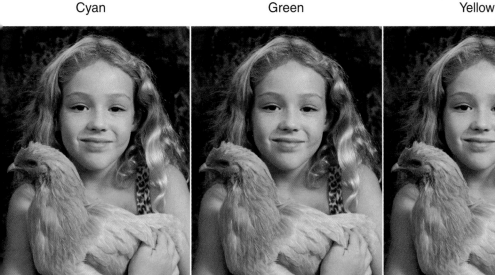

| Cyan | Green | Yellow |
| Red | Magenta | Blue |

6-37

6-38

The ring around is a handy guide to help memorize what the six basic color primary trend errors of flesh tones look like. Another aid is keeping a good standard flesh tone sample open on the desktop while you try to determine a decent flesh tone correction. Flesh tones vary a great deal, but a standard guide is a big help, especially when your eyes are tired from long hours of editing.

A great sample file is the Adobe *Ole No Moire* file, which is available for download from Dry Creek Photo (www.drycreekphoto.com) or the high-resolution image on your CD installer back in version 4 of Photoshop. Just crop it down to the famous lady and keep it handy. She has vivid flesh tones and they are a good reference for a saturation guide. Her flesh tones are about as saturated as you can get without reproduction problems (see Figure 6-38).

Any other digital file you come across, whether your own or even something on the Web (when you have a right to use it) that really has a great flesh tone quality can be saved to use as a desktop reference. The human eye is very poor at determining exact color properties as a measurement tool, but unsurpassed as a color comparison tool. Even a complete novice eye can identify a bad flesh tone when compared side by side with a perfect flesh tone.

One last reminder: Do your best to adjust for a normal saturation level before making any final judgment on flesh tone colorcasts. A slightly undersaturated image is easier to work with than an oversaturated image when trying to create a good quality flesh tone. If balancing the flesh tone causes the rest of the image content to appear out of color balance, use one of the selection methods described to isolate the flesh tones for a custom edit.

Identifying a flesh tone colorcast is the first step in your color-correction process, but it doesn't mean anything unless you know how to precisely go about correcting color problems. The Curves and Levels dialog boxes contain a gray eyedropper, and it does a fine job of producing a perfect gray by simply clicking the cursor in any part of the image where you desire a perfect gray tone. Wouldn't it be nice to use the Eyedropper tool and click on skin to fix an off-color flesh tone? Well, your wish has come true! The steps ahead offer you your very own Mason Pat Pending method for using a custom flesh tone picker where you can turn that gray eyedropper into your own custom flesh tone eyedropper!

The gray Eyedropper tool in the Curves dialog box has always had the capability to custom set the midtone gray to any color you want to use. The only problem with setting it to a flesh tone is finding a proper color source to sample. Flesh tones vary a lot, so just one sample color won't do. Unfortunately, the Photoshop color swatches don't have any worthwhile flesh samples. The solution is to create your own set of flesh tone swatches where that gray Eyedropper tool can work wonders at helping you find the proper skin correction without a lot of hassle.

Skin comes in many different tone values from very dark to very light. You need a set of samples that covers this range so you can pick the one that's appropriate for the subject at hand. You do this by first creating a flesh tone gradient and then posterizing it into a set of discrete steps. We number the steps so it's easy to remember where you sampled in case you need to repeat your pick or change the sample in a predictable way.

1. Start with a blank new document. Because this is a color reference file it doesn't have to be a large file — just large enough to use easily at a 72 ppi screen resolution.

   Choose File ⇨ New to open the New dialog box. Type **12** for the width and **2** for the height, using inches as your unit of measure. If you use millimeters, set the width to 300 and the height to 50. Type **72** for the Resolution and select Lab Color from the Color Mode drop-down menu. Select 16-bit from the drop-down menu adjacent to Color Mode, as shown in Figure 6-39. Click OK to create the new file.

6-39

PRO TIP

We prefer our picker appearing horizontal to place the document at the top or bottom of our monitor while working on correcting skin tones. When we want to view the file in a portrait view, we just choose Image ⇨ Rotate. If you prefer viewing the gradient picker in a portrait view by default, set the width to 2 inches and the height to 12 inches in the New dialog box.

2. Create a gradient ranging from very dark flesh tone values to very light. Start by identifying the foreground and background colors.

   Click on the foreground color square in the Tools pallet to open the Color Picker. Set the foreground color to a very light flesh tone value. Surprisingly, you are going to use Lab values, even though you are working in RGB mode. There's a very good reason for this. The RGB number values of flesh tones can vary a great deal in RGB mode depending on the working color space you're using. The Lab values are much more standardized because the values are device independent. After you finish identifying your colors, convert the file to RGB color mode.

   With the Foreground color picker open, look to the Lab values in the top-right corner (see Figure 6-40). Type the following values in the L, a, and b text boxes: L: **88**; a: **13**; and b: **15**. Click OK to set the foreground color.

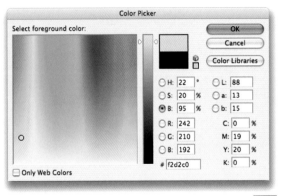

6-40

3. Click on the background color swatch in the Tools pallet. Type the following values in the boxes:

- L: **26**

- a: **4**

- b: **10**

Click OK and the background color is set to a darker flesh tone.

4. Select the Gradient tool in the Tools palette. In the Options Bar make sure the Linear Gradient item is selected (far-left icon) and the Opacity is at 100 percent. Use the default Foreground to Background gradient style. By default the Black, White style should be selected in the Gradient Picker.

Draw a gradient from one end of your open file to the other. If you want the gradient to appear from light to dark, draw from right to left in the new document window. Alternatively, you can press X and draw left to right. The direction of the gradient is a personal choice. We use a dark-to-light gradient (see Figure 6-41), but you can use what works best for you.

Choose File ⇨ Save to save the file; name it FleshPicker or some descriptive file name you can easily recognize. Use either Photoshop's native file format (PSD) or use TIFF.

5. Turn the gradient into a step tablet. You can't go directly to Posterize to create steps because the file dithering creates a very strange looking result. Use the Lightness channel in Lab Color mode to create the steps to render a much better result.

Click the Channels palette and select the Lightness channel. Choose Image ⇨ Adjust ⇨ Posterize, and type **21** in the Posterize dialog box. Click OK (see Figure 6-42).

You see the gradient turn into 14 separate steps, not 21. Why? It's a math thing. The lightness channel in Lab has fewer discrete brightness values, and the posterization setting is based on standard RGB 8-bit values.

6. Choose Image ⇨ Mode ⇨ RGB. Your file is converted to RGB and remains in 16-bit mode.

7. At this point, boost the saturation a bit. Choose Image ⇨ Adjustments ⇨ Hue/Saturation, or press Command/Ctrl+U to open the Hue/Saturation dialog box. Type **10** in the Saturation text box or drag the Saturation slider to +10 to boost master saturation by 10 percent, as shown in Figure 6-43.

8. Convert the file to 8-bit RGB color by choosing Image ⇨ Mode ⇨ 8 Bits/Channel. Save the file again to preserve your edits.

9. For convenience, number the patches with the Type tool. Small white numbers across the top are all you need. It makes it easier to remember which patch you sample for the gray eyedropper when using the Curves or Levels dialog box.

Click the Type tool in the Tools palette. Select an easy-to-read font like Arial in the Options Bar. Press D to return to default colors, and press X to swap the colors making white the new foreground color. Type numbers from **1** to **14** across the patches.

Flatten the layers created by typing numbers on the patches, and save again to update the file.

Your flesh tone color picker is complete and should look something like Figure 6-44.

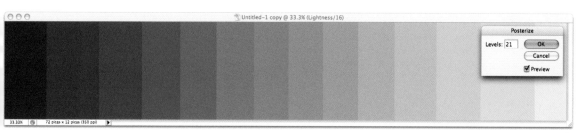

6-41

6-42

6-43

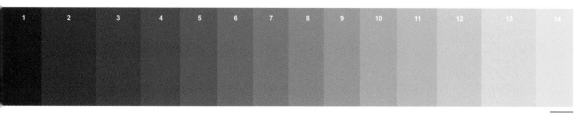

6-44

After spending time creating your flesh tone picker, you now want to use it. Just as you perform other color corrections on images, make sure you begin with a file you have already edited for normal brightness and contrast. Equally important is to be certain you have also edited your file for proper saturation.

To use a custom flesh tone picker, follow these steps:

1. Open a file or multiple files with flesh tones you want to color balance. Open the flesh tone picker and keep it where you can see both the picker and the file to be corrected.

   Set the Eyedropper tool option to 5 x 5 pixel sample. To easily change the point sample for the Eyedropper tool, select the tool in the Tools palette. Open a context menu (Control-click on the Mac, right-click on Windows) and select 5 x 5 Average. Alternatively, you can select 5 x 5 Average in the Options Bar.

   This makes the Curves Eyedropper use a 5 x 5 sample size, too. The larger sample size works much better. Skin has a lot of micro variation, and the large sample helps to even out the stray pixel values in the sample area.

2. Click the title bar on the file you want to edit to make it the active document window. Press Command/Ctrl+M to open the Curves dialog box. Double-click the gray Eyedropper tool in the Curves dialog box. When the Color Picker opens, click on a swatch in the flesh picker that's the closest match to the tone value of the skin color to be corrected. It's not critical to be exact, but closer is better.

   Click OK in the Color Picker. The gray eyedropper is now set to a flesh tone. In Figure 6-45, you can see an active document window with the flesh tone picker vertically positioned on the right side. After opening the Curves dialog box, double-click

the midtone Eyedropper tool and the Color Picker opens. Moving the Eyedropper to the Color Picker and clicking a color patch samples that color in the Color Picker.

3. With the Curves dialog box open and the flesh color selected, move the cursor over an average flesh area. Try to avoid makeup areas, lips, eyebrows, and so on. Click on a flesh tone and watch the result. Chances are, the first click won't balance the image. Skin varies a lot because of texture, freckles, blemishes, and so on, but just click around a few times, and voila! You'll hit a sweet spot and the image pops into balance. When you see what you like, click OK in the Curves dialog box.

In Figure 6-46, we first sampled the right forehead and the results appeared too cool as you see in the left image. We clicked again, this time on the chest above the chicken. The result was a little closer but the color appeared still a little cool as you see in the middle image. A third effort was made by clicking on the subject's right cheek (our left side) and the image came into perfect color balance as shown in the right photo.

Once the color balance is what you want, it's also okay to tweak the image tones with the RGB curve in the Curves dialog box if you desire.

What could be easier than using your custom flesh tone picker?

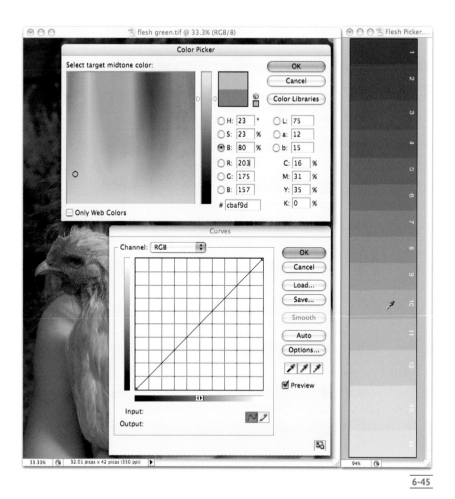

6-45

6-46

I saved a file with a custom halftone screen and the file printed at the default the prepress technician printed all other photos. What did I do wrong?

Assuming you added a custom halftone frequency and saved your file as EPS while checking the box for Include Halftone Screen in the EPS Options dialog box, you didn't do anything wrong. The problem may well have occurred in the prepress department of the publication.

Many imagesetters and platesetters have a variety of different screening options that can be selected when files are printed. Agfa Avantra Imagesetters, for example, use a screening technology developed by Agfa for printing files with balanced screens. The balanced screens option is used to insure that color separations are printed at the correct frequency and angles of the dots. If the dot angles are not correct, the film or plate can show an obvious moiré pattern. When you embed a custom halftone frequency, Agfa's balanced screens override your embedded screening. The way to solve the problem is to have the prepress operator turn off the screening when your file is printed. Other imagesetters have similar kinds of screening that can override your embedded halftone frequencies. The only way to be certain that these kinds of errors don't occur is to talk to the prepress technicians before your files are prepared for delivery. Set the guidelines set forth by those who print your files and keep your lines of communication open.

I do a lot of wildlife photography and often find my photos get blurred when tracking wildlife. What can I do to keep my camera steadier?

One important consideration is to use telephoto lenses with a stabilizer. The lenses are much more expensive, but if this is an area where you do a lot of photography, using one of these lenses will help you steady your camera and lens.

Assuming you do have a lens with a stabilizer and you use a tripod and your images are still getting blurred from the camera movement, try using a monopod. A monopod gives you much more freedom for fast-tracking wildlife and sports actions than a tripod. If you don't have a monopod you can retract two of the legs on your tripod or bring all the legs together to create a monopod-type rig. Use a monopod/tripod with a quick release so you can go to handhold when needed.

Chapter 7

FIXING SNAPSHOTS

"While there is perhaps a province in which the photograph can tell us nothing more than what we see with our own eyes, there is another in which it proves to us how little our eyes permit us to see."
— Dorothea Lange

In Chapter 6, we talk about location shooting for advanced amateurs and professional photographers where the use of a studio and controlled lighting is part of taking great pictures. We talk about professional methods and techniques using professional equipment and how photographers plan a photo shoot.

The photos always look great in books and magazines presented by professional photographers, but sometimes these images don't quite look like the photos taken at home on Christmas day or on the trip to Disney World.

Snapshot photography inherently presents a lot of problems if you need to perfect that image of Uncle Albert when the flash didn't fire or one of those great shots of the kids playing with Mickey Mouse at dusk. Snapshots are often taken in lighting conditions that are less than desirable for quality photography.

There's only so much you can do with Photoshop and the Camera Raw dialog box. Sometimes images just can't be optimized for good output. Snapshot photographers can, however, rescue an image containing a number of common problems and make it worthy of showing off to the family.

In this chapter, we present some worst-case scenarios to give you an idea for how far you can push Photoshop's controls for color correction and tonal editing. Mark this chapter for reference, and you can compare images when you occasionally find photos on your media cards where you may have encountered flash firing problems or shooting in uncontrolled lighting. If your images don't look as bad as some of our examples here, you'll have a ballpark idea for whether you can correct the images before you start opening files and examining histograms.

CORRECTING FLASH EXPOSURE PROBLEMS

Invariably, we all have one of those shots where a flash doesn't fire or the flash is insufficient to properly expose the scene. The result is an either partially or completely underexposed image.

For these kinds of images you have to be careful to get as much brightness correction without posterizing the image or showing extraordinary amounts of noise. Dragging the Levels slider to an extreme lightens the image, but you see a lot of loss in the tonal gradations resulting in severe posterization and noise. You want to add enough brightness and contrast without destroying the tonal curve. Obviously, there are limits and you won't be able to rescue some images.

Often you come across two sets of circumstances when shooting flash photography. Upon occasion, the flash doesn't fire; or if it does, the subject is so far out of range the photo appears as though the flash didn't fire. These kinds of photos are generally beyond any repair — at least to the point of producing a quality image.

The other situation you find when shooting snapshots with flash is that the flash unit fires, but is insufficient in terms of throwing out enough light to produce an image with a good tonal range. At first glance, the image may appear lost. But after careful examination you may find enough data to work with to produce a worthwhile image.

WORKING WITH THE BEYOND-REPAIR PHOTOS

Figure 7-1 shows an example of an underexposed JPEG file shot with a low ISO setting. The file has heavy noise throughout most of the dark, captured tones where the flash wasn't sufficient, and the lighting is so low, the image is beyond rescue.

Open the Levels dialog box and look at the histogram. The histogram for the image in Figure 7-1 appears in Figure 7-2. As you can see, no data appears all along

7-1

7-2

the highlight and midtone range. The data doesn't begin to show up until around level 40. An examination of both the image and the histogram appears to show this image is beyond rescue. You can adjust the tone levels, but the eventual result shows a lot of noise and problems with the tonal distribution after remapping the tones.

To check how much noise appears after making a tone adjustment, drag the white point slider to the left until you reach the beginning of the data somewhere after the noise levels. In this example (see Figure 7-3), the white point slider is moved over to level 40.

It's best to just toss this photo and try again next time. But what happens if your camera was the only one pointing directly at the book depository shown in Figure 7-4 on November 22, 1963? Assume for a moment that you were alive then and old enough to hold a camera. You took a shot that was underexposed by 6 stops, and it was the one shot that can

7-3

solve the mystery of the modern era. You waited more than 43 years for Photoshop CS2 to appear so you could resurrect your photo, appear on Larry King, and claim your rewards. All you need to do is get some reasonable detail out of the photo knowing it could very well become the next Pulitzer Prize winner. We call this method the Mason Pat Pending Mixed Mode Image Save.

7-4

The problem that results when you try to save an image by repeatedly reapplying screen modes, using a single Levels edit, or using the Shadow/Highlight command at maximum settings is that color saturation is out of control and you get super color noise and massive tone haloing — quite a dilemma.

The solution is to use multiple duplicate layers with the Apply Image command using Screen mode, while alternating between Normal and Luminosity modes in the layer stack at 50 percent opacity. Once a reasonable (or maximum possible) image tonal recovery has been achieved, you can finish with a few tweaks from the standard Photoshop tools. Follow the steps below to improve one of your own images with a similar exposure problem:

1. Open the image and convert it to 16-bit depth by choosing Image ⇨ Mode ⇨ 16 Bits/Channel.

Choose Image ⇨ Image Size to open the Image Size dialog box and reduce the width (or height) to 71 percent. Make sure the Constrain Proportions and Resample Image check boxes are selected. Choose Bicubic for the Resample Image mode.

2. Drag the Background layer to the Create a new layer icon to duplicate the layer. Select Luminosity for the Blending mode and adjust the Opacity to 50 percent as shown in Figure 7-5.

7-5

3. With the Background copy layer selected, choose Image ⇨ Apply Image to open the Apply Image dialog box (see Figure 7-6). From the Blending drop-down menu, select Screen. Leave Opacity at the default value of 100 percent.

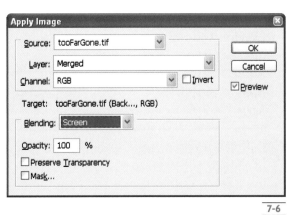

7-6

4. Drag the new layer to the Create a new layer icon to duplicate the layer. With the new layer selected, choose Image ➪ Apply Image. From the Blending drop-down menu select Normal, and leave the Opacity in the Apply Image dialog box at the default 100 percent setting.

5. Repeat the steps for duplicating layers and alternate the Apply Image settings between Screen and Normal. The layers blend their modes together while keeping saturation under control. After duplicating five layers and alternating the Blend mode in the Apply Image dialog box, the image appears as shown in Figure 7-7. Although you need to make adjustments to the color, you

7-7

can immediately see a much better result than the edit in the Levels dialog box back in Figure 7-1.

6. Usually you see a heavy red saturation when correcting images with similar problems as those in this example. Choose Layer ➪ New Adjustment Layer ➪ Hue/Saturation to open the Hue/Saturation dialog box. To reduce the oversaturation of reds in this image, select Red from the Edit menu in the Hue/Saturation dialog box. Reduce an image like this example 33 percent by dragging the Saturation slider to -33%, as shown in Figure 7-8. If you wish to reduce or increase overall image saturation, select Master from the Edit menu and drag the Saturation slider to adjust overall image saturation.

7-8

PRO TIP

If your image needs a gross color balance correction, you can create a Curves adjustment layer and handle the color imbalance in the Curves dialog box. See Chapter 5 for more detail on adjusting color with the Curves dialog box.

7. Flatten your layers and drag the flattened Background layer to the Create a new layer icon in the Layers palette. As a final step, you may need to adjust the shadow/highlight detail. Recognize the fact that an image like this example has much gross noise, and at this point, you can't avoid it. Notwithstanding the noise problem, you can make adjustments for the tonal balance.

8. Select Luminosity for the layer blend mode in the Layers palette. Choose Image ➪ Adjustments ➪ Shadow/Highlight. In the Shadow/Highlight dialog box set the Shadow amount to somewhere between 10 and 25 percent — where you set the Shadow amount depends on how much noise you are willing to tolerate. As you brighten the shadows (increase the Shadow amount), you introduce more noise. In this example, we use 25 percent, which results in the right tone quality but produces an image with a great deal of noise as you can see in the final edited image in Figure 7-9.

X-REF

For more information on using the Shadow/Highlight dialog box, see Chapter 4.

7-9

WORKING WITH INSUFFICIENT FLASH

Quite often, images are insufficiently lighted by an internal flash, but they aren't quite as bad as the photo shown in Figure 7-1. You may have a file that appears as a gross underexposure because the flash isn't strong enough to properly light the image, but the data in the file is enough to work with to create a reasonable-looking final image.

The vacation snapshot shown in Figure 7-10 is a good example of an underexposed flash-lit capture. Most of the tones are quite dark, but the image contains more data than the example used to create the final image in Figure 7-1.

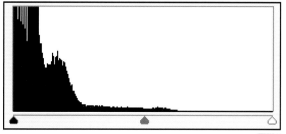

To get an idea of the tonal information available, open the Levels dialog box and drag the right-hand highlight slider most of the way to the left to make the existing dark tone information more visible as shown in Figure 7-12. Don't worry about blowing out the highlights because you are not going to save this edit.

7-10

To correct the image shown in Figure 7-10, we used the following steps:

1. The first thing to do with images where flash is insufficient is to look over the histogram and study the image. Your first determination is to understand if the image is worth editing or if it's beyond repair. In Figure 7-11, you can see the histogram for the photo shown in Figure 7-10. Even though the light in the original photo is insufficient, the image isn't beyond rescue with a little Photoshop work.

7-12

You can see that there is a great deal of detail lurking in the dark shadow tones. The noise level is relatively low, so you can recover this detail and fix the underexposure.

2. First, add some bit depth to the unedited file to allow heavy editing without posterization problems. Perform the same steps to convert to a 16-bit image as described in step 1 of the section "Working with beyond-repair photos." (Convert to 16-bit and resample the image at 71 percent.)

3. Choose Image ➪ Apply Image and select Screen from the Blending options drop-down menu and leave the default Opacity setting at 100 percent, as shown in Figure 7-13. Just one application of the Screen mode brightens the image considerably (see Figure 7-14).

7-14

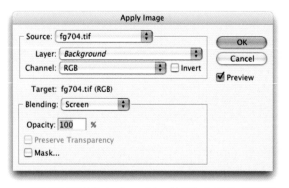

7-13

4. The dark image background still contains recoverable tonal separation that opens up the background and gives a more natural look to the snapshot. The best tool to use here is the Shadow/Highlight command utilizing only the shadow recovery feature. This tool works by auto-masking the dark tones and brings out tonal separation without affecting local contrast in the midtones.

Choose Image ➪ Adjust ➪ Shadow/Highlight to open the Shadow/Highlight dialog box. Easy does it is the keyword with this tool. A little goes a long way. For the example image, an amount setting of 15 percent of the shadow slider (see Figure 7-15) opens up the darkest tones and brings them to a more natural relationship with the foreground subjects (see Figure 7-16). High amount settings of the shadow slider cause severe haloing and a generally false look to the shadow tones. Apply the tool sparingly.

7-15

7-16

5. The image still lacks a full black or white tone. This is intentional. The initial edits with the Apply Image and Shadow/Highlight tools bring the image tones into a much more reasonable overall visual relationship and allow some fine-tuning for best quality.

The overall color balance of the image is pretty close to normal, but the red hues are oversaturated and too magenta compared to the rest of the colors. Choose Image ⇨ Adjust ⇨ Hue/Saturation. In the Hue/Saturation dialog box select Reds from the Edit drop-down menu. Reducing the red saturation by 15 percent normalizes the red saturation to the rest of the image colors — this is an eyeball judgment. But the reds are still too cool (magenta), so the Hue slider is dragged right by 5 percent to add a little yellow to the reds and warm them up as shown in Figure 7-17.

7-17

PRO TIP

To predict the hue change provided by the Hue slider, look at the color gradient on the bottom of the Hue/Saturation dialog box. Moving the slider slightly to the right when Reds are selected adds yellow to the red hues. Think of the bottom gradient as a standard color wheel lying flat on the bottom.

6. The image is still somewhat low in overall saturation, but you make the final adjustment if needed after you finish tone editing. A quick check of the Info pallet allows you to check the white and black point color balance, as well as determine absolute black and white point tone levels. In this image, the woman is wearing white pants, making highlight color balance easy to measure. For black, read the darkest tones in the background.

By default, the Navigator window is in the foreground of the Info Pallet. Either click the Info tab or press F8 to bring the Info Pallet into the foreground. Select the Eyedropper tool and then click on the lightest area of the image to assess the white point. Click the Eyedropper tool again on the darkest area of the image to assess the black point. The results show that both the white point and the black point are very close to neutral, as shown in Figure 7-18.

7-18

7. For a snapshot type of file, white and black assessment is close enough, but the white values are a little dull. The woman's white pants measured about level 225 at their brightest parts. You can't use Auto Contrast successfully on this file, because of some highlight clipping in the image on the planter light sources. Because you know the pants measure 225, you can simply open Levels and clip off some additional levels in the highlights to give a brighter white. Dragging the

NOTE

Neutral gray is composed of equal parts of red, green, and blue. When all the RGB channels read the same value, perfect neutral gray is confirmed.

Highlight slider 15 levels to the left (a setting of 240) places the highlight values right where you need them (see Figure 7-19).

7-19

The Highlight slider move adds that last bit of highlight sparkle. Because of file noise in the blacks, three additional levels of black are clipped off to give the file a more solid look, and the Gamma slider is dragged slightly to the left to add a little more overall image brightness.

PRO TIP

It's usually a good idea with noisy, underexposed files to leave black a little shy of Level zero to preserve all possible shadow detail.

The addition of the extra image contrast brings the overall saturation right on target — quite an improvement over the original file as you can see comparing the original (left) to the edited image (right) in Figure 7-20. The editing steps to fix a file like this take us less than one minute.

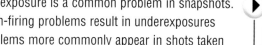
WHEN EXPOSURE IS NOT ENOUGH

Underexposure is a common problem in snapshots. Flash-firing problems result in underexposures but problems more commonly appear in shots taken at dusk outdoors, indoor shots where the flash is not sufficient to light all the background area, flashes that

7-20

fire outdoors in low-level light and don't provide sufficient lighting, and other similar shooting problems. In
many cases you know you won't get a great image
after editing, but that one vacation image shot at dusk
that happens to be too dark is one you want to show
the family.

Figure 7-21 shows an underexposed image shot
with a point-and-shoot camera. Because the camera
doesn't have an adjustable ISO range, the exposure
setting can't be controlled. This image is a typical
example of an urban twilight photo. The overall illumination level is low, and the street and building lights
are starting to show, which overpowers the ambient
illumination in a very short time. Commercial pros
have always called this time of day "magic hour."

7-21

Because of the urban subject matter, this photo contains a full mix of colors, unlike a traditional landscape, which is composed of mostly earth-tone
colors. You aren't able to control the noise problem,
but this image allows you an easy fix of the underexposure and color balance. Here's how:

1. To make your adjustments on a JPEG image shot
   with a point-and-shoot camera, first sharpen the
   image then shove it up to 16-bit mode. Choose
   Image ⇨ Mode ⇨ 16 Bits\Channel. Next, resample the image by choosing Image ⇨ Image Size to
   open the Image Size dialog box. Resample the
   image by reducing the size to 71 percent and set
   the resample mode to Bicubic.

X-REF

For more information on editing in 16-bit mode
and converting JPEGs to 16-bit, see Chapter 4.

The histogram (see Figure 7-22) shows that most
of the image tones are recorded below middle
gray. Notice the thin histogram line that extends
all the way to the White Point slider. This is the
image data of all the little bright light sources in
the picture along with the raindrops close to the
camera that are lit by the built-in camera flash.
The histogram reflects the fact that these little
highlights comprise only a tiny percentage of the
image. Holding detail in these little highlights is
irrelevant to the overall image quality, so the following fast edit works just fine.

7-22

2. Drag the White Point slider left (see Figure 7-23)
   until it just touches the main histogram hill. This
   brightens the image (see Figure 7-24) considerably, and avoids losing any highlight detail in the
   main image area.

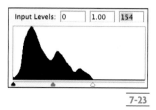

Input Levels: 0   1.00   154

7-23

7-25

7-24

3. Choose Image ➪ Adjust ➪ Levels. When the dialog box opens, click Options. Select the Enhance Per Channel Contrast radio button as shown in Figure 7-25. This step sets histogram clipping to work independently on the individual RGB color channels.

NOTE

If you follow the recommendations in Chapter 4, your Auto Levels Clip settings for Shadows and Highlights should already be set at .01 percent. Making the adjustment in the Auto Levels dialog box sets the Auto Color Correction Options to the same values.

4. An underexposed digital capture contains a great deal of noise. The histogram can't tell the difference between real image information and random noise, so you have to increase the clipping values to blow through the noise to allow Photoshop to recalculate the real image information. The new clip settings can vary a great deal depending on the image type and the result desired. Luckily, the monitor shows you the results of any new settings in real time without having to commit to the setting, so you can experiment a bit to get the visual appearance that you like.

The shadow tones of this image are very noisy, so start by typing **0.5** in the Shadows Clip box. The red tint in the shadows disappears right away (see Figure 7-26).

7-26

219

5. Set the Highlights Clip value to 0.5. The image lightens and the blue colorcast is eliminated, as shown in Figure 7-27.

7-27

Click OK in the Auto Color Correction Options box, and then click OK in the Levels box. (Try a higher number in the Highlight clipping box if the file shows little change.) Very noisy files might require a setting of 1 or higher. Play around until you get a result that you like. A setting of 0.5 is usually a good starting point. Do not click Save as Defaults, however. This is an independent adjustment you make for this image, as you can see in our edits shown in Figure 7-28. When editing other images for levels and color, you want to use your default settings where the Clip value is set at .01.

7-28

6. Your adjustments leave you with just one problem — the full correction eliminates the evening mood of the image. You can fix this problem by using the Fade command to fine-tune the overcorrection and replace the cool mood of the photo. Choose Edit ➪ Fade and the Fade dialog box opens (see Figure 7-29). Drag the Opacity slider left to reduce the amount of the Auto Color Correction.

7-29

PRO TIP

Dragging the slider all the way to the left (0 percent opacity) undoes the edit. This is a handy tool to decrease almost any kind of tonal or filter overedit.

A 75 percent Opacity setting seems to give the best look to the photo as you can see in the final image shown in Figure 7-31.

7. As a final little enhancement, do a Hue/Saturation edit to give the image more of a picture postcard look. Chose Image ➪ Adjust ➪ Hue/Saturation. For this image, add 25 percent overall saturation. In the default Master channel, drag the Saturation slider to +25.

Ted's haunted point and shoot sure likes those red tones! Decrease the Red saturation by selecting Reds from the Edit drop-down menu and decrease the Saturation setting to -40, as shown in Figure 7-30.

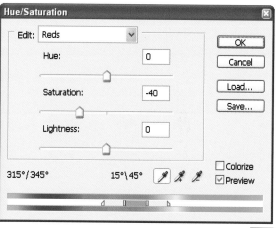

7-30

8. As a final edit, you may need to clone out some artifacts or spots in the image. The raindrops are knocked out of this image, and the final result appears in Figure 7-31. As you can see in the final image, the photo suffers from a large noise problem and the contrast is not as snappy as a shot taken in a studio with controlled lighting. However, for those snapshots where you have similar problems, you can see that the final result at least gives us an image that we can show off to the family.

7-31

REDUCING NOISE

Although you can rescue pictures that suffer from tonal loss, the result is usually an image with a lot of noise. That is what happened with the example images that were shot with insufficient flash, including the twilight image shown in the previous section. It's a perennial tradeoff between good tonal reproduction and image sharpness. Unfortunately, Photoshop can't offer both when your original photos are shot with severe lighting and exposure problems. You have to make choices individually for how much of one you have to sacrifice for the other.

One of the added features in Photoshop CS2 is a new Noise Reduction filter. The manual noise reduction methods used in older versions of Photoshop are time consuming and tedious. The new filter reduces noise automatically, but it works relatively slowly. The more processing power you have on your computer the more you'll enjoy using this feature for faster editing.

Because we work with snapshot-type files here, we want to fix them quickly. The Noise Reduction filter can be fine-tuned to give a custom result, but we aren't going there with snapshot files. The following method fixes the noise quickly and still allows you to fine-tune the amount of reduction in one step.

Figure 7-32 shows a great deal of noise. The multicolored noise is the most distracting. This kind of noise is referred to as *chromatic noise. Luminance noise* concerns tonal speckling. For our purposes, it's all just noise and no matter what noise you see in your file, the noise reduction method described here works well. Follow these steps:

1. Open a file where you see noise after making corrections similar to the corrections made on files in all the previous sections in this chapter. Choose Filter ⇨ Noise ⇨ Reduce Noise.

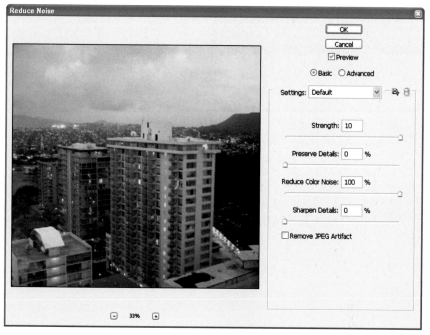

7-32

The Reduce Noise dialog box has four adjustment sliders as shown in Figure 7-32. Set them as follows:

> **Strength:** 10

> **Preserve Details:** 0%

> **Reduce Color Noise:** 100%

> **Sharpen Details:** 0%

Next, click OK.

2. You just turned the filter up to a full blast. It does an amazing job of eliminating all the noise. The only problem is, it also wipes out a lot of image detail and sharpness (see Figure 7-33). Just zoom in on the image and you can see how much detail.

3. Depending on your image and the effect you want, you may be satisfied with sacrificing some image sharpness to eliminate noise. In this example, we want to regain a little sharpness so you increase the sharpness by applying less noise reduction.

7-33

Choose Edit ⇨ Fade. Drag the slider toward zero Opacity until the image seems to have the best compromise between noise and lost detail. It's your call. There's no *perfect* setting. This image uses a setting of 50 percent. It seems like a good compromise, the result of which is shown in Figure 7-34.

7-34

You might want more local control of the noise reduction. In this image, the sky area has no real detail, so the noise is the most visible in the sky. It would be great to give the sky full noise reduction, while maintaining the same 50 percent for the foreground.

1. The easiest way to decide which areas to give full strength and which areas to hold back noise reduction is to use a duplicate layer and the Eraser tool. You have to be careful how you set up the duplicate layer, so you can erase to less detail. The first step is to drag the Background to the Create a new layer icon in the Layers palette to duplicate the layer. As yet, there is no noise reduction in these steps.

   Before you use the Noise Reduction filter, you want it to act on the bottom (Background) layer. The top layer has to be invisible or you won't see

anything happen when you run the filter. Hide the top layer by clicking on the eyeball icon (see Figure 7-35).

7-35

2. You're ready to run the filter. Choose Filter ⇨ Noise ⇨ Noise Reduction. Use the same settings for the Strength (10), Preserve Details (0), Reduce Color Noise (100), and Sharpen Details (0) used in the first example in this section. The result looks exactly like it did before you ran the Fade filter — very soft.

3. This time, instead of using the Fade filter, activate the top layer (which still holds the noisy version of the image). Click the layer and click the eyeball icon to show the layer.

4. Drag the Opacity slider on the top layer to 50 percent. The resulting image looks exactly like it did when you used the Fade slider and faded the adjustment to 50 percent.

5. Leave the top layer activated and select the Eraser tool. Make the brush size large, and leave Hardness set to zero. You want a nice soft edge on the brush. Leave Opacity set at 100 percent. For this 7MB file, a brush size of 200 pixels works well.

   Move the Eraser over the sky area to bring back the full noise reduction effect. Erasing to the horizon finishes the layer edit. The result is a much better-looking cloudy sky. You can also erase away more noise in any local area of the image. It just depends on the image, and the result you'll like best. The final image appears in Figure 7-36.

Figure 7-1 that we corrected back in the first section of this chapter had a lot of noise. In Figure 7-37 we used noise reduction on a layer and set the Opacity to 50 percent. We then created two more layers adding more noise reduction with 100 percent opacity and merged the two 100 percent opacity layers. We used the Eraser tool to remove areas around the face, hands, badge, and on some of the table items in the photo to help sharpen them up a bit by erasing the noise reduction merged layers. The background textures and table curtain don't really require a sharp look so we left the noise reduction from all three layers at full strength.

As you can see in Figure 7-37 the original corrected image appears on the left with the noise reduction image on the right. The end result is really a testimony to Photoshop's power in rescuing very bad images.

7-36

7-37

CORRECTING RED-EYE

You know that picture of Aunt Sarah you shot on Christmas Eve is going to be great. But when you open the file in Photoshop, poor Aunt Sarah's eyes have red rings. The red-eye effect that is so common with flash photography is something you need to handle on most indoor pictures taken with built-in flash.

Because this problem is so common in flash photography, almost all cameras sold today have a built-in red-eye correction function. From low-end point-and-shoot cameras where red-eye correction is a fixed feature to DSLR cameras where you have a setting you can turn on and off, red-eye correction is a standard on many digital cameras. However, some of these automated red-eye correction tools found in cameras, and some quick fixes you find in Photoshop, can cause more problems than fixes.

We could talk about using the Red Eye tool or using the Channel Mixer or a number of other different fixes for red-eye problems, but we'll stick with a method that tends to work best when the red eye is so severe that you can't return to a natural eye color by simply removing the red from the eye. You may need to restore a little eye color after you eliminate the red. Try this:

1. Create a selection around the eye and feather the selection at least 5 or more pixels. In some cases, you may need to increase the feather amount to 15 pixels. The amount you apply for feathering depends on your image resolution and the severity of the red-eye problem. If at first you don't succeed, revert your file and try another feather amount.

In Figure 7-38, the red eye is so severe you can't determine what the original eye color should be. In this example, you need to remove the red eye and restore the eye to its natural color.

7-38

2. Choose Image ⇨ Adjust ⇨ Channel Mixer. In the Channel Mixer dialog box, you see the Red Channel slider at +100%. Drag the slider to 0 (zero) or simply type 0 (zero) in the Red channel text box. Drag both the Green and Blue sliders to 50%, as shown in Figure 7-39.

7-39

Generally, a 50% adjustment takes care of any problem with too much cyan appearing in the edited area. This takes the red out of the image (see Figure 7-40).

3. To restore the eye color, you may need to open a second file where you can see a good sample of the natural eye color. If you shot many images of your subject, you most likely have some images where the red-eye problem is not as severe and which shows a good sample of the eye color. Open such an image and then click the Eyedropper tool to lift the color and to make it your new foreground color.

4. Close the second file and select the Color Replacement tool in the Tools palette.

7-40

5. Paint with the Color Replacement tool around the iris in the eye to restore the natural eye color. In Figure 7-41, we fixed the red-eye problem, then moved on to make other color and tonal corrections for brightness and color correction as discussed in Chapters 4 and 5.

7-41

CORRECTING UNEVEN OVEREXPOSURES

Uneven exposures often occur when shooting indoors when daylight spills in through a window and creates an overexposure in the background and an underexposure of the foreground subject. Additionally, many overexposures occur in bright sunlight when your meter is focused on a foreground subject against a bright background.

In working with overexposures, you typically have one of two goals to accomplish. One goal is to try to bring the underexposed background area to normal brightness where you can see detail in the highlights — something that you can't always accomplish. The other goal might be to let the background stay washed out a bit and diffuse the background to work the image a bit so the foreground subject stands out in the photo. This objective might be something like having a very shallow depth of field where all the background detail is out of focus.

One thing you might consider when shooting scenes where you know you are going to have strong contrast in lighting between the foreground subject and the background is to be certain to meter your scene for the detail you want to capture.

You have three choices:

> Meter the foreground subject when you don't care about the background.

> Meter the background when you don't care as much about the foreground.

> Average the exposure between foreground and background knowing you have to do work in Photoshop to adjust the brightness and contrast.

When you don't want a silhouette, you want the foreground subject to be properly exposed or you may want the entire picture to be properly exposed. It is unlikely that you are more concerned about the background detail than the foreground.

NOTE

Unless you have manual controls for your camera's meter, the camera's sensor provides an average exposure of the field of view. With point-and-shoot cameras, you may not be able to control exposure. DSLR cameras have all the manual controls you need to override the camera's meter.

1. If shooting with a DSLR or a point-and-shoot with manual exposure control — where you can manually control exposure — move in close to the foreground subject so the meter can assess only the subject without background light. If your subject is people, have your subject hold out a hand or use your own hand to meter flesh tones in the light in which you intend to expose your image.

2. Lock down the exposure and use your manual overrides to shoot at the shutter speed and f-stop recorded by your camera's meter.

3. Shoot the image. When you open the file in Photoshop, you should have a correct exposure for the foreground subject while the background may be washed out.

One method you can use with washed-out backgrounds is to apply some adjustments to strengthen the tonal range of the background a little and then edit the image for a very narrow depth of field and blur it to subdue the background. In this regard, you use the background to help bring the foreground subject forward where it receives the most attention.

If your exposure is neither appropriate for the background nor foreground, and you want both areas to appear with the best tonal ranges, you may have to mask the areas and adjust color independently. For the purpose of the discussion in this chapter, we first discuss making brightness and contrast adjustments for an uneven exposure; masking and color correction are covered in Chapter 10. To first make adjustments for uneven exposures before you make color adjustments, follow these steps:

1. In the snapshot in Figure 7-42, the camera meter calculates an average exposure setting from the dark foreground and the bright background. The resulting image shows what happens in this kind of lighting situation. Neither the foreground nor background is properly exposed.

7-42

Lightening the dark foreground wipes out the remaining detail in the background, and recovering the detail in the background leaves you with just silhouettes of the main subjects.

There are a number of ways to deal with this kind of image. It all depends on how much time you want to spend on the edits and the level of quality you desire. In Figure 7-42, you want to take your time and try to bring out as much as you can in both shadows and highlights. A quick check of the histogram tells you that most of this image is recoverable (see Figure 7-43).

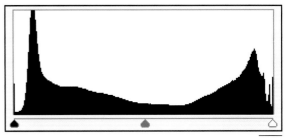

7-43

Another quick way to check for tonal highlight and shadow clipping in this type of file is the Threshold command. This confirms quickly if the file is worth trying an aggressive tonal recovery. The Threshold command is actually designed to create an edit of a single tonal level and displays the chosen level in the image preview. You are just using it to check Level 1 (Black) and Level 255 (White) to see how much tonal information is missing from the file. To make this assessment, choose Image ⇨ Adjust ⇨ Threshold. The image and the Threshold dialog box are shown in Figure 7-44.

X-REF

For more information on using the Threshold command, see Chapter 9.

By default, the adjustment slider is centered when the dialog box opens. The preview shows all middle gray pixels (Level 128). It looks like an old-fashioned litho negative from the old days — like way back in 1990! Interesting to play with, but you are just using it for a fast preview.

Drag the slider all the way to the right, and all full-white pixels are displayed (see Figure 7-45). Drag the slider all the way to the left to see just the full-black pixels (see Figure 7-46). The black and white pixel previews show that very little of the image is completely clipped, so a great deal of correction can be achieved.

2. Most of the image tones are segregated on the left and right sides of the histogram. In other words, the file has mostly very dark and very light tones. A single global edit can't really do a very good job of fixing the tonalities; but if you're in a hurry, just use the Shadow/Highlight command. The Shadow/Highlight command works by creating shadow and highlight masks to isolate tonal areas and attempts to repair the problem tones separately. If used with care, a reasonably good result can be obtained.

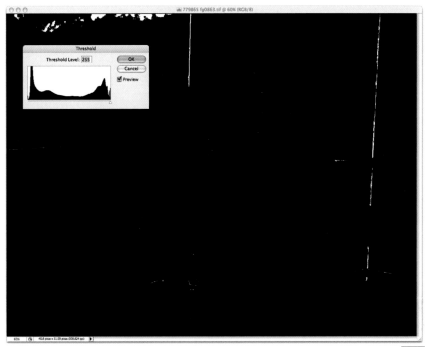

7-45

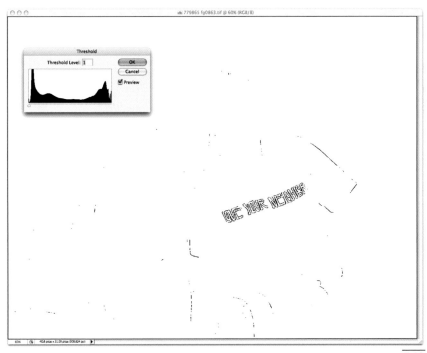

7-46

Choose Image ⇨ Adjustments ⇨ Shadow/Highlight to open the Shadow/Highlight dialog box. Be sure to select the More Options check box to expand the dialog box as shown in Figure 7-47. The Amount sliders determine how much change to make to the highlight or shadow tones, but selecting the More Options check box allows finer control.

7-47

The Tonal Width control determines how far the correction is allowed to bleed into the midtones. The Default setting of 50 percent is a good starting point. Lower the setting if the middle tones are lightened more than you want. Very low settings affect only the darkest tones, but result in excessive graying out of the darkest tones if pushed too far.

The Radius setting tells Photoshop how far to sample around the dark pixels to determine the local tonal limits in the correction. A low setting can result in smearing of the tones.

For this image, the Shadow Slider Amount is set at 40 percent. Tonal width is boosted to 80 percent to walk the lightening into the darker midtones. Radius is left at the default setting of 30 pixels.

Notice the Black and White clipping options on the bottom of the dialog box. This works just like a pass through Levels right before or after the Shadow/Highlight edit. It's like two edits in one. Lightening the shadows can result in loss of any full-black pixels and makes the image look flat. The Black Clip is set to 1.5 percent, which darkens the blacks somewhat, but doesn't wipe out needed shadow detail. A Clip setting that is too high can eliminate the detail you're trying to recover, so take care not to overdo the clipping.

For the Highlights correction, the Amount is set at 50 percent, but set Tonal Width to just 20 percent. Because a Shadow setting is used that allows lightening of midtones, make sure to limit the highlight correction to just the lightest tones to avoid a double correction in the midtones. The Highlight clipping amount is left at default, because the image view in Threshold shows highlight clipping in the brightest parts of the background.

3. Click OK and observe the result. Using the Shadow/Highlight command is a great improvement (see Figure 7-48) over the original file, but foreground and background color balance and saturation still don't match each other as well as they could.

7-48

4. To finish up the image you need to make some color corrections. However, for finer control over correcting the color in the image, create selection masks for the foreground and the background, and edit the color separately for the highlights and shadows. All the steps for creating the selection masks and adjusting the color are detailed in Chapter 10. After making the color corrections as explained in Chapter 10, the final image appears in Figure 7-49.

X-REF

For a continuation of the steps to produce the final image where more advanced masking methods and color correction are discussed, see Chapter 10.

7-49

WORKING WITH FLUORESCENT LIGHTING

Standard fluorescent lighting has always been a big problem for quality color photography. As explained in Chapter 1, the color rendering index (CRI) of an average fluorescent light is far from ideal. The most common fluorescent tube used in commercial interiors is still the ubiquitous Cool White. The spectrum is awful for photography and always contains a number of green and yellow spikes in the output spectrum. The resulting photos shot under this type of light source will always have a green cast when shot with daylight balance.

There isn't a fix for those fluorescent green pictures that doesn't involve some eyeball color balancing, unless there's a known white or gray in the capture. The most important work you need to be concerned about, as is the case in most photography, is to set up the shots correctly. That means using a white balance adjustment on your camera — if it exists — and shooting with a gray card to help deal with the tonal corrections once you get the files in Photoshop. One simple solution is to tape a .30cc green filter over the flash and leave the camera in auto white balance. Even if the auto guess is a bit off, the resulting picture will have the same general color balance throughout.

The low CRI makes a high-quality final result impossible, but careful color correction allows acceptable results. So, with the understanding that there is no easy solution, here's how to fix up your snapshots:

Figure 7-50 is a typical capture in a mall store using the Auto White Balance setting under fluorescent lighting. The camera comes fairly close considering all the different types of tubes used in the light fixtures. Beth looks a little jaundiced, but almost passable.

7-50

If your camera is set to daylight balance, the problem is obvious when you open the image in Photoshop. As you can see in Figure 7-51, we turned poor Beth into a Martian. If your images appear like this figure you know that your camera's white balance was set to daylight when you shot the picture.

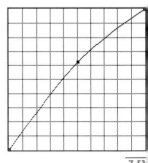

7-52

7-51

The colorcast is overwhelming, and the only remedy for this image is some custom color correction. Use this example for your correction steps here and try the easy method of correction first.

1. Choose Image ➪ Adjustments ➪ AutoColor. AutoColor can be hit or miss, but in this case it results in quite an improvement, as you can see in Figure 7-52. With such a strong cast to begin with, even a near-miss helps a lot.

2. The image is too dark. Use Curves to lighten it up some. This is a basic lighten curve adjustment (see Figure 7-53).

X-REF

For a detailed description of the six common Curves adjustments, see Chapter 4.

7-53

As you can see in Figure 7-54, the Curves adjustment brightens up the image, but it can be a little better.

7-54

7-55

3. There's a lot of what seems to be white and near-gray objects in the background. You can't be completely certain, but you can always take some guesses.

The Curves dialog box contains three eyedroppers. The one in the center changes any color in the file to gray just by clicking it in the document window. In many cases, you can obtain a good color correction just by clicking around until you hit a genuine neutral value somewhere in the image.

Three places look like good candidates, as shown in Figure 7-55.

Click on position 1 in Figure 7-55. This sample turns the image to cyan blue (see Figure 7-56, left). That pile of paper must have been an orangish color. Click position 2 in Figure 7-55 and the result is much better (see Figure 7-56, center). However, the flesh tones look a bit too warm. The papers must have had a cool tint. But with this temporary correction it's a lot easier to see what's really in the background. That pile of books above her left shoulder looks like a good target. Click the eyedropper in the gray seams of the books (see Figure 7-56, right). This sample is very close but the image is still too dark.

7-56

4. With the Curves dialog box still open, lighten the image by moving the midpoint up to a similar position as shown in Figure 7-53. This adjustment is just about the right correction (see Figure 7-57).

7-57

The other big problem under fluorescent lighting occurs when you activate your camera flash. The fluorescent light is far greener than your camera flash, and the two don't mix well at all. If you use your camera with a flash in auto white balance setting, you're likely to get a result something like the one in Figure 7-58. The camera tries to compromise the color balance, and Beth turns magenta while the background, which is out of flash range, turns green. You cannot fix the problem without a lot of time-consuming masking, but there is an easy fix while shooting. It's nice to be able to use the flash, especially if the interior lighting is spotty and uneven, but weird colors will never do. The solution is to filter the flash to match the fluorescent lighting — or at least get it much closer.

7-58

Point-and-shoot cameras have very small flashguns, so a tiny filter is all you need. The Rosco Laboratories Inc., makers of correction filters for movie production, has just the filter you need. It's called Rosco Tough Plus Green #3304. This filter is designed to change daylight to cool white. The daylight balance flash then matches the cool white lamps. In other words, all the light becomes goose green. The filter can be purchased at Calumet Photographic (www.calumetphoto.com) for $7.49 as of this writing.

The filter is huge, 20 inches x 24 inches, so you'll have plenty for years to come. The filter is designed for light sources only and is made of tough polyester. You can use a .30cc green camera gel filter if you want, but a tiny 3-inch x 3-inch filter is the same price because it's designed to be placed on a camera lens.

Just cut a piece of filter slightly larger than your camera flash, and affix it with tape, or use a special photographic grade copolymer cross-linked matrix, hot extruded, catalyst-hardened attachment band as shown in Figure 7-59. This configuration works great with no glue residue to worry about. If the filter gets dirty or damaged, just cut another piece from your giant filter stash.

7-59

When shooting close-ups of people or objects, the soft overcast light can be quite flattering. The lack of harsh shadows gives an open look to the tones when working in close and can create a soft serene mood if used appropriately.

The snapshot in Figure 7-61 is an example of overcast lighting that flatters the subject matter.

7-61

In Figure 7-60, you see the result of shooting with a .30cc green camera gel filter and using a fluorescent white balance setting on the camera. As shown in the photo, the color balance is much improved over the original photo.

7-60

On the other hand, wide landscape views that include a lot of sky can look just awful on an overcast day. The camera's metering system averages out the brightness values. Because the sky is the actual light source for the entire photo, the result is a gray, dreary capture lacking in contrast and snap.

The landscape view of Chairman Mao in Figure 7-62 is the kind of result to expect on a heavily overcast day when the image includes a great deal of sky. The image quality could use "a great leap forward."

Some complex and time-consuming masking, combined with custom edits, can greatly improve this kind of photo; but in this chapter, the fast fix is what you're after. Here's a revolutionary method that takes little time to improve a flat overcast image:

WORKING ON CLOUDY DAYS

Days with overcast lighting can be a blessing or a curse, depending on the subject matter you're trying to capture and the total image content. A full overcast turns the sky into a giant soft box light. The result is a nearly shadowless top light and low image contrast.

7-62

7-64

1. Open the Shadow Highlight command by choosing Image ➪ Adjustments ➪ Shadow/Highlight. Leave the shadow setting at or near default as shown in Figure 7-63.

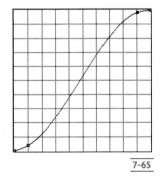

7-63

The shadows look somewhat overcorrected. Move the Highlight Amount slider to the right until the highlights darken to near the values of the original image. The image is still flat, as shown in Figure 7-64. The shadows are overcorrected, but this is the appearance you're after for the second and final step.

2. Open the Curves dialog box by choosing Image ➪ Adjustments ➪ Curves, and create a classic contrast increase curve (see Figure 7-65).

7-65

A little extra bump is added to the highlight end of the curve for the sky. The midtone portion of the curve adds a great deal of midtone contrast, as shown in Figure 7-66.

7-66

By overcorrecting the shadows with the Shadow/Highlight command and darkening the sky at the same time with the Highlight Amount slider, you leave plenty of tonal headroom for the Curves edit to boost midtone contrast. The usual darkening of shadows and brightening of highlights by the contrast curve is compensated by the first editing move. This also gives you far more tonal control than using the Midtone Contrast option in the Shadow/Highlight edit.

As you gain experience with Photoshop, you'll find that editing becomes far easier when you always try to think one step ahead of each editing move you make and visualize the final result of multiple editing moves. One might seem to contradict the other until you see them as a whole.

"The analytical method is dialectical. By analysis, we mean analyzing the contradictions in things. And sound analysis is impossible without intimate knowledge of life and without real understanding of the pertinent contradictions." — Mao Tse-Tung

SHARPENING SNAPSHOTS

Sharpening? Wasn't that covered in Chapter 4, you ask? Yes, sharpening guidelines were covered in Chapter 4, and for a good number of Photoshop edits, the methods described in that chapter work well. But for point-and-shoot cameras capturing JPEG images, it is necessary to offer yet one more method for sharpening. As you know, Photoshop has about a dozen different ways to perform any given task, so here's a consideration for the point-and-shooters.

Most point-and-shoot digital cameras made in the last few years automatically sharpen (edge enhance) image captures when the JPEG file is created from the camera data and stored on the memory card. The default sharpening is usually adequate for the vast majority of snapshots.

Sharpness problems can arise when working with noisy and underexposed files similar to the typical examples used in this chapter. In many cases, the camera's auto exposure system uses a very slow shutter speed in its attempt to capture as good a file as possible. A very wide aperture setting is also very common in this kind of situation. The result in many cases is a soft image that lacks sharp detail. The slow shutter speed amplifies camera shake during capture, and the wide aperture setting can make any focusing errors far worse than a smaller aperture with a wider depth of field. In addition, the noise problem is also of great concern. Sharpening adds more noise to your files.

If the file is very noisy, like the urban scene example used for noise reduction, it's best to leave well enough alone and use the file as is. On the other hand, if a soft file can tolerate a little sharpening, the following method gives you the best result with the least enhancement of noise.

Keep in mind that the following method is an abuse of the Unsharp Mask filter. Unsharp masking can't replace lost detail: It can only enhance tonal edges to create the illusion of more sharpness.

1. Return to the snapshot of Danielle and Drew used earlier in the chapter (see Figure 7-42). The file requires an aggressive tone recovery, and the image also suffers from camera motion with a narrow depth of field. The resulting image is very soft with moderate noise.

   Noise artifacts are difficult to see at the image magnification required for printing in this book, so the examples are tight crops that are upsampled with Genuine Fractals Print Pro to simulate a 100 percent size monitor view (at least we tried anyway).

X-REF

For more information on Genuine Fractals Print Pro, see Chapter 1.

We always advise downsampling a defective snapshot before you begin editing. Because you are willing to take a resolution hit to recover the file, it is advantageous to presharpen an out-of-focus file before editing begins. Use a wide radius setting with the Unsharp Mask filter to sharpen the soft edges, and noise is greatly enhanced. By sharpening before downsampling, some of this noise is averaged out by the bicubic interpolation. The difference is fairly subtle, but you need every advantage you can get with a soft, noisy file.

PRO TIP

When examining file noise for final output on inkjet and commercial printing, a 50 percent monitor view gives a more realistic impression of final output noise.

Techniques described for sharpening antique photos (see Chapter 9) are more useful for recovering very blurry pictures, but this method is fast and adds little time to your bad snapshot edits.

In Figure 7–67, the unedited file looks very soft at 100 percent screen view. Edges are not well defined. We use the final image after color correcting it, which we discuss in Chapter 10.

2. Use a wide-radius Unsharp Mask to force some crispness back into the tonal edges. For this image, use an Amount setting of 500 percent, a Radius setting of 2.0, and a Threshold setting of 2 (see Figure 7-68).

7-67

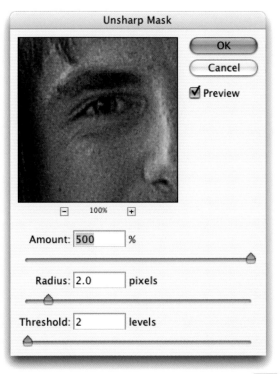

7-68

Don't panic when you see the Amount of 500 percent appearing like your file is much too over-sharpened. You take care of that when you down-sample the image. You also use a lower Threshold amount than recommended in Chapter 4. A slight bit of Threshold is a good idea, but easy does it. Be certain to not push the Threshold slider down too far when using this method.

3. Downsample after the edit. This may be contrary to what you frequently hear about sharpening after downsampling. After all, downsampling soft-ens the image. However, because you exaggerate the sharpening, your downsampling averages out the noise and reduces the exaggerated edge sharpness.

Notice the visible haloing of tones in Figure 7-69 after you apply the Unsharp Mask filter. The amount shown is about right for a very soft file. Turn down the Amount setting if noise looks any worse than this example.

7-69

Choose Image ⇨ Image Size to open the Image Size dialog box. Type **71%** in the Width or Height item after changing the units to Percent for the best results. Be certain to select Bicubic from the Resample to drop-down menu.

4. Click OK. That's all there is to it. Proceed with the rest of your edit. If the image looks oversharpened when you view the file at 50 percent on your monitor, you can use the History palette to return to the Unsharp Mask adjustment. Apply a lower Amount in the Unsharp Mask dialog box and try again.

Figure 7-70 shows the file unsharpened (left), sharpened before downsampling (center), and sharpened an equivalent amount after downsampling (right). The difference in dark tone noise is noticeable at the same perceptual sharpness.

7-70

I'm confused about when to sharpen my images during my editing process.

As a general rule you want to sharpen images as one of the last steps in your editing process. This works well for Camera Raw images where you always perform sharpening tasks while in 16-bit mode before you reduce the file to 8-bit mode for printing or screen viewing.

The exception to the rule is when you convert an 8-bit image to 16-bit to perform your color correction steps, reduce noise, and perform all your tonal adjustments. When you make 8-bit to 16-bit conversions, first sharpen your images before downsampling them.

Why do my very dark photos turn red when I make brightness and contrast adjustments?

Dark, underexposed images adjusted using Levels and Curves can produce oversaturation, excessive color noise, and massive tone haloing. A simple brightness and contrast adjustment using the Levels, Curves, or Shadow/Highlight isn't the best way to make tone adjustments on these kinds of images.

You need to use multiple duplicate layers with the Apply Image command using Screen mode, while alternating between Normal and Luminosity modes in the layer stack at 50 percent opacity. By building up the image data in this manner, you avoid producing images with overly saturated reds and a lot of color noise. To help you out with these kinds of corrections, you can record an action that creates the layers needed to make your adjustments and fine-tune the results after adding about five different alternating layers.

A lot of my images appear a little too cool or a little too warm. Is there an easy correction method I can use to change the mood of my images?

In many cases, a simple application of using a Photo Filter can warm up an image or cool it down. You don't always need to use the Hue/Saturation dialog box to make these kinds of corrections. Look over our discussion in Chapter 10 on using the Photo Filter adjustment layers to learn more on how to change the mood in your images.

I'm never quite sure where to move my Levels sliders to adjust brightness and contrast. Is there a standard rule of thumb I can follow to make these kinds of adjustments?

Remember that once you make a destructive adjustment on a Background you can't regain the image data you lost. You can always use a Levels adjustment layer and return to the Levels dialog box to fine-tune your adjustment without destroying any image data.

As a general rule of thumb, look over the Levels dialog box histogram and study it to determine where you have no data appearing in the highlights and shadows. Try to observe the distinction between tonal absence and noise. Usually noise appears as a straight line at the base of the histogram from the last hill on either end to the 0 or 255 tone levels. When you move the white point and black point sliders, don't position them adjacent to the last (or first) appearance of image data. Fall short of the histogram hills slightly and make your other tonal adjustments.

If you need to return to the Levels dialog box you can easily do so when using an adjustment layer. Double-click the adjustment layer and the Levels dialog box opens. You can then move your white point and black point sliders a little to tweak the adjustment. Get used to using the eyedropper to assess the white and black points to find a neutral balance, and you'll know exactly where to move the sliders.

When I have an image with blown-out highlights and shadows I always have a problem adjusting brightness and contrast. How do I make adjustments in these kinds of images?

You can't always make a global adjustment on an image. Sometimes you need to isolate the highlights and shadows and make the adjustments independent of each other. First, try the Shadow/Highlight command and see if that does the trick for making a good tonal adjustment.

If the Shadow/Highlight command doesn't work, you need to create a selection mask and apply Levels and Curves adjustments to the shadows and highlights independently. To make your selections, try using the Color Range command, and select Highlights for one selection and Shadows for the other. If you have a lot of mid-tone data, you may not be able to make one selection and inverse it, but it's worth a try.

After making one selection, use the Levels and Curves dialog boxes to make your brightness and contrast adjustments. Inverse the selection and see if making similar adjustments does the job. If not, return to Color Range and select the Shadows, and follow the same steps for brightness and contrast adjustments.

Chapter 8

PHOTOCOPYING

"If your pictures aren't good enough, you're not close enough." — Robert Capa

Photocopying, in digital camera photographic terms, is a broad topic that can encompass everything from traditional photocopying using a copy stand to using your camera as a substitute for a scanner. When you think about it, if you have a DSLR camera, you have an instrument much superior to ordinary consumer-grade desktop scanners, and you can often achieve results as good as scanners costing hundreds of dollars.

As a measure of just the quality of photos taken with a digital camera, look at Figure 8-1. The photo on the left was shot with the Canon 20D DSLR. The photo on the right was a 4 x 5 transparency scanned on a drum scanner. As you can see, the quality of the images compared to each other is quite respectable.

You may find yourself engaged in a number of different kinds of photocopying assignments. Fine artists are finding their way to digital-imaging centers for inkjet output for creating limited-edition prints. The art prints first need to be acquired in digital form,

and what better way to capture them than with your camera?

You might have photos, slides, 3D objects, documents that need to be converted to text using optical character recognition (OCR) software, printed pieces where the copyright owner of the piece doesn't have the original photo, and a host of other source material that needs to be captured as digital files. In most circumstances, a good-quality digital camera can handle all your photocopy jobs.

Using your digital camera for copy work is a blessing when compared to using a scanner. You can crank off ten or more shots for every pass a scanner performs. So if you find that your camera does a good job, tuck the scanner away in the closet and use the tool that saves you time.

Photocopying, however, brings its own problems regarding brightness/contrast, tonal corrections, and some new dilemmas not yet addressed in earlier chapters. As is the case with all digital photography, the better your source material and lighting, the better

8-1

the images you can expect to open in Camera Raw and Photoshop. In many cases, however, expect to spend some time in Photoshop editing your files. You may have printed pieces that need to be edited to prevent moiré patterns from appearing on your prints. You may see various tones on photocopies that need to be neutralized. You may need to do some heavy editing in Photoshop to repair anomalies captured from the source material. All in all, photocopying is a fast, easy way for shooting material that was once a job handled by a scanner; but in digital photography terms, it presents a new set of problems that can take some editing time.

CREATING A MAKESHIFT COPY STAND

Digital copy work is generally set up the same way you approach analog photography. If your source material is small enough to fit on a table within the camera's field of view, you need a *copy stand.* Professional photographers have copy stands in their studios. You can purchase a stand from a photo supplier, or you can make your own stand after picking up materials from sources such as eBay or a local home-improvement store.

If you don't have a copy stand, you would be wise to invest a few dollars to make your own stand. Critically important, of course, is the lighting arrangement you assemble to light your source material.

Readymade copy stands are still manufactured today, but a high-quality stand can cost $1,000 or more. It's hard to justify this expense unless you plan to do enough copy work to amortize the cost of the stand in a reasonable period of time. As an alternative, with a little ingenuity, you can make your own quality copy stand with all the basic features of the professional models.

A copy stand is nothing more than a chassis that holds the camera in alignment over a horizontal flat surface and a balanced light source to evenly illuminate the copy area surface. The easiest and cheapest solution for the chassis is an old photo enlarger. Photo enlargers are, by design, nothing more than a device to hold an optical flat bed in perfect alignment with a flat surface under the optical bed. A light source is included on top to provide illumination for the transparent original to be projected onto the board.

You simply remove the projection module from the chassis, attach your camera, and your stand is ready for use. Of course, enlarger designs varied greatly over the years, so you need one that allows easy attachment of your camera without a lot of fuss. In Figure 8-2, you see our homemade copy chassis. It started life as a Bogen 6 x 7 Color Enlarger purchased on eBay for $50.

We don't have the room in this book to outline all the steps to make your own copy stand. For the mechanically inclined, you can no doubt discover the few pieces of hardware needed to attach your camera to the stand and set up the lights. Search around the Internet and check eBay for an old photo enlarger, and you can play around with it to create your own stand much cheaper than buying a copy stand from a photo supplier.

8-2

COPYING PHOTO PRINTS

Shooting photo prints with your camera has at least one great advantage over scanning prints. You can use polarizing filters on your lights and camera to reduce reflections off your source material. You don't have the same latitude when scanning prints. The only way you can eliminate any unwanted reflections is to make a copy negative of a print using a polarizing filter or muddle through a number of gyrations of twisting and turning your original print on the scanner platen — quite a nonsensical series of steps considering your digital camera and some filters can save you a lot of time.

The challenge you face when shooting older photos is that older papers tend to curl, and you can't lay them flat on a copy stand or mount them on a wall. This condition is good for neither shooting with a digital camera nor scanning. If you lay a severely curled photo print on a scanner platen and plop the lid down, you run the risk of adding more cracks and creases in the print. The objective henceforth is to remove the curl so you can lay the print flat in order to shoot it.

Vintage photos were printed on papers with a gelatin base that, for all intents and purposes, remains in a liquid state. If the gelatin dries, it turns to powder. The thing that prevents more modern papers from curling is that they have a resin coating that secures the paper and prevents it from curling. Because moisture is already part of your source material, the best way to get the curl out is to add a little moisture to the print. You don't want to bathe the print or spray a solvent on the emulsion, but add a gradual amount of moisture over a long period of time.

Adding the moisture is where you need a little help from Grandma. Remember the cake plate and the cake cover grandma used to serve and store her desserts? If you can get hold of that same kind of cake cover, you've just added a valuable piece of equipment to your photo studio.

Place a print on a flat surface and add room temperature water to a cup (see Figure 8-3).

8-3

Place the cake cover over the print and cup of water and walk away (see Figure 8-4). After three to seven days, pull the cake cover and see your print laying flat with the curl removed.

If the above method doesn't work and you are willing to take a risk, submerge your print in distilled water with Photo Flo (Photo Flo can be purchased from you photo supplier). In many cases you won't damage the print, but there are times when the emulsion falls off. If you have a precious print you need to preserve and you don't want to risk damaging the photo, place the print under glass and shoot it.

8-4

Photo Restoration Resources

Photo restoration is an art form in and of itself. Covering all the methods and techniques for restoring photos is beyond the scope of this book. The same tonal and color corrections you use with underexposed photos and tonal limitations found in photos throughout this book can be used when restoring photos. Other things that you have to be able to edit in Photoshop like removing dust and scratches, reconstructing parts of a photo, and photo compositing are left to other authors. You can find an excellent book by Katrin Eismann on photo retouching and restoration at any of the online resellers or your local bookstore. In addition, many other Photoshop books have chapters specifically covering restoration and compositing. Search through books at your local bookstore to find the book that suits your needs.

Once your print is prepared for shooting, use a copy stand as we described earlier in this chapter. Use a clear piece of window glass that is clean and dust free. Don't worry about the reflection because you take care of that with the polarizing filter on the camera lens. Use your camera and arrange your lights to shoot the image as you see in Figure 8-5.

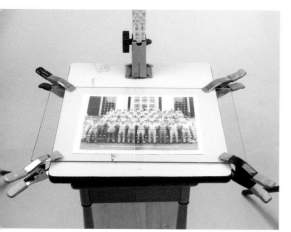

8-5

COPYING ART PRINTS

Among the most common items that won't fit on your copy stand that you may be called upon to shoot are art prints. Paintings and drawings of all sorts from fine artists represent a tremendous growing market for professional photographers and amateurs alike. Not too many years ago, before the days of archival inks, artists ran limited editions at high-end print shops producing lithographs. Because the cost was so high, an artist needed to get at least 100 to 1,000 or more prints to make the order affordable. With the advancement in digital methods, artists can now order prints on demand. No longer is there a need to store unsold prints in a garage. The fine artists can order prints as they sell them.

Before the advancement of oversize inkjet machines and development of high-grade substrates and archival inks, vendors used $100,000-plus Iris printers that were out of reach of small photo studios and amateurs who wanted to start a business out of their garages. Today, impressive machines that produce excellent quality prints can be purchased for less than $5,000. Used machines that are not very old can be found for well below $2,500.

It's not so much the setup you have to be concerned about when shooting fine art prints. Sure, you need to follow the same principles for lighting as we've discussed in this chapter and earlier in the book, and a wall suffices where you can lay a print flat to shoot it. Your biggest concerns with shooting art prints are what you can realistically duplicate and working with the expectations of your client.

Some of the issues include:

> **Saturation.** Art prints can include heavily saturated colors (see Figure 8-6). It may be difficult to get those colors to match on your monitor let alone on your printer. Adjusting saturation is likely to be one area where you need to spend some editing time.

8-6

> **Color matching.** If you're a very critical individual in terms of color reproduction, you haven't seen anything like the critical eye of the fine artist. Unlike traditional photography, where you can let some hues slip to try to control the more important hues such as skin tones, fine artists know every color they plopped down on a painting, and they expect to see those colors reproduced — especially if they don't have a lot of experience with digital prints. In Figure 8-7, the original image that was opened in Photoshop appears on the left; the final print appears on the right after a lot of editing. Unfortunately, we can't show you precisely all the differences between the original and the final edited version in this book, but realize that a lot of editing time is required to get the photo from the original capture to its final form.

> **Disclaimers.** Due to the fact that you can never expect to get an exact color match between a fine art print and a digitally reproduced print, it's essential that you let your client know what to expect before you take on a job. Don does fine-art reproduction in his studio on Epson oversized inkjet printers. As a disclaimer, he warns each client that he can generally come within 95 percent accuracy on reproducing artwork. He warns that there is not a possibility to reproduce the artwork exactly. If clients don't like what you say, then by all means walk away from the job.

> **Substrates.** If you currently work with commercial art reproductions or you intend to offer the service, be careful to choose a limited line of papers. If you have a small shop with one or two inkjet printers, don't try to print on 15 different substrates. The constant changing of material and the calibration issues you have to contend with will severely eat into your profits. Leave the widespread support for all the papers produced today to the large commercial shops that have many different printers. By all means, however, be sure you have an accurate color profile for each paper you use.

Original

Color Corrected

X-REF

To learn about working with color profiles, see Chapter 1.

> **Output size.** If you shoot a large art print, poster, sign, or other such item that may be outfitted for a trade show booth or commercial business signage, you may not be able to capture the entire original with a single shot with sufficient resolution. You may need to take two or more shots and piece them together in Photoshop.

USING A COPY LIGHTING CORRECTION MASK

Flat art copy lighting has one very important criterion — it has to be perfectly even for the entire image area being copied. If you are to achieve a perfect reproduction, tone for tone, uneven lighting makes this impossible.

Some kinds of original art are more forgiving than others. Graphic art that consists of just solid colors can be easily corrected for any unevenness with simple selections and digital paint editing. Fine art or museum-quality reproductions have no leeway for errors. Lighting falloff in any part of the image area renders the reproduced tones darker than the original,

and correcting the problem by trial and error is enormously time consuming. In addition, optical limitations can also cause reproduction problems. Most lens designs have a certain amount of illumination falloff toward the corners. The problem is so common, that Photoshop CS2 includes a special filter function specifically for the correction of the optical falloff problem, commonly referred to as *vignetting*. Combine some uneven copy lighting with lens vignetting, and you've got a real problem!

X-REF

For more information on using lens correction filters, see Chapter 10.

We have been called on occasion to shoot artwork to produce high-quality results in far less-than-perfect conditions. Clients don't understand the problems involved but they expect flawless results.

The remainder of this section describes a technique that corrects both lighting and lens falloff problems with a single tonal edit. We create a correction mask that combines all illumination errors at the capture plane to use later on the flat art shot under the same lighting conditions.

For this example, we use an antique poster Don shot on location in a small conference room. For insurance reasons, the work could not be taken to Don's studio. To make matters worse, there was not enough room to use a four-light setup so Don had to use two lights (one on each side) and plan on correcting the captures during editing. The only thing needed to make this technique work was a solid-colored wall for the copy work.

Here's how it works:

1. After lighting your artwork as best you can, shoot the needed captures. Without changing the crop, focus setting, or moving the camera in any way, remove the art, and shoot the blank wall behind the artwork you shot. Be sure to capture your photos as Camera Raw for 16-bit files to use during your editing steps. Figure 8-8 shows one of the posters shot for this assignment and the capture of the blank wall behind it.

   In Figure 8-9, you can see a contrast-enhanced view to make the lighting problems more obvious. Notice the dark corners and the illumination falloff toward the bottom of the image.

   The capture of the off-white wall contains all the tonal information needed to correct the problem. You just have to create a correction mask from the blank wall capture to use as a selection to fix the problem on the artwork capture.

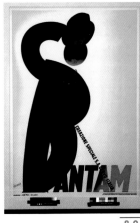

8-9

2. Open the blank wall file in the Raw converter and move the Exposure slider to produce an overall gray file. The exact amount isn't critical. Drag the Saturation slider in the Raw converter to zero. You don't need any color for a selection mask. Your mask file appears as you see in Figure 8-10.

3. You are going to make a huge contrast boost on the image file. Blur the file using the Gaussian Blur filter, set the Radius to 4 pixels, and select the Monochromatic check box. Click OK. Choose Image ⇨ Adjustments ⇨ Auto Contrast.

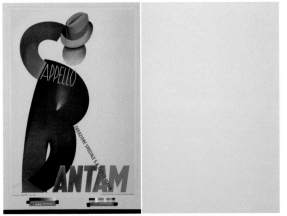

8-8

8-10

4. The file appears darker with strong contrast. If you have any dust or debris on your camera sensor, it will show up on this image. Clean up any spots on the file with the Clone Stamp or Healing Brush tool before continuing.

Next, blur the mask after the contrast boost and the cleanup. For captures of 6 to 12 megapixels, use a Gaussian Blur filter with the Radius set to 125 pixels. The mask should appear completely smooth.

Again choose Image ➪ Adjustments ➪ Auto Contrast and your image should appear something like Figure 8-11.

8-11

5. Invert the mask by pressing Command/Ctrl+I. Drop the bit depth by choosing Image ➪ Mode ➪ 8 Bits/Channel. Convert the color mode to grayscale by selecting Image ➪ Mode ➪ Grayscale. The correction mask is now completed. Notice the density pattern on the mask shown in Figure 8-12. Both lighting errors and lens falloff have been incorporated into a single correction mask.

Note that the mask should be used to correct the file before you perform any custom color correction.

8-12

6. Because the file dimensions of that mask are the same as the art image, it can be loaded into the art file as a selection. Just make sure both files are open. While the art file is active, choose Select ➪ Load Selection. By default, you see Gray listed for the Channel in the Load Selection dialog box if you don't have an alpha channel or layer mask in your art file. Click OK when you see Gray appear for the channel, and the selection from the mask file is loaded into your art file. Note that the Document drop-down menu should report the mask filename and your image mode for the mask file needs to be grayscale.

7. With the selection loaded, create a Curves adjustment layer and set the blending mode to Luminosity. To create the adjustment layer and choose a blending mode in one step, press Option/Alt when you select Curves from the Create a new fill or adjustment layer menu in the Layers palette. The New Layer dialog box opens for creating a Curve adjustment layer. Select Luminosity from the Mode drop-down menu and click OK.

You need to use the Luminosity blend mode so that only the tones change but not image saturation. Otherwise, areas of the image that are more affected with the edit gain saturation and lead to reproduction errors.

8. Create the curve shown in Figure 8-13. Simply drag the white anchor point to the left to the first grid intersection. If your auto contrast clipping defaults are set at 0.01 and you use the blur amounts we recommend, this curve setting will be very close every time.

View the Info pallet and check the sides and edges of the image while the Curves dialog box is open. Use the matte board in the frame (when shooting matted art prints) for a reference because it's supposed to be the same tone overall. A small adjustment might be needed to get the evenness just right. If the art has no easy reference areas, use the default correction curve shown in Figure 8-13.

9. Once finished, click OK, deselect, and your corrected file is ready for fine-tuning the color balance and tonal qualities. Compare the edges of Figure 8-9 to the final file with the edge correction in Figure 8-14.

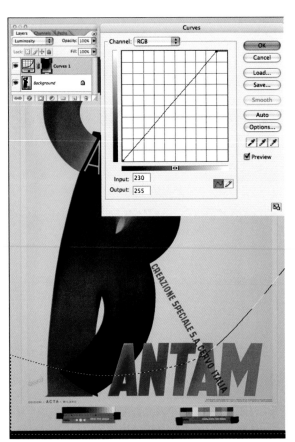

8-13

8-14

RAW CALIBRATIONS FOR COPY WORK

As mentioned in Chapter 3, you can't rely on a single calibration in the Raw converter to handle all your photography. At best, we offer an eyeball view of color calibration in the Raw converter to help sweeten memory colors in Chapter 3.

One area where color calibration in the Camera Raw dialog box can help you is when shooting copy work. If you don't have too much variance in the source material, such as great changes in hues or problems with changing between light and dark samples, you can create a calibration to fit all your copy work for a given session. Note that this is not something you can expect to apply to all copy work, but something you can do when shooting many prints that have similar visual attributes.

Rather than using the eyeball method we mention in Chapter 3, you can employ a more sophisticated approach by downloading a calibration utility from the Web. Visit http://fors.net/chromoholics/, where you can find a free download to fine-tune Adobe's Camera Raw built-in profiles. The Chromoholics Web site provides the free download utility and guidelines to perform the calibration. In addition, it provides an online video showing step-by-step how to use the ACR-Calibrator script.

1. View the instructional video on the Chromoholics Web site for how to use the ACR Calibrator.

2. Download the ACR-Calibrator.jsx file.

PRO TIP

If you have trouble downloading the file by clicking the link, press Control and click (Mac) or right-click (Windows) and choose Save Linked File to Desktop from the context menu.

3. The file you download is an ASCII text file containing a script. Copy this file to the proper Photoshop folder in order to run the script. Drag the ACR-Calibration.jsx file to `Adobe Photoshop CS2/Presets/Scripts` on both Mac and Windows.

4. If Photoshop is currently open when copying the script to the Scripts folder, you must quit Photoshop and restart it. Open your test file shot with your camera and your lens in the lighting conditions of the images you intend to shoot. This test file should be a shot of the GretagMacbeth Color Checker chart. Because the file should be a Camera Raw image, the file opens in the Camera Raw dialog box, as shown in Figure 8-15. Be sure you use your default Camera Raw settings as described in Chapter 3 for the white point and adjustment sliders.

X-REF

See Chapter 3 for setting up your Camera Raw defaults.

PRO TIP

You can order a Gretag Macbeth Color Checker chart online by visiting http://usa.gretag macbethstore.com. As of this writing, the chart is $74. This is a worthwhile investment, and you will have many uses for the chart not only when calibrating Camera Raw, but also for every other calibration you make and when shooting pictures.

5. Select the smallest file size from the Size drop-down menu (see Figure 8-15). Also select 8 Bits/Channel from the Depth drop-down menu. The calibration you perform takes one to three hours depending on the speed of your computer. You can significantly reduce the time by selecting the smallest file size and setting the bit depth to 8 bits in the Camera Raw dialog box. The script opens the Camera Raw test file many times. The smaller file size takes less time to open, thereby reducing the overall time to run the complete script.

6. Select the White Balance tool in the Camera Raw dialog box (first Eyedropper tool), and click on the second-whitest point on the chart. In Figure 8-15, the second-whitest point appears on the bottom row, second from left. Clicking on this color swatch sets the white balance. Click Open to open the file in Photoshop.

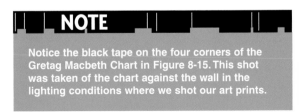

NOTE

Notice the black tape on the four corners of the Gretag Macbeth Chart in Figure 8-15. This shot was taken of the chart against the wall in the lighting conditions where we shot our art prints.

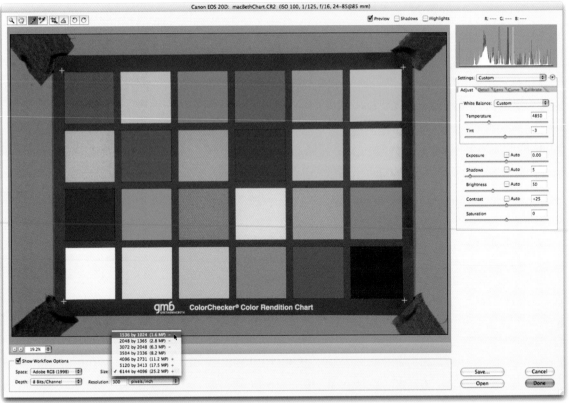

8-15

7. Select the Pen tool and click in the center of each corner swatch, starting with the brown swatch in the upper-left corner. The order is important. Click the white swatch next, then the black swatch, and finally the blue-green swatch in the upper-right corner to plot the last point on the image (see Figure 8-16).

8. Run the script. Choose File ⇨ Scripts ⇨ ACR-Calibrator. Soon you see the original Raw file open and a new Photoshop document window is automatically created reporting the calculations for the calibration. Do not interrupt the script; let it run until it finishes.

9. Add the results to your calibration setup. Open the Camera Raw dialog box on any Raw image. In the Adjust tab, type values reported for settings identified by the ACR-Calibrator. Click the Calibrate tab and add the values also reported by the ACR-Calibrator. In Figure 8-17, you can see the results added to the Calibrate tab for a calibration we performed.

10. Save the new settings as a subset. Open the fly-out menu adjacent to the Settings drop-down menu (right-pointing arrow) and select Save Settings Subset. The Save Settings Subset dialog box opens. Leave all check boxes selected and click Save to open the Save Raw Conversion Settings dialog box. Type a name for your settings — something descriptive to identify your photo shoot. Click Save.

Figure 8-18 shows the original unedited image from a commissioned job for copy work on the left. The file opened with a calibration created for this assignment and various tonal corrections were made. The final corrected image appears in Figure 8-18 on the right.

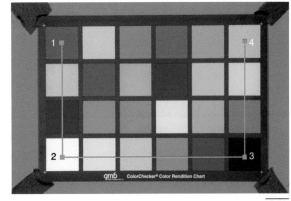

8-16

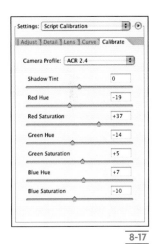

8-17

This particular assignment involved shooting 44 photos. Because the editing on these images would be tedious and time consuming, creating a calibration that took several hours turned out to be a wise time investment and ultimately saved much editing time.

Once again we emphasize that the ACR-Calibrator doesn't work with all photos — especially where you have variances in lighting. But for a job where you use consistent, controlled lighting, it works wonders when it comes to color correct your images.

WORKING WITH MOIRÉS

When you shoot any published print, be sure to inquire about copyright ownership. You're responsible for ensuring that what you shoot can be legally reproduced. In some cases your client may own the copyright of the prints and have a need for duplicating images where original negatives and photographs have been lost. If in doubt about the copyright ownership, acquire a release from the original photographer or other copyright holder.

If you shoot printed pieces of 75 years or older, the prints may be in the public domain — but not always. Generally, magazines and books fall under the fair-use

umbrella of commentary, criticism, or parody. But you should make an effort to check out the legality for duplicating anything carrying a copyright just to be sure what you shoot is fair game. Many universities have published Web pages for copyright guidelines when duplicating materials for their students and faculty. You can find information on the Web for help in understanding more about copyright laws.

When you scan a print run off a press, your image suffers from a moiré pattern. Printed pieces are halftone images comprised of tiny dots. They result in an image that appears with rhythmic distracting moirés that really mess up a continuous tone photograph, as you can see in Figure 8-19.

8-19

When you photograph a printed piece with your digital camera, you get much better results and the moiré pattern is less pronounced. Look at the same image shot with a Canon 20D camera (see Figure 8-20). Notice the zoom level is different between Figure 8-19 and 8-20 because we took a screen capture of Figure 8-20 at a 100 percent view to show you how the file would print. If you zoom out on photos that have a moiré pattern, the pattern isn't as pronounced or perhaps not seen at all when in zoom views less than 100 percent.

The less obvious moiré pattern shown in Figure 8-21 is not a function of the Raw converter but a function of your camera at the time of capture. Digital cameras have a special antialiasing filter mounted in the camera to help reduce moiré in your photos. Moiré patterns can appear in your photos due to certain lighting situations, with certain focal lengths, camera position relative to the subject, camera angle, and the content of your image. Shoot something like a gray shirt or other cloth material at a certain angle and you may see red and blue wavy lines in areas that should be

8-20

solid gray — this too is a moiré pattern. When shooting printed material, the patterns are more or less visible depending on the effectiveness of your antialiasing filter.

Assuming you have permission to shoot printed pieces, your task turns to editing the image(s) to eliminate or reduce the obvious moiré pattern.

8-21

For this example we use the scanned photo shown in Figure 8-19 to illustrate how much the moiré pattern can be eliminated in Photoshop. The same methods can be employed where the pattern is obvious in a digital camera image.

1. Shoot a print with your camera in a studio with balanced lighting following some of the suggestions in Chapters 3 and 6. Do not use incandescent or fluorescent lighting. You don't want to add the extra work for color correction for additional problems you add to the original source material.

2. Open the image in Photoshop and examine the three channels by pressing Command/Ctrl+1, Command/Ctrl+2, Command/Ctrl+3, and press Command/Ctrl ~ (tilde) to return to the composite channel. As you can see in Figure 8-21 and common with most images, each channel is affected to a different extent. Typically, the Blue channel requires the most work.

3. Fixing moiré patterns is handled by blurring pixels to eliminate the pattern and soften the image no matter what tools or commands you use. If you go to the RGB composite channel and apply the Dust and Scratches filter, the pattern disappears, but the image blurs up so the crisp detail from your camera image is lost. The same can be said when using the Gaussian Blur filter. The objective is to eliminate the pattern with a minimal amount of blurring and softening. To do this, apply different blur amounts to the separate RGB channels.

Start with the Blue channel and apply a Gaussian Blur. Use a fair amount of blurring like 3 pixels for the Radius, keeping an eye on the preview as you make adjustments. After applying the Gaussian Blur filter, add a little noise to the channel using the Median filter (choose Filter ➪ Noise ➪ Median). Use the same value in the Median dialog box as you use for the Radius in the Gaussian Blur filter — in this example 3 is used. The results of the Blue channel at this point are shown in Figure 8-22. As you can see, the moiré pattern has been eliminated, but the image appears with a gob of blurred pixels that creates severe loss of detail.

4. While still in the Blue channel, sharpen that blob of fuzziness to bring back a little detail. Oversharpening can be a problem here so be careful when sharpening the image. Choose Filter ➪ Sharpen ➪ Unsharp Mask. In the

8-22

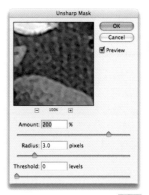

8-23

Unsharp Mask dialog box (see Figure 8-23) type the amount of sharpening you want to apply to the channel while keeping an eye on the preview. Be certain you are working at a 100 percent view to see a more precise view of the sharpening effect. The amount of sharpening depends on the resolution of your image. For a 240 ppi image opened from the Camera Raw dialog box, try applying 200 for the Amount, 3 for the Radius, and 0 for the Threshold, as shown in Figure 8-23. The Radius value is a match for the amount of the blur applied in the Gaussian Blur dialog box. If you change amounts and the radius, be certain to keep the Threshold at 0. Higher Threshold values limit sharpening of moiré pattern edges.

5. The Green and Red channels require less attention. Start with the Green channel and apply half the Amount in the Gaussian Blur dialog box. In this example, 1.5 is used for the Radius. Use the Median filter and set the Radius to 1 — also a lower value than what is applied to the Blue channel. Sharpen the image using the Unsharp Mask filter again adding the same amount as applied to the Blue channel. In this example, 200 is used for the Amount. For the Radius, again match the same value as the blur radius used in the Gaussian Blur dialog box. In this example, 1 is used; the Threshold remains at 0.

6. The Red channel typically displays the least amount of moiré. For this channel apply a Gaussian Blur and Median filter using 1 for the Radius. Sharpen the channel using the same sharpen Amount (200 in this example) and a radius of 1, again matching the same Radius used in the Gaussian Blur filter.

7. View the RGB composite channel to see the results in the RGB image. The results of the blurring and Median filters will undoubtedly show a softer image. You can discretely sharpen the image using lower values of the Unsharp Mask filter and preview the results. Try applying an Amount of 50, a Radius of 1, and a Threshold of 4 to the RGB composite image. If you haven't oversharpened the image, try applying the same amount again. At some point you begin to see problems on the edges showing high contrast. Reduce Opacity in the Layers palette to back off the sharpening while previewing the image at 100 percent view.

8. Downsample the image by choosing Image ⇨ Image Size. Downsample the image to the desired output resolution using the Bicubic method in the Image Size dialog box. When you downsample the image, you greatly improve the appearance of the final result (see Figure 8-24). This step goes a long way in reducing the appearance of moiré patterns.

8-24

As stated earlier, moiré patterns can also appear on images you shoot that aren't copies of press pieces. These moirés are the result of the capture chip and its capture of textures in your photographs. Although this chapter relates to copy work, we are talking about moiré patterns so we thought we would mention handling moiré patterns for any kind of noncopy work photo you take.

1. Open an image you have that appears as though there are wavy lines appearing as a moiré. Select the Brush tool in the Tools palette; from the options bar pick a large brush tip with a 100 percent hard diameter. Pick a tip of 60 to 80 pixels in size to paint over a large area.

2. In the options bar, select Color for the blending mode.

3. Sample a color with the Eyedropper tool on the color where you see the moiré. If you have the Brush selected, press Option/Alt and the cursor changes to an eyedropper. Click to sample a color, then release the modifier key to return to the Brush tool.

4. Scrub over the moiré. Be careful to not encroach on other colors as you paint. Generally, a large brush tip can move close enough to remove the moiré without having to select smaller tips to paint delicately in the affected area.

SLIDE AND FILM DUPING

If you've evolved with photography from the traditional film cameras to the modern digital cameras, you are likely to have storage containers filled with transparencies and negatives. At some point you'll want to convert many of your film images to digital files.

The traditional way to get transparencies and negatives into digital form has been to scan the film with a film scanner or flatbed scanner with a transparency adaptor. Anyone who has used either a film scanner or a flatbed knows that scanning slides is a painfully slow process. As an alternative, you can use your camera to copy transparencies and negatives.

There are some slide-copying adapters developed for digital cameras that can be used for 35mm slide copying. A variety of different kinds of slide duplicators are springing up all the time. You can find generic duplicators that can be outfitted on

almost any kind of DSLR camera. Among them are the Specialty Photographic SP-A52 Copier (www.specialtyphotographic.com) or the Opteka Pro Digital Slide Duplicator (www.opteka.com) shown in Figure 8-25. The unit fits on your camera lens. Prices for these units range from $69 for the Opteka unit to $99 for the Specialty Photographic unit. We recommend the Opteka unit because it accommodates slides and filmstrips without purchasing additional attachments, and overall it is easier to copy slides.

PRO TIP

If you have a point-and-shoot camera you might be able to find a slide copier adapter for your camera. There are a number of different point-and-shoot cameras such as the Nikon Coolpix 900 and 950 series, Sony Mavica, Sony Cybershot, and others that currently support slide duplicators. These cameras don't support Camera Raw, however, which is very helpful when color correcting negatives.

8-25

What can you expect from digital camera slide copying?

Low-end film scanners start out capturing 35mm slides at 2750 dpi. That image capture produces a file that can offer you a quality print up to about 8 x 10 inches. Going a step up to the moderately priced 4000 dpi scanners produces files that can give you quality prints up to 12 x 18 inches. You can go higher, but the prices increase in direct proportion to the resolution you can capture with the film scanner. If you get into the 9000 dpi resolution scanners and higher, the film scanner ultimately gives you much better results than you can hope to achieve with your digital camera and with higher resolutions.

If you have a point-and-shoot camera, you can be certain a film scanner will give you the best results. If all you are interested in is producing 4-x-6-inch prints of reasonable quality, then you can achieve acceptable results with a point-and-shoot camera using an adapter for slide duping. If you have a 6-megapixel camera, you can capture 35mm slides with sufficient resolution to print 8-x-10-inch prints. If you have an 8-megapixel camera you can capture files with enough resolution to print up to 16-x-20-inch prints. A 16 x 20 file will be over 200 ppi and much less than 300 ppi, but pushing the print size to 16 x 20 often gives you good results.

Deciding when to use a slide duplicator with your digital camera and when to use a scanner all depends on the end product you want. For prints up to 8 x 10, almost all DSLR cameras work well. In terms of speed, you can generally capture slides with your camera much faster than scanning them. The speed of shooting a roll of Ektachrome in slide mounts or film strips with your camera is five times as fast as a film scanner.

Shooting transparencies

By far, the easiest captures to correct are from transparency film. If your film is dated, you may need to do quite a bit of correcting in Photoshop. Faded films, colorcasts on films, and other anomalies associated with film degradation over time are harder to balance

for color, and you may need to play with the brightness adjustments. If the condition of the film is well preserved, then your correction edits won't be much different than original captures taken with your camera. Likewise, newer films with good lighting and brilliant colors provide for easier adjustments in Photoshop.

For all transparency and film shots taken with your camera, you can use the bright sky (not pointed directly at the sun) for your lighting source. Shoot outside or indoors through a window. Shoot your slides using aperture-priority with an f-stop of f/11 or greater and use your camera's autofocus. Be certain the vertical and horizontal planes of the slide copy unit are parallel to the film plane. You shouldn't see a tilt either vertically or horizontally.

1. Once you set up the accessories and optics for capturing images from 35mm film slides, the real challenge awaits. You've got to adjust the Raw capture properly to open the file and complete your edit in Photoshop.

   We begin with slides, because it's a positive image to start with and the edit is more visually intuitive. A slide is, of course, a small color transparency. Color transparencies have a wide tonal range — somewhat wider than most real-world camera captures. From brightest highlight to the last of the usable shadow detail, this range is about eight f-stops, or LOG 2.40 — to be technical. Although the D-max of a transparency can be as heavy as LOG 3.0, visual detail is really not viewable when darker than 2.40 — these values assume a properly exposed slide.

   This tonal range requires you to manipulate the Raw converter to bring out all, if not most, of the data captured. The color balance of the slide, at least when captured, looks reasonably close to the actual slide if the white balance for the light source is set properly when the slide is shot with your camera.

   Open the file in the Raw converter, and click off all the Auto adjust options, as shown in Figure 8-26.

8-26

2. A color slide by nature has plenty of contrast and tonal compression in the highlight and shadow tones, so the first edit to make in Camera Raw is to open the Curves pane. From the Tone Curve drop-down menu, select Linear (see Figure 8-27).

3. Click the Adjust tab. Drag the shadow slider all the way to zero to include all the deep shadow detail captured by the camera chip. It's very important to give the maximum exposure possible without clipping during your slide copying to realize the maximum captured dynamic range.

4. Play with the exposure slider to bring the slide to normal brightness without clipping. Observe the histogram as you make your adjustments to insure no clipping appears in the highlights or shadows.

5. If the image is still too dark when clipping begins, back off the exposure slider a bit and add brightness with the Brightness slider. You might have to move back and forth to get it just right. The idea is to center the histogram in the Camera Raw window while getting the best tonalities you can in the preview image.

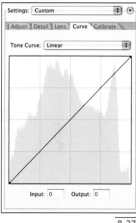

8-27

X-REF

For more information on clipping in the Camera Raw dialog box, see Chapter 4.

6. If the color balance of the original has a pronounced colorcast, take the white balance eyedropper and try clicking it on the image where a known neutral tone in the original scene appears.

You can also try setting white balance to Auto and see if you get lucky. If the image color mix isn't too biased, auto white balance can make a fairly good guess.

The white balance eyedropper is clicked on the girl's white top and the highlights clean up nicely. The other adjustments made in the Adjust tab appear in Figure 8-28.

7. With the image looking as good as it can and with full data preserved across the histogram, open the file by clicking Open in the Camera Raw dialog box.

The image looks reasonably good when opened in Photoshop. Open the Levels dialog box to check the histogram (see Figure 8-29).

The histogram shows the image has a few levels short of a full tonal range, but the overall balance looks very good. Choosing Image ⇨ Adjustments ⇨ Auto Contrast changes the image slightly and brings up the full tonal range. The final image, copied with the Opteka Slide Copier, of a 35mm transparency shot over 30 years ago, appears in Figure 8-30 after making the corrections outlined here.

8-28

8-29

8-30

At this point, if the image needs any color balance, saturation, or tonal changes, the edit can be handled just like any other file modifications covered in Chapters 4 and 5. Depending on the condition of the slide, you may need to do some cleanup in Photoshop to remove dust and debris, repair scratches, and so on.

WORKING WITH BLACK-AND-WHITE NEGATIVES

Black-and-white negatives can also be captured with your DSLR camera using an adapter that accommodates filmstrips. The capture you make from negative film results in a negative image you either need to invert in Photoshop for JPEG images or invert negatives in the Raw converter for Camera Raw images. When you shoot negatives in Camera Raw you have more conversion options than you do with JPEG, and you can expect much better results. The raw images enable you to choose to invert the negatives to positives either in the Raw converter or in Photoshop. Using the Raw converter is your best option because you can easily apply the same Raw conversion settings to a folder of photos, make some tonal adjustments in

the Raw converter before opening the files, and remove colorcasts that often appear when shooting black-and-white film in RGB color.

Editing negatives is a little more challenging because all the tones are backward when you open a negative in either the Raw converter or Photoshop. In Figure 8-31, a number of photos shot with Plus-X film over 25 years ago appear in the Adobe Bridge window prior to converting the raw images.

When your capture of a negative opens, it still looks like a negative! You can edit it as a negative and invert it later in Photoshop, but it's a lot easier if you invert the image in the Camera Raw converter.

1. First, look at a raw negative capture when opened in default mode in the Raw converter. Upon opening a slide copy of a negative (see Figure 8-32), you see the image as a negative and the capture has a slight greenish cast. This isn't unusual when capturing a silver-based film image, even if the light source white balance is correct.

8-31

8-32

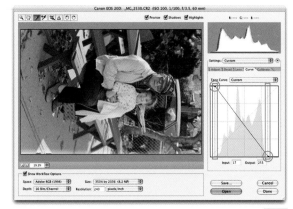

PRO TIP

The edits you make while the image appears as a negative are reversed from edits you make on positive images. If you search for the white balance, you're looking for blacks in the image while it remains as a negative.

Start by neutralizing the cast with the white eye-dropper to line up the histograms of all three color channels. In this image, click the eyedropper on the midtone of the man's coat. Notice that all three histogram color channels are aligned in the histogram area, as shown in Figure 8-33.

2. Turn off all of the Auto adjust options in the Adjust pane. You don't want the auto adjustments to work in the background when you make manual adjustments in Curves.

3. Click the Curves pane in the Raw converter, and select Linear from the Tone Curve drop-down menu.

4. Invert the curve by dragging the bottom-left anchor point to the top of the box and the upper-right anchor point to the bottom. While you reposition the curve settings the image view in the Raw dialog box may disappear or look strange, but just keep going.

   Once the curve is inverted, your preview turns into a positive image.

5. While still in the Curves pane, drag each of the anchor points horizontally to the base of the light-colored histogram appearing inside the Curve box (see Figure 8-34). As you drag, a light-colored guideline appears to help you determine when the upper-left anchor point intersects with the base position of the histogram. The right-side anchor point is on the bottom of the box, but the guide-line will appear.

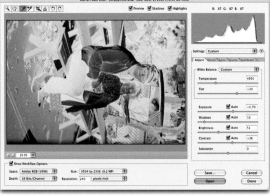

8-33

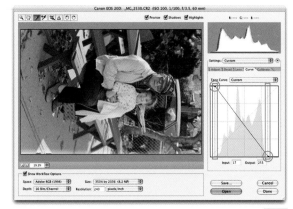

8-34

This sets the black and white points to the ends of the histogram, just like you would using Levels. Try not to clip the file data. If you want to readjust later, you can do so in Levels after the file opens in Photoshop. The image preview displays clipping as usual if you overedit the image in the Curves pane in the Raw converter.

6. The image looks a little too dark. Placing another anchor point on the curve center and raising it lightens the image nicely, as shown in Figure 8-35.

7. With your adjustments made in the Raw converter, open the file and convert to grayscale mode by choosing Image ⇨ Mode ⇨ Grayscale.

PRO TIP

For more information on converting RGB files to grayscale, see Chapter 7.

8. A final check in Levels shows the image is a bit shy of a true black, so clip an additional nine levels from the left side of the histogram. The final result is shown in Figure 8-36. The entire edit took less than one minute.

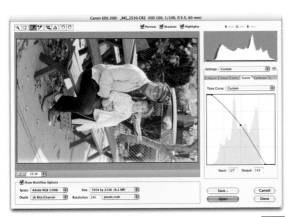

8-35

8-36

PRO TIP

You can also change the curve shape with additional anchor points to change overall contrast just as you can do with the Photoshop Curves dialog box.

Working with negative color film — or welcome to Bizzaro World

When editing color negatives captured with your digital camera, just about everything in the Raw converter works backward, but with a little practice, you can quickly get used to the initially strange editing method.

Scanning and editing color negatives for a high-quality positive output result has always been a challenging endeavor. A color negative film is designed as an intermediate step toward the creation of a positive color print on a three-color primary multilayer paper. Certain special criteria are required of the color negative material for this task. The two most important criteria, (the only ones that matter for our editing task), are the high dynamic range captured by most color negatives when properly exposed and the wide unmatched density range spread of the CMY (Cyan, Magenta, Yellow) dye layers in the film.

Color negative film is designed to capture a high dynamic range to allow for a wide exposure latitude. During the printing step, the print paper exposure determines what part of the captured dynamic range

is used, and tones outside that range are rendered as full black or full white in the print. To think of it another way, the film might capture as much as a nine-stop range from a contrasty scene if heavily exposed, but the paper can only render about six stops of that captured range. The rest is blown out to white or prints down to full black. On the other hand, a color negative capture that is underexposed, or a capture of a low-contrast scene, contains a much lower density range and results in a low-contrast final print.

Why does this matter? Well, the inversion and editing of the image can lead to very strange results from all this variability in the original color negative. If we use standard editing methods based on the histogram view, as we do with digital captures of a standard scene, only a tiny percentage of the color negatives edited have a normal appearance after the standard edit. We have to edit by eye and not necessarily by the numbers to obtain a result with a pleasing appearance. Editing by eye is difficult when you attempt to perform your edits on a negative image in the Raw converter as shown in Figure 8-37.

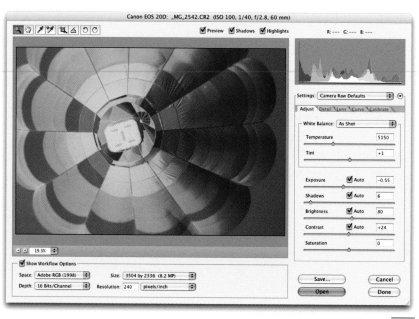

8-37

The wide density difference in the film's CMY layers poses another problem. In all color negative films, the yellow layer carries the highest density followed by the magenta layer, and the cyan layer has the least of all. Why? The color paper it's printed on has no yellow barrier filter like the film has. That's because color print papers need to have the yellow dye layer on the bottom, and a barrier filter doesn't allow the yellow layer to receive any exposure at all. To get around this problem, the negative is designed to have widely spaced primary dye layer densities to white light. The yellow layer carries far more density than the other two layers. In the print paper, the yellow dye layer is much more light sensitive than the magenta or cyan layers. This allows the blue sensitive layer to receive full exposure levels before the green and red sensitive layers *see* any exposure at all. This wide difference in the color layers makes color balancing the color negative capture a bit tricky to say the least.

If you ever wondered why the Blue channel in Photoshop, from a color negative scan, always has the worst noise, now you know. The blue-sensitive layer in the film has a relative ISO speed at least two stops faster than the green and red sensitive layers.

Because of all these complexities when trying to edit a color negative capture, we have decided to show you a basic edit using the Raw converter to get you in the ballpark with your image inversion to a positive because it is easier to demonstrate than trying to edit a basic negative capture in Photoshop. We could write an entire book the size of this one concerning all the fine points of editing color negatives for digital use — but unfortunately, we can't double the size of this book.

To make this exercise fair play, we use a pair of color negatives that Ted shot so many years ago he can't remember what the final images are supposed to look like. Therefore, we make the best edit we can by guesswork.

The first negative, captured with the Canon 20D and the Opteka slide copier, seems to be a hot air balloon shot from underneath. Ted can't remember standing under it, but he does know he took the shot.

1. Open the file in the Raw converter. As you can see in Figure 8-38, the image is indeed a negative.

2. The first task to perform in the Raw converter is to change the negative preview to a positive. Click the Curve tab in the Raw Converter dialog box and select Linear from the Tone Curve drop-down menu. Invert the curve by dragging the black point straight up to the top left and the white point straight down to the lower-right corner, as shown in Figure 8-38. At this point, everything in the Raw converter works backward.

3. Because of the orange dye correction mask on the negative and the varied dye layer densities, the image looks very blue when inverted. When the image is opened in the Raw converter the white balance is at the default As Shot setting.

   To correct the color, get creative with the White Balance and Tint adjustments. Leave all the tone correction sliders set to Auto for the time being. For a first editing move, try setting the White Balance drop-down menu to the Auto setting. In many cases, this brings the color balance much closer, as shown in Figure 8-39.

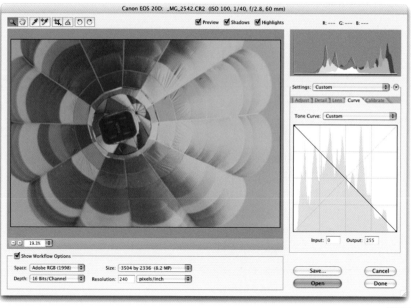

8-38

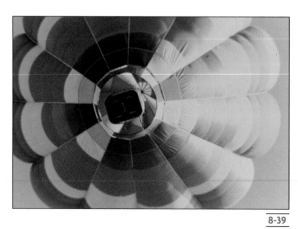

8-39

8-40

4. Auto white balance removes a great deal of the cast. It appears that the balloon has some white panels mixed with the colored ones. Great! You have some kind of color reference now.

Try clicking the White Balance Eyedropper tool on one of the left-side white panels. Select the White Balance tool in the Raw converter and click on the white in your image. In this example, we get a little closer with our color balance, as shown in Figure 8-40.

5. The overall balance is much closer, but the highlight (right side) whites have a somewhat cyan cast. Try clicking on a right-side white panel near the gondola. This edit cleans up the whites nicely, but the left-side whites now have a magenta red cast.

At this point it's time for a little custom adjusting with the Tint slider. The Tint slider, when used in this way, adds magenta to the image when moved to the left and green when moved to the right (just the opposite of how it normally works because the tone curve is inverted).

Moving the slider right by two values from -33 to -31 cleans up most of the residual cast in this example file, as shown in Figure 8-41.

6. The image lacks contrast. The black and white points need to be reset. Because the curve is inverted, the Shadow slider has traded places with the Exposure slider. Set highlight clipping with the Shadow slider and shadow clipping with the Exposure slider! This is where Bizzaro World comes in.

Reset the Exposure slider right to 0.75 to darken the shadow tones. The Shadow slider is moved right to 19 to brighten the highlights.

The Brightness slider is moved left to 55 to lighten the image. (It works backward, too!) The Contrast slider is moved right to 33 to add a little more contrast (it works normally).

The Saturation slider is moved left to subtract a little saturation (it works normally, also). If you forget which way to move a slider, try a move and see what happens. Figure 8-42 shows the result of the custom edits.

7. We clicked Open after making all the adjustments we could in the Raw converter and decided to leave the rest to Photoshop. We used Auto Levels to set the black point to neutral and used the White eyedropper tool in the Curves dialog box set to R 245, G 245, and B 245 (we double-clicked the White Eyedropper and typed 245 for the RGB values in the Color Picker), and clicked it on one of the bright white balloon panels on the far right side.

The file (see Figure 8-43) can now be custom edited like any other digital image.

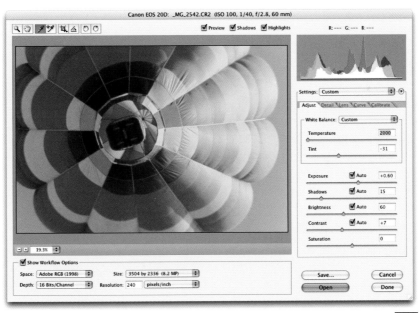

8-41

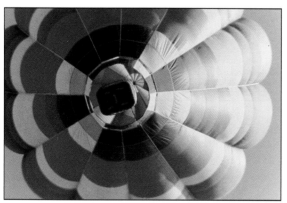

8-42

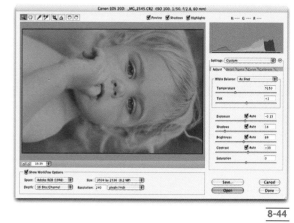

8-44

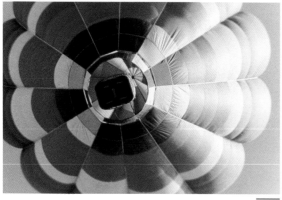

8-43

This second negative presents a bigger challenge. The close-up of a little child has no real neutral tones for reference, and the only memory color is the flesh tone. The negative is a little overexposed, so the capture has more visible grain. Some of the dye in the negative has faded from age (this shot was originally taken over 25 years ago), so the color is not as clean as that obtained from freshly processed film.

1. The image is already opened and inverted in the Raw converter as previously described. Do your best to balance color, density, and contrast.

   After inverting the image in the Raw converter the file displays the usual heavy blue cast, as shown in Figure 8-44.

2. Change the White Balance setting to Auto but the image is still very blue. There are two reasons for this: The image is almost all warm tones so the auto white balance algorithm is fooled a bit, and the photo is probably originally shot in a cool tone lighting environment like open shade.

   There's nothing obvious to use in the image for the white balance eyedropper, so work manually. The image still has a heavy blue cast; add yellow by moving the Temperature slider to the left. Go for it and move it far left. The edit result shows an overly yellow flesh tone, with a bit of green cast, as shown in Figure 8-45.

8-45

8

Photocopying

3. Flesh tones are mostly composed of yellow and magenta, so next try moving the Tint slider left to add some magenta to the image. This edit brings the image to a much closer color balance, as shown in Figure 8-46. Notice also that the image darkens because all the auto tone adjustments are enabled, forcing the Raw converter to make tone changes as you work on the color balance. It's okay. Just be aware of that as you work.

Next, move the Shadow slider to the right from 27 to 38 to brighten the image. (Remember that the slider is functioning as the Exposure slider.) The image now brightens up.

4. Move the Brightness slider left to 40 from 53 to brighten the image and add a little more saturation. Move the Saturation slider from zero to 5. The results of these edits are shown in Figure 8-47.

5. The file is now ready to open. Click Open in the Raw converter and choose Image ⇨ Adjustments ⇨ Auto Contrast. Add a single custom edit in the Hue/Saturation dialog box (as shown endlessly in this book) to tweak the flesh tones, and the file is complete (see Figure 8-48). Not bad for a 25-year-old faded negative and a $69 slide copier.

8-47

8-48

8-46

Balancing Light with Copy Attachments

If you plan to capture color negatives with heavy color balance problems that trend toward blue and cyan, use a light source on your slide duplicator that is cooler than daylight. By doing so, the white balance slider won't run out of steam when trying to neutralize heavy blue casts in the negative captures. A great solution is a Rosco Cinegel 3204 1/4 Tough Booster Blue correction filter available at Calumet Photographic for $7.49. The filter is 20 x 24. Just place a piece of it over the end of the slide duplicator attachment and use a daylight-balanced light source. Remember that the converter is working in reverse. More blue in the light source results in a more yellow capture.

Q&A

Wouldn't it be best for me to have a scanner to reproduce photo prints?

Your choice of tools is related to how much you want to invest in equipment and how much time you want to spend doing one series of edits or another. If you already have a scanner and the scanner delivers the results you desire, it may not be so wise to change your methods or your tools. If you find your scanner not producing the results you want or if scanning many prints is a slow process, then look into shooting your prints with your camera and test the results. Quite often you find a camera properly set up on a copy stand will not only deliver better results, but the process moves much faster.

Why does my slide copying produce slides needing a lot of touchup work?

When you shoot small 35mm or even medium- or large-format film, you are magnifying the size up to the frame size of your capture. Any tiny particles of dust and debris are also magnified resulting in a capture that most often needs some cleanup work. You can help minimize the amount of cleanup on film captures by keeping your slides clean in glassine sleeves or other protective material. When you copy film, use a white glove and be certain to handle your film on the edges. Use a lint free cloth or air compressor to remove loose particles before capturing your film using your camera or scanner.

Is there any way I can determine if a slide-copying unit will work with my camera before I buy one?

Unfortunately, many providers claim great results in marketing literature that may not measure up when you receive your unit. One thing you can do is take your camera to your equipment supplier and see if you can take a test shot with a copy attachment. Take a few good quality slides and don't use antiquated film with a lot of loss in saturation to run a fair test on a copy attachment unit. Bring your camera home and be certain to open the file in Photoshop and not judge the quality by the image appearing in the camera's LCD. If the image looks good you can return to your supplier and purchase the unit.

If you don't have a supplier near you that carries any attachment units, try to search for mail order suppliers with return policies with little to no restocking fees. Instead of placing an online order, telephone the supplier and talk about your concerns and ask about a return policy. Try to choose a low-cost unit specifically designed for a digital camera. There are many units out there designed for use with film cameras that just won't work satisfactorily on your digital camera.

Try to avoid spending money on rails and bellows systems costing several hundred dollars. You really want to see some reviews or test any equipment before spending serious money. The low-cost $69 unit from Opteka (www.opteka.com) can do a respectable job. Start with one of these units to see how much copying you really end up doing. For those special photos where you need an enlargement, you can always use a service center with a high-end drum scanner.

Chapter 9

BLACK-AND-WHITE PHOTO EDITING

"Let us first say what photography is not. A photo-graph is not a painting, a poem, a symphony, a dance. It is not just a pretty picture, not an exercise in con-tortionist techniques and sheer print quality. It is or should be a significant document, a penetrating statement, which can be described in a very simple term — selectivity." — Berenice Abbott, 1951

Much of the true photographic art of the great mas-ters had its origin, and to a certain extent remains, in black-and-white photography. The names of Berenice Abbott, Ansel Adams, Margaret Bourke-White, Robert Capa, Henri Cartier-Bresson, Alfred Eisenstadt, Dorothea Lange, and Edward Weston bring visions of excellence to the minds of the informed photography historian. When we think of the great photographic masters, our minds are filled with not only great scenes but also all those wonderful transitions of gray tones, the rich blacks, and the snowy whites that were part of so many artworks of earlier years. Whether it be extraordinary compositions of the human condition such as those captured by Capa, Cartier-Benson, and Lange, or the spectacular natural scenes shot by Adams and Weston, the rich tonal transitions of the black-and-white photos of the masters are truly great pieces of artwork.

The forefathers of artistic black-and-white photogra-phy were not only photographers; they were also chemists, mathematicians, researchers, physicists, and scholars seeking methods to perfect their photo-graphic prints. Shooting the scene was just a part of the time and preparation needed to produce a great photographic print. Choices for films, filters, papers, and chemistry were also part of the photographer's toolkit and required knowledge of what was needed to attain the results they were seeking.

Today's digital photographers have fewer decisions to make when evaluating materials, but the post-image processing requires much talent and knowledge to reproduce black-and-white photos with the rich tonal transitions of the great masters. It's not a matter of

shooting digital and performing an RGB-to-grayscale conversion that produces the contemporary black-and-white art piece. You need to invest time and exer-cise care in making tonal adjustments to produce images that can stand against the wonderful photo-graphic prints you appreciate in art galleries.

CONVERTING COLOR TO GRAYSCALE

Photoshop pros use a variety of different methods to convert color images to grayscale. The one thing that rarely happens is using the Image ⇨ Mode ⇨ Grayscale command as the only step in the conversion process. This method uses an algorithm to combine percentages of the three RGB channels and push it all into a grayscale space. The percentage mix of the channel information is fixed and you have no control over how that information is mixed to form the grayscale image. This can be a problem if infor-mation in one channel is noisy or less than optimum in one respect or another. If you have a part of your image such as the background that appears better in one channel while the foreground appears better in another channel, converting to grayscale doesn't take the best of separate channels into account when mak-ing the mode conversion.

The one thing Photoshop pros do most often when examining images, particularly color images to be converted to grayscale, is to look at each individual channel to find out what's going on with the channels, which ones have more noise, more artifacts, better tonal quality, more contrasting edges, and so on. It stands to reason then that one of our grayscale con-version methods is to take charge of the channel mix-ing to produce the best grayscale image we can get.

If converting to grayscale is one step in a multiple-step process where you're not interested in producing a final grayscale print, you might use simpler methods for converting to grayscale when you don't have to mix the channel information to get the best-looking tonal range; for example, converting to grayscale then converting to bitmap for some sort of effect, creating high-contrast images, and so on. In this regard you have a choice for using a destructive or nondestructive method of conversion. In other cases, you may need to convert many images to grayscale quickly, such as providing image files for wire services and newspapers, and not want to bother with more complex methods. Yet a third condition is the fine-art photographer who wants to take advantage of all Photoshop has to offer to produce the best quality images for fine-art prints. With all these various needs to satisfy, Photoshop provides many different methods you can use to convert your RGB images to grayscale.

SIMPLE CONVERSIONS TO GRAYSCALE

A simple conversion method uses just one step to convert color images to grayscale. In production environments where the conversions need to be performed routinely and rapidly you find artists who typically favor one channel and use it for the conversion. When you delete a channel, you use a destructive method for your conversion. Whatever color information was in the image is lost and can't be regained.

Follow these few steps to create a simple RGB-to-grayscale conversion:

1. Open an image and look at the three RGB channels. Press Command/Ctrl+1, Command/Ctrl+2, and Command/Ctrl+3 to toggle between channels and view them for what appears to be the best grayscale information. Typically, the best choice is the Green channel and the worst the Blue channel. Sometimes the Red channel is a better choice; the only way you know is to view each channel on your monitor.

2. After viewing all the channels, click the one that has the best grayscale appearance in the Channels palette. Choose Image ⇨ Mode ⇨ Grayscale. The grayscale conversion uses only the selected channel to create the grayscale image. The other two

channels are deleted. In Figure 9-1, you can see how each of the three channels in a composite color image appears when using each channel for converting to grayscale. On the bottom left is the Red channel conversion, in the middle is the Green channel, and on the right is the Blue channel.

3. Using this method is destructive because after the two channels are deleted, you lose the color information and can't regain it. This is okay if you happen to be a photojournalist and need to get a fast image out to a wire service for reproduction in black and white. If you later need to use a color version of your photo, then you need to save two versions — one RGB and the other grayscale.

Another destructive method of converting color to grayscale is deleting just the channels that contain color. Go back to your RGB image and choose Image ⇨ Mode ⇨ Lab Color. Open the Channels palette and select the Lightness channel, as shown in Figure 9-2. Choose Image ⇨ Mode ⇨ Grayscale and the mode conversion is made using only the selected Lightness channel. (Alternatively, you can delete the a and b channels and then convert the mode to Grayscale, but why take the extra steps?)

As a simple conversion to grayscale, using the Lightness channel in Lab Color mode provides you a better result than selecting one of the RGB channels. This method of conversion ignores the color in the image and coverts the file using just the brightness information.

A nondestructive method for converting to grayscale keeps your color information in a file while you create the grayscale image — also in the same file. If you want to avoid saving two files of the same image — one in grayscale and the other in color — you can print either grayscale or color, or pass off the file to a graphic designer who can choose from either color mode to use in a design.

Red

Green

Blue

9-1

9-2

To perform a simple nondestructive RGB-to-grayscale conversion, follow these steps:

1. Open the Create new fill or adjustment layer drop-down menu in the Layers palette. Select Hue/Saturation.

2. In the Hue/Saturation dialog box, move the Saturation slider all the way to the left to -100, as shown in Figure 9-3. The adjustment layer eliminates all the color in the image.

The advantage for using this method is that the adjustment layer can be turned off or deleted to return to the RGB color image. You can select either layer and make it visible to print either in grayscale or color. However, just desaturating the image may provide the same quality that you may find in selecting a channel to use for your grayscale image. If you choose this method, observe the results and see if the resulting file is what you have in mind.

9-3

COMPLEX CONVERSIONS TO GRAYSCALE

A more complex method for converting to grayscale involves using multiple Hue/Saturation layers or a Hue/Saturation layer and a Channel Mixer adjustment layer where you can strip the color in an image and adjust the Hue (or mix channel information) in another layer to bring the tones you want to appear with more or less brightness values. These methods are nondestructive, and you can retain both grayscale and color in the same image.

To perform an RGB-to-grayscale conversion using Hue/Saturation and Channel Mixer adjustment layers, follow these steps:

1. Add an adjustment layer to an RGB image. From the Create new fill or adjustment layer drop-down menu select Hue/Saturation. When the Hue/Saturation dialog box opens, click OK to accept the defaults. For now, leave this adjustment layer alone, and come back later to make your conversion after adding another adjustment layer.

2. When you return to the document window, open the Mode drop-down menu in the Layers palette and select Color.

3. Create a second Hue/Saturation adjustment layer. When the Hue/Saturation dialog box opens, move the Saturation slider all the way to the left to -100 to eliminate the color on this layer. Click OK to return to the document window.

4. Double-click the middle layer (the first adjustment layer you created) to open the Hue/Saturation dialog box. Note that you need to double click the Layer thumbnail and not the Layer mask thumbnail to open the Hue/Saturation dialog box.

5. You have a number of options for deciding how the color values are treated when converted to grayscale. As a simple adjustment, you can move the Hue and Saturation sliders to globally change the brightness values in the image. For much more precise adjustments, you can target different color primaries in the color background and determine how you want those values converted to grayscale. Open the Edit menu in the Hue/Saturation dialog box and select a color, then move the Hue and Saturation sliders to make your refinements (see Figure 9-4).

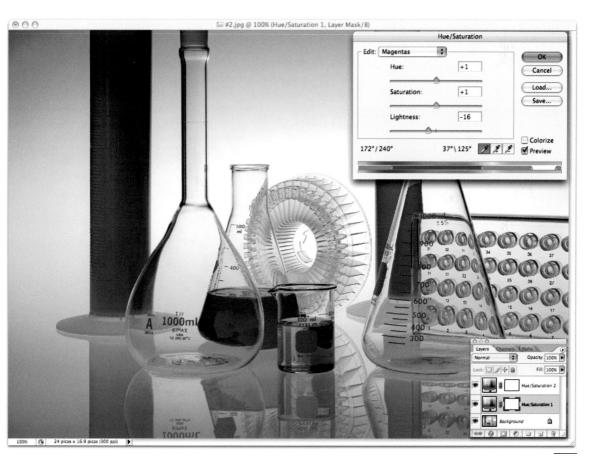

9-4

You can use the Channel Mixer to perform another complex nondestructive conversion to grayscale. For a simple conversion, you can use the Channel Mixer to blend the overall R, G, and B channels together to create the composite grayscale image using your own custom mix.

Where the Channel Mixer and Hue/Saturation adjustment layers really help you is when you mask areas in a document and use multiple adjustment layers. For example, suppose the background area needs a different mix than the foreground area. You can create a selection in either the background or foreground and apply a Channel Mixer or Hue/Saturation adjustment layer to the selection. Inverse the selection, and you can apply different Hue/Saturation adjustments or a channel mix to the selection.

Take a look at the following steps to see how RGB-to-grayscale conversions are applied to selected areas in an image:

1. Create a selection in a file for a background or foreground. Any area you want to isolate to apply two separate adjustments for grayscale conversion will do. Save the selection as an alpha channel.

2. Load the selection and create a new adjustment layer. Select Channel Mixer from the Create new fill or adjustment layer drop-down menu. When the Channel Mixer dialog box opens select the Monochrome check box, and your image preview shows a grayscale image. Move the RGB sliders to create the mix you want to appear in the selected area, as shown in Figure 9-5.

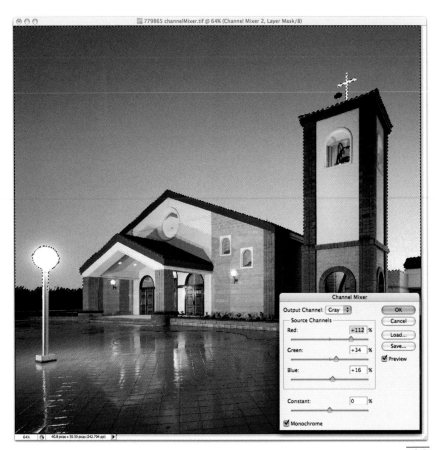

9-5

3. Click OK to return to the document window. Your
   selection is inactive so you first need to load the
   selection saved to the alpha channel. First, click
   on the background in the Layers palette then
   choose Select ⇨ Load Selection, and load the
   alpha channel. In the Load Selection dialog box,
   select the Invert check box to inverse the
   selection.

4. Create a new adjustment layer. Open the Create
   new fill or adjustment layer drop-down menu, and
   select Channel Mixer again. When the Channel
   Mixer dialog box opens, again move the Red,
   Green, and Blue sliders to create the mix for the
   current active selection.

   In this example, a simple Image ⇨ Mode ⇨
   Grayscale conversion produces the image shown
   in Figure 9-6. When you open the Levels dialog
   box, notice the balance of the tone values are to
   the right of the midtone 128 value.

9-6

You can use the Channel Mixer and two adjustment layers to lighten the sky a bit and adjust the foreground by blending the channels. The end result is a much more even distribution of tones as you notice in the histogram that appears when you open the Levels dialog box after the conversion (see Figure 9-7).

Using a similar approach with the Channel Mixer you can create a partial grayscale image while leaving a portion of your photo in RGB color. A number of different effects can be applied simply by creating a selection and converting the selected area to grayscale. The remaining portion of the image stays in RGB color.

Figure 9-8 is a simple selection that is saved as an alpha channel. It's always a good idea to save a selection even if you plan to only use the selection one time in your editing sequence. You may never know if you want to return to the selection or not when you first use it. After saving the selection as an alpha channel, an adjustment layer is created using the Channel Mixer. Apply a monochrome mix to the selection.

9-7

9-8

FINE-ART BLACK-AND-WHITE CONVERSIONS

For the best color-to-grayscale conversion, we recommend this method over all the other methods described in this chapter. This method of grayscale conversion provides a real-time black-and-white proof preview while maintaining the color in an image. Rather than mixing channel information, you can target colors and control how the color primaries are converted to grayscale, apply Hue/Saturation adjustments, and tweak your brightness values using Curves, all while working in your target profile color space. For the photographer interested in critical fine-art black-and-white reproductions, we recommend using this method of conversion from RGB to grayscale.

1. Open a file you want to convert to grayscale. First, convert the RGB image to your output profile color space. Ideally for fine-art black-and-white photography you would have color profiles designed specifically for black-and-white printing. If you don't have custom color profiles for black and white, use a profile created for your output material and printer.

PRO TIP

For more information on obtaining profiles for black-and-white photography, see Chapter 11 where we discuss QuadTone RIP (www.quadtonerip.com).

Choose Edit ⇨ Convert to Profile to open the Convert to Profile dialog box. Open the Profile drop-down menu, and select your output profile, as shown in Figure 9-9.

PRO TIP

For more information on using color profiles for printing see Chapter 11.

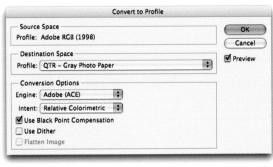

9-9

2. You work on a grayscale view as you add adjustment layers and adjust tones in the image. If you want to see a color view of your file, you can add a second window and observe the color file while working on a grayscale view. Choose Window ⇨ Arrange ⇨ New Window for *<file name>* where file name is the name of the file you currently have open in Photoshop.

Choose View ⇨ Proof Setup ⇨ Custom to open the Customize Proof Condition dialog box. Open the Device to Simulate drop-down menu, and select Gray Gamma 2.2, as shown in Figure 9-10. If you have a color profile specifically created for black-and-white printing such as the QuadTone RIP profiles, choose a gray profile designed for your printer and paper.

Click OK, and you see a grayscale view of your image. Your photo is still in an RGB color space but the view you see soft-proofed on your screen is grayscale, as shown in Figure 9-11. You now see the grayscale image soft-proofed in the color

9-10

space for your output device and paper. Theoretically, all the corrections you now make on your image show you a soft-proof for how your printer will output the file.

PRO TIP

For these steps, we apply linear tonal adjustments to our image. If you want to make adjustments individually to different areas such as foreground and background you can create a selection mask like we discussed when using the Channel Mixer in the "Complex Conversions to Grayscale" section earlier in this chapter. Load a selection, and then create the adjustment layers as we explain in this series of steps. Inverse the selection and create new adjustment layers.

3. If you convert your image from Camera Raw and preserve the 16-bit mode, leave the file in 16-bit. If you work with a JPEG captured image, choose Image ⇨ Mode ⇨ 16 Bits/Channel then choose Image ⇨ Image Size, and downsample the image 71 percent using Bicubic interpolation. Perform all your tonal adjustments while in 16-bit mode.

4. In the Layers palette, select the Create new fill or adjustment layer icon to open the drop-down menu and choose Selective Color. In the Selective Color Options dialog box, open the Colors drop-down menu, as shown in Figure 9-12. Select one of the channels (Reds, Yellows, Greens, Cyans, Blues, Magentas), and move the Black slider to adjust the tonal range. Be careful to not make your adjustments too radical or you end up clipping the image.

The Neutrals option in the dialog box is a Gamma adjustment. If you proof the image using a 2.2 Gamma, you can back off a little to brighten the overall look in the image by selecting Neutrals and moving the Black slider to the left. Use the Whites option for adjusting the white point and Blacks for adjusting the black point.

9-11

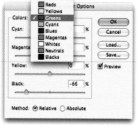

9-12

Click OK and you return to your document window. Keep in mind you have an additional option on an adjustment layer for adjusting Opacity in the Layers palette as well as using a blending mode.

5. Create another adjustment layer using Hue/Saturation. When the Hue/Saturation dialog box opens, you can make additional adjustments to the RGB color primaries, as shown in Figure 9-13. Click OK, and you again have more options by adjusting Opacity and blending modes.

6. Create a third adjustment layer, and select Curves from the drop-down menu in the Layers palette. For an adjustment to brightness and contrast, add a little contrast to the final view using the Curves settings shown in Figure 9-14.

9-13

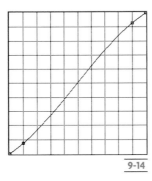

9-14

To print the file, you need to flatten the layers. Open the Layers palette fly-out menu. Select Flatten Image, or open a context menu on one of the layers and select Flatten Image. You're still in a proof view, and the original document is still RGB. Before printing, convert the file to grayscale. Use the Image ⇨ Mode ⇨ Grayscale command, and the grayscale conversion is based on the view you see in the document window. After converting, you won't see a difference between the proof view and the converted image.

Print the file using the color profile you use for printing to the target substrate. This profile should be the same profile you use when using the Convert to Profile command.

7. Save your file in the native Photoshop format while preserving the layers. In Figure 9-15, you can see the Layers palette containing the three layers we use to produce our final image. After saving as a Photoshop file you can always open the file and make adjustments to the adjustment layers by double-clicking on the adjustment layer icon in the Layers palette.

9-15

X-REF

For more information on printing with profiles,
see Chapter 11.

A quick look at the histogram shows where the data falls along the 256 gray curve. In Figure 9-16, you can see the histogram on the left from the Levels dialog box opened on the same file using the Image ⇨ Mode ⇨ Grayscale command. On the right is the

histogram using the Levels dialog box on the file we converted using these steps. As evidenced by the histograms, you can add a little more to the blacks in the image, create a better midtone range, and brighten the whites a little. The original image has a little clipping on both ends of the histogram, but the black can be brought under control while leaving a very tiny clip in the highlights. In Figure 9-17, you can see the comparison between using an Image ⇨ Mode ⇨ Grayscale conversion versus the method used in these steps.

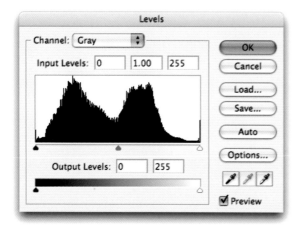
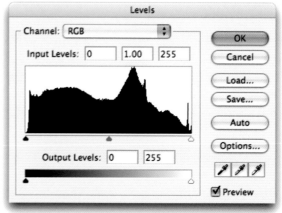

9-16

9-17

SHOOTING INFRARED PHOTOGRAPHY

Traditional infrared (IR) photography is shot with films that are sensitive to the light you can see and infrared light that you cannot see. This broader range of sensitivity to light records waves that fall below our visual spectrum. The human eye can only see light in wavelengths from 400 nm (nanometers) (deep violets) to 700 nm (deep reds). Ultraviolet light falls below 400 nm while infrared is in the 700 nm and longer waves. Near-infrared (NIR) falls in the 700 nm to 1200 nm range.

Some film photographers experiment with IR film, shoot a roll or two and then give up, while some others get hooked and specialize in infrared photography. These IR junkies like the effects of the areas of intense light that appear to glow, darker skies, and unusually light vegetation (because chlorophyll and other pigments in greens are transparent to infrared radiation). The overall grainy quality that produces an impressionistic type of image having an exotic and antique look is typical of IR images. In Figure 9-18, you can see some of these effects shot by Schaf of Schaf Photo Ventura, California with traditional IR film, scanned, and reproduced here.

Your DSLR camera's sensor is capable of capturing what we refer to as near-infrared light (NIR). The CCDs and CMOS chips used in virtually all digital cameras and camcorders are sensitive to 1000 nm and higher. You may or may not have the capability of capturing infrared photos with a little help from filters that block out all visible light, while letting infrared wavelengths pass through. Some cameras may not be capable of capturing IR images due to a blocking mechanism in your camera that prohibits IR light to hit the image plane. More than likely, your DSLR camera is incapable of capturing IR images due to more sophisticated construction compared to the lower-end point-and-shoot models.

9-18 — Photo Courtesy Schaf Photo
(www.schafphoto.com)

If you want to shoot IR images with your digital camera you'll need to use a cutoff filter and be certain the camera is capable of capturing IR wavelengths. There's much to learn about the filters you need to use and the cameras that can shoot IR images. If you want to shoot IR photos, search the Internet and you'll find information on shooting digital IR.

Shooting IR images is beyond the scope of this book. We can, however, talk about simulating an IR effect with any photo you take with any digital camera. To learn how to create a photo with an IR effect, follow these steps:

1. Select an image you want to use for simulating an IR shot. You can use an RGB or grayscale image and you can perform almost all your work while in 16-bit mode. In this example (see Figure 9-19), we use a photo that was created using the Merge to HDR command.

X-REF

For more information on using Merge to HDR, see Chapter 1.

2. The first step you'll want to make is adjusting image tones for the right brightness and contrast whether you use a grayscale image or an RGB image. Be certain to adjust Levels and Curves as we described in Chapter 4 to obtain the best looking image you can get while in your default color mode. If you start out with a grayscale image skip down to Step 4.

If you work with an RGB image such as we use in this example, open the Channel Mixer by selecting Image ⇨ Adjustments ⇨ Channel Mixer. Move the Red slider in the Channel Mixer dialog box to the far left to reduce the Red channel to -200%. Move the Green channel slider to the maximum 200% as shown in Figure 9-20. *Note: Do not check the Monochrome checkbox.*

3. Convert the RGB image to Grayscale using Lab color and the Lightness channel. Select Image ⇨ Mode ⇨ Lab Color. Open the Channels palette and select the Lightness channel. Select Image ⇨ Mode ⇨ Grayscale to convert to grayscale.

9-19

9-20

4. Click the Layers tab and drag the Background layer to the Create a new layer icon in the Layers palette to duplicate the layer. (Note: be certain to duplicate the layer and not the Black channel). Select Overlay for the blend mode in the Layers palette and open the Gaussian Blur dialog box by selecting Filter ⇨ Blur ⇨ Gaussian Blur.

In the Gaussian Blur dialog box add a hefty Radius for the blur amount — somewhere between 20 to 40 works well for these kinds of images. In this example we use a Radius of 30 as shown in Figure 9-21.

5. Create a new fill layer. Press the Option/Alt key and click the Create a new layer icon in the Layers palette. (Pressing the modifier key opens the New Layer dialog box). In the New Layer dialog box select Overlay for the blend mode and check the box for Fill with Overlay-neutral color (50% gray). Name this layer Grain and click OK.

Select Filter ⇨ Artistic ⇨ Film Grain. Don't worry about the Film Grain filter applying too much noise. You can always reduce the amount by adjusting the Opacity slider in the Layers dialog box.

6. Reduce your image to 8-bit mode by selecting Image ⇨ Mode ⇨ 8 Bits/Channel. Everything up to this point can be performed in 16-bit mode. The next step where we use the Diffuse Glow filter, however, can't be performed on a 16-bit image.

7. If your image gains too much contrast or the overall brightness appears too dark, create a Curves adjustment layer and adjust the brightness and contrast as we described in Chapter 4 then

9-21

select Image ⇨ Mode ⇨ 8 Bits/Channel. When the image appears correct for brightness and contrast, open the Layers pop up menu and select Flatten Layers.

8. Create a duplicate layer of the new Background by dragging the Background layer to the Create a new layer icon in the Layers palette. Select Filter ⇨ Distort ⇨ Diffuse Glow to open the Diffuse Glow dialog box shown in Figure 9-22

This adjustment is a matter of personal choice. Set the Graininess, Glow Amount, and Clear amount sliders according to your personal preference. Make your adjustment a little more than you want the results to appear and you can back off a little by adjusting the Opacity slider in the Layers palette. To get a reasonably fair rendition

of a simulated IR image, you'll want to see some obvious grain, glowing highlights and even have some highlights approaching burn out. You might want to experiment a little and make choices for settings then view your results. If you want to make changes, use the History palette and return to the Diffuse Glow settings.

PRO TIP

If you want to return to a filter dialog box showing the last settings you made and open it from keyboard shortcuts, press Command/Ctrl+Option/Alt+F.

9. Click OK and flatten the layers. The final image is shown in Figure 9-23.

9-22

9-23

High-Key Darkroom Techniques

High-key images are a classic style in black-and-white photography, although high-key photos are not limited to black and white. You can produce high-key color images as well. High-key photos are images with most of the gray tones lighter than middle gray with just a touch of black. Ideally, you would plan to shoot a high-key photo especially if the photo is in color. If you haven't planned a shot for a high-key image you can create a high-key effect in Photoshop (see Figure 9-29 for an example of a high-key photo).

When creating a high-key effect in Photoshop for a black-and-white image, most often you find using the Red channel as the best method for converting RGB to Grayscale. Much like a photographer uses a red filter and increases exposure by two f-stops to shoot a high-key photo, start with the Red channel and then apply brightness adjustments to emulate the high-key effect a film photographer can achieve.

If you try to use the Channel Mixer to create your high-key image, make sure all the percentages add up to 100 percent or less or the highlights will be clipped. Mix channels for the best tonal separation, and then use Levels or Curves to adjust for contrast.

In some cases you can create a respectable high-key photo when your original image lacks the proper tone levels for producing a good black-and-white photo. For example, Figure 9-24 is an image shot with a point-and-shoot camera with the internal flash. The light shut down quickly, and the background appears quite dark. Even if the background is well lit, the photo would be less than interesting. The image might look much better as a high-key photo, where you get rid of that disturbing shadow and the distracting background.

1. Look at the individual channels. Typically, it is best to use the Red channel for your grayscale conversion. Select the channel then choose Image ➪ Mode ➪ Grayscale to convert the file to grayscale, or you can leave the file in RGB color

9-24

and duplicate the channel you want to work with. If you duplicate the channel, perform all your brightness and contrast adjustments in the channel, then copy the finished image in the channel and paste it into a new layer. If you expect to use the grayscale version and never return to the RGB image, then converting to Grayscale while deleting two channels is best.

2. Select the area you want to appear with a range of grays up to a little bit of black. In the example, we created a selection mask using the Lasso tool because the image tonalities didn't lend themselves to any shortcut methods. We isolated the foreground subject so we could apply different tonal adjustments to the subject and the background separately. The selection is saved to an alpha channel, as shown in Figure 9-25.

3. Load the selection from the alpha channel by choosing Select ➪ Load Selection. Choose the alpha channel for the selection in the Load Selection dialog box and click OK. This creates a selection on the background, which is the original selection created. You can make your brightness adjustments on the Background layer, but using layers and layer masks provides much better tweaking because you can return to a layer and readjust settings or move the layer Opacity slider.

To create a copy of the selected background area, choose Layer ⇨ New ⇨ Layer Via Copy or press Command/Ctrl+J. Only the selected background is copied to a new layer. Notice the selection isn't feathered.

4. For the tonal adjustment, choose Image ⇨ Adjustments ⇨ Curves to open the Curves dialog box, and adjust both the white and black points. The white point anchor is moved left until the background whites reach a level of 245 (almost white). The black point slider is raised until the darkest tones in the background are at a level of 200, as shown in Figure 9-26. The background

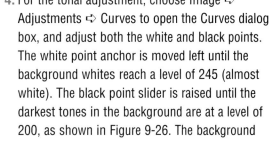

should be adjusted so that it appears very flat and very light. Note that the selection is loaded on the copied layer. When the Curves adjustment layer was created, the adjustment layer created the layer mask.

5. To diffuse the background, apply a slight Gaussian Blur. Choose Filter ⇨ Blur ⇨ Gaussian Blur, and use a Radius of 12. This helps eliminate that unattractive shadow caused by the flash and takes the detail out of the distractions in the background.

6. For the foreground, load the selection again and select Invert in the Load Selection dialog box.

Press Command/Ctrl+J to copy the selection to a new layer. Select the layer and make another Curves adjustment (see Figure 9-27). This adjustment needs to lighten up the overall layer while still keeping a little black in the image.

7. The veil presents a problem. That part of the image still needs to be lightened a little. For this step, another selection on the veil is created and the layer duplicated where we lighten the foreground subject. Soft Light is selected from the Layer blending modes, and the Opacity slider in the Layers palette is pushed to the left to 50 percent (see Figure 9-28).

9-27

9-28

The default color for the foreground is set to white and a large, soft brush for the Brush tool is selected. The veil is painted over, and it lightens up nicely.

8. We flatten the image and add a little edit using an oval feathered selection and lighten it a little to produce the final high-key image in Figure 9-29. As you can see, the end result is quite an improvement over the original poor snapshot. High-key effects like this can sometimes produce a quality photo from a poor shot in addition to creating a more dynamic-looking image.

9-29

COLORIZING BLACK AND WHITE

Black-and-white photos can be colorized in Photoshop to provide a number of different effects. You might want to add a tint for vintage photos such as a sepia tone, a tint for simulating IR images, colorizing selected areas in a black-and-white photo for artistic effects, or adding a slight tint for reproducing some richer tonal values. The possibilities are endless, and a number of avenues open to you are all a matter of personal preference and choice. We cover a few here to give you an idea on how to colorize images in Photoshop.

X-REF

For more information on colorizing black-and-white photos, see Chapter 10.

CREATING A SEPIA TONE

A sepia tone is a monochrome image appearing in shades of reddish brown. The sepia tone was originally produced by adding a pigment from a marine cephalopod in the order of Sepiida known as cuttlefish. Cuttlefish have ink, much like squids, from which the sepia dye was originally added to the chemical baths during photographic printing. The chemical process for producing these prints converted metallic silver to a sulfide, which was much more resistant to chemical decomposition and breakdown over a period of time. As such, sepia tone prints have survived years over other photographs processed without sepia toning.

When we see a sepia tone print we immediately equate that print with antiquity — primarily because the color appears in so many antiquated prints that were sepia toned and have survived so many years. When we look at vintage photographs that were sepia toned, we immediately recognize the print as being timeless more because of the color then the image content.

As a natural application in photo retouching, photographers have applied sepia toning to images that are restored from original vintage photos. But sepia toning is not necessarily an effect you need to restrict to vintage photographs. You can add sepia toning to contemporary prints, which adds rich tonal transitions and improves the dynamic range of photos when printing them. The mistake some photo editors make is adding too much color to grayscale images in an effort to emulate a vintage photo. Vintage photos appear with deeper reddish-brown tints because of inconsistencies in the original print processing and discoloration through natural aging. In many cases, a slight toning of your grayscale images can provide a nice attractive print with rich tones.

Fortunately, you don't have to shorten the one- to two-year life span of the cuttlefish to create a sepia tone. Photoshop has a number of different tools that can help you create sepia tones. You can use the Variations dialog box, use a Hue/Saturation adjustment layer, or use the preinstalled Action in the Actions palette. Any of these methods can easily lead to applying too much toning on certain prints. For a more delicate sepia tone, use the Curves adjustments and carefully finesse each channel without overdoing it.

Follow these steps to apply a sepia tone to an image:

1. If you have a grayscale image currently in Grayscale color mode, change the color mode to RGB. Open your black-and-white photo, and choose Image ⇨ Mode ⇨ RGB Color.

2. If it's a one-time edit before printing, Don tends to favor applying a color tint to an image directly to the Background layer with a no-fuss, no-muss-type of approach. Ted tends to favor using adjustment layers just in case he wants to tweak the opacity a little. Either method works fine. If you apply a tint to an image on the background, you can always undo if you don't like the effect.

Because Ted has his hands on the keyboard, go ahead and use an adjustment layer for this procedure while Don's off shooting an image for the next chapter.

Assuming all the contrast and brightness in the image require no adjustment, choose Layer ➪ New Adjustment Layer ➪ Curves, or click the Create new fill or adjustment layer icon in the Layers palette to open the drop-down menu and select Curves.

3. This is a one-step method (one step being you make all your adjustments in the Curves dialog box) for sepia toning a photo. Look at each of the three channels in the Curves dialog box, and apply a slight Curves adjustment to each channel.

   Select Red from the Channel drop-down menu. Keep the Input level at 128 for all curve adjustments, and move the Red Output point up to 141. Select Green from the Channel drop-down menu and move the Output point to 131. Go to the Blue channel and move the output point to 119. The three channels should be set as shown in Figure 9-30.

4. Click OK and look over your final image to be certain the effect is as you want. If the tones look

good and you want to use the same settings again, double-click the Curves adjustment layer, and click Save in the Curves dialog box. Note that you can also preview the image on-screen before leaving the Curves dialog box when you first apply the adjustment if you're working on the Background layer. If you have enough room on your monitor to comfortably see the Curves dialog box and your image, you can click Save before you exit the Curves dialog box.

Digital Darkroom Techniques

PRO TIP

While the Curves dialog box is open you can't use the menu commands or tools in the Tools palette to zoom in or out of your photo. You can, however, use keyboard shortcuts to zoom in (Command/Ctrl++) or zoom out (Command/Ctrl+-).

Save the Curves adjustment to a location on your hard drive where you keep your settings files for Photoshop. This can be a folder inside the Photoshop folder or any convenient location where you can easily find your files.

Curves is used to apply a sepia tone to the snapshot image in Figure 9-31. The results of the sepia tone appear in Figure 9-31.

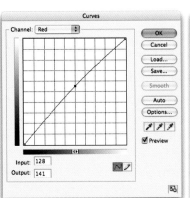
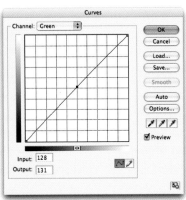
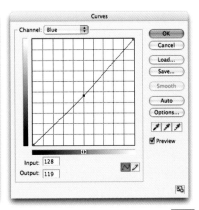

9-30

9-31

COMBINING TINTS AND **RGB** COLOR

Tinting photographs is another technique originally used by old-time photographers. Hand tinting photographs has been around almost as long as photography itself. Somewhere around the 1840s, photographers began hand tinting black-and-white and sepia-toned images with oils and dyes. The art of hand tinting almost ceased to exist when color films became commonplace during the 1950s. Today, there are a number of photo editors who have revitalized hand tinting to produce nostalgic and retro-type photo prints.

For many professional photographers, the art of hand tinting has moved from the traditional mechanics of using Marshall's Photo Tinting Oils, Spot Pens, cotton balls, Q-Tips, toothpicks, and wax paper to the digital world of Photoshop. Photographic tinting is used for creating moods, a sense of nostalgia, surreal impressions, and so on, as well as adding more tonal range to your photos.

Some digital image editors combine sepia toning with tinting and/or RGB color. The work of professional photographer PJ Leffingwell of Melbourne, Florida, for example, combines sepia toning and a touch of RGB color so evident in many of his prints, such as the one in Figure 9-32. This effect accentuates a mood in his wedding photographs and adds romanticism in contemporary photos with a vintage impression.

PJ shoots his images with a Nikon D2X DSLR in RGB color in Raw format. Rather than let Photoshop do the work for sepia toning, he uses a sepia effect applied with the Nikon capture software. In Photoshop, he takes the original RGB image and adds the sepia image as a new layer. He then paints back in the RGB color using a layer mask to create the final image.

To combine a sepia tone with a tint or add two or more tints of different colors, start with a selection or several selections saved as channel masks. Use any number of tools you want to create your selections, and save the selections as alpha channels. From that point you're ready to apply tints in adjustment layers with layer masks.

We start out with an image that was created as the background for a double-page catalog spread. The

9-32 — Photo courtesy PJ Leffingwell
(www.photosbypj.com)

client produces rose plants for commercial growers and has a multigenerational family background dating back to the early 20th century. Old photos of the original family founders needed to be incorporated with a contemporary rose variety for the spread. A selective sepia look was deemed the best type of visual for this image and would be far more interesting than a simple multiphoto page layout.

The setup is reasonably simple. All the vintage photos were placed in period-style frames and placed on a dark wood coffee table. An antique-style lacy curtain created a simple background. Lighting consists of a large, soft box top light, with a gridded head high to the right to add some highlights to the curtain. A

small mini spot high to the left is aimed at the foreground roses to add brilliance and illumination to the front of the blossoms. The original capture appears in Figure 9-33.

PRO TIP

We're starting with an RGB file in this series of steps to illustrate how you might approach applying a tint to a selected area in an image while keeping the remaining area in RGB color, much like the image shown in Figure 9-38. If you have a grayscale image and convert it to RGB color, then add other RGB image data to your files that are in RGB color, you can follow the same steps to produce the exact same results.

Follow these steps to produce an image with a sepia tone while keeping a portion of the photo in RGB color:

1. To give the image the mood and look needed for the layout, a selective sepia tint is required. The foreground flowers are left in natural color to bring them forward from the background and ensure that they are the dominant visual element in the image. Using Curves and a careful selection of the background only is the easiest way to create the needed image edit.

   The first step is to create a selection for the roses. The Lasso tool is used to create the selection, which is then inversed and feathered by one-half pixel. The selection is saved as an alpha channel.

2. Before moving on, we make sure the Swatches palette is in view and the default color Swatches are loaded. With the background selection loaded, press Command/Ctrl+M to open the Curves dialog box. Double-click the white point eyedropper to open the Color Picker; with the Color Picker open, move the eyedropper to the Swatches palette and click the light-brown color swatch, as shown in Figure 9-34.

3. Click OK in the Color Picker, and you return to the Curves dialog box. Keep the Curves dialog box open, and move the cursor to the document window. When the cursor leaves the Curves dialog box and you move it to the document window, the cursor changes to an eyedropper. Move the eyedropper to the brightest area in the photo on the sleeve in the photo in the top-right corner, as shown in Figure 9-35. Click to sample the white point, and the light-brown color is applied to the

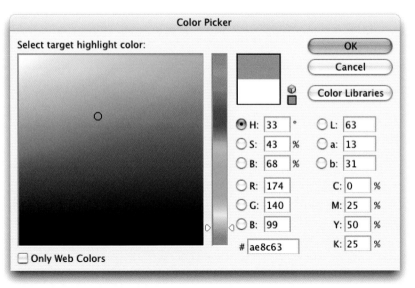

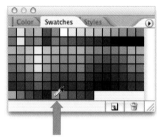

9-34

9-35

selected area. We use the white eyedropper here in the Curves dialog box to keep a low-key result, which helps highlight the foreground roses.

4. A quick check of the individual color channels in the Curves dialog box reveals the new white point settings by the eyedropper set to light brown, as shown in Figure 9-36. The Curves adjustments in the separate channels demonstrate how the highlights carry such a deep brown.

5. Go back to the composite channel by selecting RGB in the Channel drop-down menu in the Curves dialog box. The white highlights are darker than we want so pull the white anchor point to the left to lighten the image, and add a black anchor point to keep the shadow area in control by moving the point slightly down, as shown in Figure 9-37 on the left. This adjustment keeps the darkest shadow tones from lightening up too much.

6. One more edit is needed before exiting the Curves dialog box. The resulting overall look is a little too red. Reduce the red in the image by selecting the Red channel from the Channel drop-down menu, and move the midpoint down, as shown on the right in Figure 9-37. Click OK, and Photoshop asks whether you want to save the new target colors as defaults. Be certain to click No to revert

the Levels and Curves white points back to the original default values.

7. At this point, there is a little too much saturation. Open the Hue/Saturation dialog box, and move the Saturation slider to the left to -20. This desaturates the overall image to a nice, warm tone without too much saturation.

As a final touch, click OK in the Hue/Saturation dialog box and return to the document window. The selection is inversed a little saturation can be pumped into the roses to make them a little more pronounced in the foreground. Visit the Hue/Saturation dialog box, and push the Saturation slider up to +10.

The final edited image appears in Figure 9-38.

PRO TIP

You have many choices for applying tints to images. You can use several different adjustment layers of different types, such as the Solid Color selection, Curves, Hue/Saturation, and Photo Filter. Whatever method works for you is what you'll want to use. Another very simple method to tint grayscale images is through the use of the Photo Filters. See Chapter 10 for some information on how we apply color tints to grayscale images using these filters.

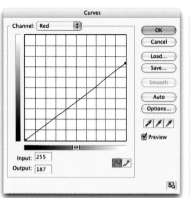
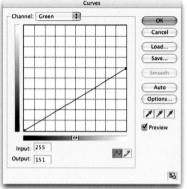
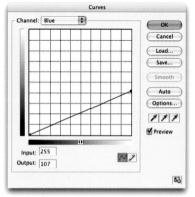

9-36

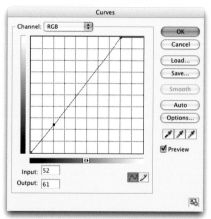
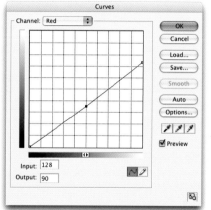

9-37

9-38

■ **When I save my final black-and-white photo for printing, what color mode should I use?**

Generally, you want to convert your images back to RGB for printing. Many newer printers have several black inks that are used to print finer tonal gradations. For richer tones in your prints with more dynamic range, apply a slight tint to your file. This is a practice common with earlier black-and-white film photographers who added toners to their development baths. See Chapter 11 for more information on printing.

My photography is equally divided between black and white, color, and infrared. What are my best options for outfitting my camera to shoot the ranges of photos I want?

It all depends on how serious you are and how much money you want to spend. For the high end, you can use a quality DSLR for your black-and-white and color shooting. Purchase another lower-end DSLR of the same brand so you can interchange lenses for your IR photography. On this camera, have the hot mirror removed and use filters on the lenses for capturing the IR wavelengths.

If you want a lower-cost solution, use the same DSLR camera for your black-and-white and color work. Search the Internet for point-and-shoot cameras that have good responses to IR light and purchase it. In addition to looking at the IR capture capabilities of the camera, look for models with more bulk that weigh more than the featherweight cameras. You'll most often use a tripod, and a heavier camera is easier to keep still. Additionally, try to find a camera using the same memory cards as your DSLR model. For the filter, your can purchase a gel that you can tape over the lens if you can't find filters that screw in front of the lens.

I want to print fine-art black-and-white photography on special papers, but I don't have a color profile for printing on the papers of my choice. How can I get color profiles for my papers?

One solution is to have a custom color profile created for you using a service. Search the Internet and try to find providers who offer profiling for black-and-white printing on various papers. Additionally, you can search for Web sites that provide information on black-and-white digital photography, and printers and papers that come closest to a traditional fiber paper visual appearance. A good place to start is `inkjetmall.com`.

Another option for you is to search the paper suppliers. Your printer manufacturer may have fewer papers than can be found with paper suppliers. Although most printer manufacturers recommend you use their papers, you can find materials from reputable suppliers who have tested their products with a variety of printers. The paper suppliers also create custom profiles for using their papers with a number of printers.

As a last resort, be certain to print your files using the RGB color mode, and choose a profile developed by your printer manufacturer for a similar paper you use. Create a viewing layer, as we describe in Chapter 11, and run tests to get your print to match your monitor. It may take you some time, but through trial and error you can find the right adjustments to print your files exactly as you see them on a well-calibrated monitor.

Chapter 10

LENS EFFECTS

"Which of my photographs is my favorite? The one I'm going to take tomorrow."—Imogen Cunningham

Film photographers have used a variety of different filters on lenses to correct problems with color, add special effects, and compensate for many different lighting conditions. The disadvantage for the analog photographer has always been the irreversibility of using a filter or an ability to change a filter after the shot. Once an image is recorded on film, you're stuck with it.

Photoshop and digital photography provide you a much better solution. You can change white balance on images shot in Camera Raw (a distinct purpose for using filters on film cameras), and you can apply filter effects on images after postprocessing or on JPEG images that don't provide you the ability to change white balance.

Photoshop even takes the application of filter effects a step farther. Inasmuch as you can purchase varying degrees of warming and cooling analog filters (the most common filters used on film cameras), Photoshop enables you to apply adjustments to filter effects using blending modes, opacity settings, and channel masks that result in an infinite number of choices. To obtain the same options with a film camera, you'd need thousands of filters.

Photoshop also provides you the ability to see your results before committing to the final image. The difficult job for the analog photographer is guessing at what filter to use when setting up a shot. Not all intuitions pan out in the final image. If a shot needs a different correction filter, your only option is to reshoot the image. With Photoshop you can see your results in real time as you apply filter effects.

The Photo Filter adjustment layer in Photoshop enables you to adjust tonal balance, make mood

changes on your images, and add special effects. For color correction, you'll want to use the methods we describe in Chapter 5. The Photo Filter, as we explain later in this chapter, isn't a good color-correction tool. However, for other applications, such as tinting photographs and changing the mood of an image, the Photo Filter works quite well.

In addition to the Photo Filters, you have a number of correction options using the Lens Correction filter to compensate for lens aberrations. Using filters designed specifically for image corrections can be helpful if other tonal edits don't get the job done. In this chapter, we explore some of the applications for using the Photo Filters, Lens Correction, and Lens Blur filters.

USING PHOTO FILTER ADJUSTMENT LAYERS

A good amount of color correction we do takes place in the Hue/Saturation and Curves dialog boxes. For color-correction work, we recommend staying with the Hue/Saturation and Curves adjustments in Photoshop and avoiding the Photo Filter for correcting color. Photo Filters are great for adding a colorcast, changing the mood of a scene, colorizing black and white, and adding tints and other kinds of additive-type edits to an already color-corrected image. A good part of using the Photo Filters in Photoshop is knowing when to use them and when not to use them.

PHOTO FILTER AND COLOR CORRECTION

Any old-timers out there who have worked with Ektachrome or Fujichrome duping films will immediately recognize the linear correction signature of the Photoshop Photo Filters when they're used for color correction. The image shown in Figure 10-1 was mistakenly captured as a JPEG in daylight balance setting under tungsten illumination.

An attempt was made to fully correct the image using just Photoshop's Photo Filter as a color correction tool. Here, we used a cooling Filter (82) with a 29 percent density setting (see Figure 10-2).

10-1

10-2

As the image example shows, the filter correction leaves a characteristic tint of the correction filter in the image highlights when the opacity setting is strong enough to correct the midtones. The same visual result could be obtained in the old days of film photography when trying to color correct a severely off-color original transparency with heavy correction filtration during the duplicating process. Although we have managed to correct the midtone colorcast, the final result is a severe color crossover in the highlights.

The Photo Filters work fine if you want to intentionally add a colorcast, but they fail miserably at providing a quality, one-step correction of an unwanted colorcast. We can still recommend using the digital Photo Filters for a fast fix, but for a high-quality result, stick with the traditional use of Curves to fix image colorcast problems. In Figure 10-3, we color corrected on the same image using only the Curves dialog box. The results using Curves adjustments provide a much better correction method than using a Photo Filter.

NOTE

We find it odd that Adobe chose to build an algorithm that mimics the poor results of a reversal film single-step duplicating correction. The rebalancing of a color negative film original to a direct transparency film, like the old Vericolor slide film, gave a far superior result with no strange color crossovers in the highlight portions of the image (but that's another reprographic issue we don't have space for here).

X-REF

For more information on correcting colorcasts, see Chapter 5.

10-3

PHOTO FILTER AND TONING

You can use the Photo Filter options in two ways. If you choose Image ⇨ Adjustments ⇨ Photo Filter, Photoshop applies any choice you make in the Photo Filter dialog box to the current active layer. Using this command permanently changes pixels on the layer. Moreover, the only control you have for specifying density after applying the filter is to use the Fade command.

The other method involves adding a Photo Filter adjustment layer. When using an adjustment layer, you can return to the Photo Filter dialog box and tweak your filter result, use any of the layer blending modes, add a layer mask to apply your filter effect to a selection mask, and adjust opacity to control density after leaving the Photo Filter dialog box. Photoshop offers you more options using an adjustment layer than when using the Photo Filter command in the Adjustments submenu. However, if you are in a hurry and you want to make a fast linear edit to print your file, you can add a Photo Filter and use the Undo command or step back in the History palette if you need to go back and apply a different filter.

The Photo Filter dialog box has several option choices you can make for applying a filter effect that include:

> **Filter.** From the Filter drop-down menu select a filter. The first three options are the warming filters. These filters are designed to be used when the white point in the image is too cool, which creates a bluish colorcast. Following the warming filters are the two cooling filters. These filters are designed to counteract yellowish artificial light. The last filter in the list is the Underwater filter, which is designed for corrections made with colorcasts in underwater photography. This filter neutralizes colors to create a greenish-blue colorcast that is typically normal for underwater images. The remaining color filters are presets for color tints that can be used to neutralize colorcasts. The intent is to use a complimentary color to make corrections for files containing colorcasts.

> **Color.** Any color in the Photoshop Color Picker can be used for a filter effect to either neutralize a colorcast or apply a tint to an image. Click the default color swatch in the Photo Filter dialog box, and the Photoshop Color Picker opens. Select a color in the Color Picker, and click OK to use that color for a new filter.

> **Density.** The Density slider enables you to adjust the amount of color toning you make to your image. As you move the slider left toward 0 percent, less density is applied. Moving to the right increases density. Regardless of the density choice you make here, when using an adjustment layer you can further control density by moving the Opacity slider in the Layers palette. However, be careful if you use the Opacity slider in the Layers palette. If you combine several filters on different layers with layer masks, you'll want to

control the density of the filter in the Photo Filter dialog box. Blending the filters may produce undesirable results.

> **Preserve Luminosity.** By default, this check box is selected. Leave this check box checked to insure that the brightness values in your image are not darkened when you apply a filter. If this option is not selected, you can mess up the tonal range in your photos. This option has the same effect as when using the Luminosity blend mode in the Layers palette where you essentially affect only the brightness values without disturbing the tonal gradations.

To apply a Photo Filter using an adjustment layer, follow these steps:

1. To apply a Photo Filter adjustment layer, click the Create new fill or adjustment layer menu icon in the Layers palette and select Photo Filter from the menu choices. The Photo Filter dialog box opens (see Figure 10-4).

2. Select a filter from the Filter drop-down menu and click OK. The adjustment layer can then be blended using a blend mode in the Layers palette, and another density choice can be made by adjusting the Layers palette Opacity slider.

The image in Figure 10-5 was edited to bring detail to both the blown-out background and the underexposed foreground. The file at this stage still needs brightness corrections and a boost in saturation. We tackle the edits to bring the tonal range into balance, and we use the Photo Filter adjustment as one of our last steps, not for color correction, but for warming up the tones a bit.

10-4

10-5

Using the example in Chapter 7, where tones in highlights and shadows are corrected using the Shadow/Highlight dialog box, we continue with that image to talk about making selections using the Color Range and Quick Mask mode. We toss in some selections and masking techniques to demonstrate the use of tone corrections in isolated areas of the image, then we move on to more linear adjustments using the Photo Filter.

1. Open an image you have corrected for brightness and contrast but also needs some color adjustment. In this example, we use a file that needs

separate corrections applied to the highlights and shadows. Choose Select ➭ Color Range to open the Color Range dialog box. Because this image has tonal variations in the highlights and shadows, we first work on the highlights and choose Highlights from the Select drop-down menu (see Figure 10-6).

Color Range selects just the highlight information in the file. The selection isn't perfect, but using this first step narrows down the selection and provides you an opportunity to refine it. In Figure 10-7, you see the selection created using the Highlights command in the Color Range dialog box.

2. Click OK in the Color Range dialog box and the selection appears in the document window. Click the Quick Mask tool or press Q to enter Quick Mask mode. The image appears by default with a red Rubylith-type appearance, shown in Figure 10-8.

We use the Quick Mask mode to paint in more mask in the image to improve our highlight selection. Note that the mission here is to add some color correction to the highlights and shadows independent of each other. If we create a selection where we pull out the foreground subjects and place them in another image for compositing photos, we can use a different selection method that creates a more precise selection on the foreground subjects. Selecting the loose strands of hair, for example, would be the task of a different set of steps using other methods. But for the mission at hand, a few loose strands of hair won't noticeably disturb the kind of edits we want to make because we create some transitions between the hair and the background to permit more gradual changes in the color adjustment.

10-6

10-7

10-8

When in Quick Mask mode, you use marking tools such as the Brush, Airbrush, Pencil, Eraser, and so on, to paint more mask. When entering Quick Mask mode, your default colors are changed from whatever colors are assigned in the foreground and background color swatches to a black foreground and a white background. Use black to paint more mask, and use white to remove mask. You can easily toggle the colors by pressing X. For example, while painting more mask in the document window, press X to change the foreground color to white and paint to remove any excess. Press X again to change back to black and paint more mask.

3. Select the Brush tool in the Tools palette. From the options bar, select a brush size from the Brush drop-down menu (see Figure 10-9). You can make selections for the brush tip, size, and the softness on the brush edge from the drop-down menu. Additionally, Opacity and Mode adjustments are made in the options bar.

Pick a brush size that enables you to accurately paint in the areas you want to add to your mask. Be certain the Opacity is set to 100 percent.

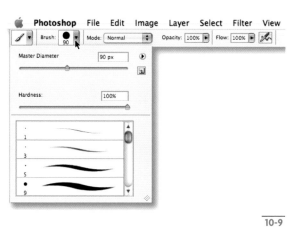

10-9

4. The bright background needs to be isolated from the dark foreground, so we start by painting using the black foreground color to paint where Color Range missed the foreground we want to select. We can later inverse our selection to select the background.

With a large brush, begin painting over the non-masked areas of the foreground. To cover the smaller areas, shrink the brush and keep painting. If you accidentally paint over the background, switch to white paint by pressing X, erase the mistake, and switch back to black. If you want to retrace some steps, open the History palette and click the step you want to return to from the recorded steps in the palette.

Paint over the hair and use the soft brush to bleed off the edge of the photo. This makes a nice smooth transition to the background. Once the foreground is finished (see Figure 10-10), switch to white paint and clean up any background areas missed by the Color Range selection.

5. After completing the mask, exit Quick Mask mode by pressing Q or click the Edit in Standard Mode tool in the Tools palette. After all the work you do creating a selection, you want to save the selection so you don't lose it. Choose Select ⇨ Save Selection to save the selection to an alpha channel. Name the selection a descriptive name such as Image Background, and click Save.

10-10

6. Load the selection and inverse it by pressing Command/Ctrl+I so the background becomes the selected area. Choose Image ➪ Apply Image to open the Apply Image dialog box. Select Multiply from the Blending mode menu (see Figure 10-11). The image background darkens nicely and gains tonal separation. Click OK to return to the document window.

7. Inverse the selection by choosing Select ➪ Inverse, or press Command/Ctrl+Shift+I. The foreground area is now the current active selection. Choose Image ➪ Apply Image. In the Apply Image dialog box, select Screen from the Blending drop-down menu (see Figure 10-12) to lighten the foreground area. Note that the Multiply blend mode darkens the image, and the Screen blend mode lightens the image. The image comes to life, and the image tones have a far more natural look. However, the foreground flesh tones still look a little off. The mixed color temperature in available lighting makes Danielle and Drew look unmatched.

8. To keep the edit simple and easy, use Hue/Saturation to clean up the flesh tones a little more. Choose Image ➪ Adjustments ➪ Hue/Saturation. In the Hue/Saturation dialog box, select Reds from the Edit drop-down menu and move the Hue slider right to +5 to add a little yellow to the red component of the flesh tones. Bump up the Saturation slider to +10 to saturate the flat flesh-tone colors (see Figure 10-13).

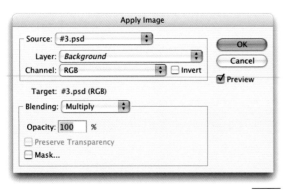

10-11

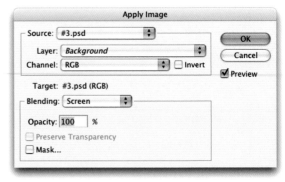

10-12

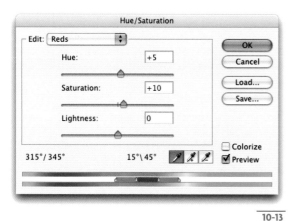

10-13

10-14

The adjustment is not perfect, but appears close (see Figure 10-14), and is much improved over the starting image.

PRO TIP

If you aren't sure about what Hue/Saturation adjustment works and you think you may need to return to the Hue/Saturation dialog box, use an adjustment layer. We chose to apply this edit to our selected area on the background because a quick eyeball view was all we needed to make the correct color adjustment. We're moving a little fast in this edit sequence to make our corrections, and we don't feel we need to return to the color adjustments to tweak the color correction. If we work on an image where several corrections need to be made, and we need to return to dialog boxes for refining adjustments, we would indeed use adjustment layers.

9. The background has a much cooler color balance than the foreground — this is where our Photo Filter can help. The background just looks wrong for the mood of the picture. This is just a snapshot, so we go for an easy edit using a Photo Filter. Because we work on the background, choose Select ⇨ Inverse to select the background area.

PRO TIP

Notice that in this sequence, we do our color correction first. We don't try to use the Photo Filter to correct a color problem in the image. We use the filter after the color appears correct, then go about changing the mood of the image by applying the filter.

What we want to do to the background is to warm it up a little bit. For a quick adjustment, choose Image ⇨ Adjustments ⇨ Photo Filter. You can use a warming filter here to change the tones from a cooler look to a warmer appearance. In this example, we use Warming Filter (81) selected from the Filter drop-down menu in the Photo Filter dialog box (see Figure 10-15).

10-15

10. The background mood looks much better after applying the filter. As a final tweak, add a little more contrast and density to the background. With the background selection still active, choose Image ⇨ Adjustments ⇨ Curves and create a darkening curve, as shown in Figure 10-16. Again, we're making a quick edit here and we're not concerned about returning to the Curves dialog box, therefore an adjustment layer is not used.

The amount of darkening needed is subjective. The amount selected seems to make the image look more normal, as you can see in the final image in Figure 10-17.

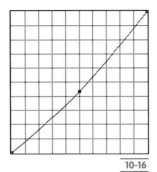
10-16

10-17

COMBINING FILTERS

In addition to making selections and applying a filter to just a part of your image, you may find sometimes that several filter effects can help you create the overall mood you desire. There's really nothing magic about making selections and applying filters, but we thought we would just toss this in to demonstrate how we use several Photo Filters on an image to create the effect you see in Figure 10-21.

Don shot three separate photos in Lone Pine, California, near the area where some of Ansel Adams's great photos were taken. The three images we started with are shown in Figure 10-18. The three shots were scanned for our composite image because all the photos were taken prior to acquiring a DSLR camera. The sky is from a stock skies folder shot on another day. This image was originally shot on Kodak VPS-3 4 x 5 color negative film. The grayscale Photoshop file for the sky was created using the Channel Mixer with Red at 75 percent and Green at 25 percent. The mountains, with Mount Whitney, were shot on Plus-X Pan film with a Hassleblad and a 150mm lens. The guy on the rock was shot on a Hassleblad with an 80mm lens, with T-Max 100 film. All tonal corrections using Levels and Curves were made prior to compositing the final image.

PRO TIP

We often shoot various sky formations for all kinds of weather conditions to use with images shot on days where the sky doesn't appear exactly like we want in our final image. When you shoot on days where the sky appears interesting, take some shots of the sky and keep them in a folder to use with other images when you want to replace a sky that doesn't have the character you want. When you shoot the sky, try to keep any foreground areas out of the photo so you won't have to spend time masking the image.

10-18

To apply Photo Filters to separate image selections, we used the following steps:

1. We first create selection masks for the mountains and rock images and save the selections to alpha channels in case we need to return to the original selections. We drag the selections to the sky image to create the composite photo shown in Figure 10-19. We keep the layers intact to easily create layer masks for the two layers where we want to apply a photo filter effect.

2. After converting the file to RGB color mode, we begin to work on adding the Photo Filters. First is the Background, where the Cooling Filter (82) is added and the density is dropped by moving the Density slider to 10 percent. Luminosity is checked for all the filters applied to each layer. Note that Preserve Luminosity is always used to maintain the tonal range, and it keeps the tinting of the image from looking like digital paint. When applying the Cooling Filter to the background,

don't create a selection. The background accepts the filter, and we use the other two layers to mask the background areas where we don't want the Cooling Filter to appear. We use the Density adjustment in the Photo Filter dialog box to control opacity and don't go to the Opacity slider in the Layers palette; therefore, whatever color you apply to a layer appearing above the background masks out the Background layer.

3. We then make a selection for the Mountains layer and create a second Photo Filter adjustment layer. By making the selection, first we create a layer mask; and when the filter is applied to the layer mask, the only area affected by the new filter is the active area within the mask. For this filter we use the Warming Filter (85) and adjust the Density to 15 percent, also keeping the Preserve Luminosity check box selected.

4. The last layer for the Rock also begins as a selection to create the layer mask. We choose the Violet filter with a Density of 15 percent and again keep the Preserve Luminosity check box selected. The results of the three layers and the adjustment layers can be seen in Figure 10-20.

The end product of the surreal photo, shown in Figure 10-21, has a certain sense of being real because the lighting patterns on the floating rock and the background mountains match perfectly.

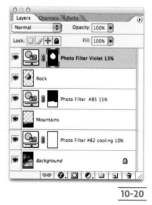

10-20

10-21

USING LENS CORRECTIONS

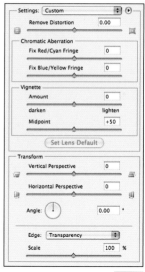

The Lens Correction filter contains settings to correct several conditions as a result of lens problems. You find settings for removing distortion, chromatic aberration, vignettes, and perspective control. For our purposes related to color and tonal corrections, stick with the middle two settings that you can adjust in the Lens Correction dialog box — Chromatic Aberration and Vignette, as shown in Figure 10-22.

To understand the first adjustment, Chromatic Aberration, travel back about 200 years and observe a little demonstration by Sir Isaac Newton. If you were in Sir Isaac's presence, he would show you that white light is composed of multiple wavelengths. White on your computer monitor is composed of three wavelengths — red, green, and blue. Blue is the shortest wavelength followed by green and then red. Your camera lens refracts (or bends) light differently according to each wavelength. What happens at the film plane is that the light is not imaged all in the same place. In Figure 10-23 you can see a lens and the R, G, B wavelengths being refracted.

The chromatic aberrations are the result of wavelength-dependent artifacts that occur because of the wavelength variations. Each wavelength is refracted according to its frequency. Hence the refractive index is greater for the blue wavelengths that change more rapidly than the longer red wavelengths.

What all this means in terms of your photographs is that these artifacts can show up in your images. The chromatic aberration is visible as color fringing close to the contrasting edges in your photos. The artifacts are particularly noticeable at the frame edges and on photos shot with wide-angle lenses.

10-22

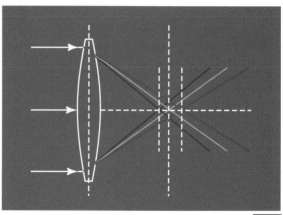

10-23

To compensate for chromatic aberration, the Lens Correction filter offers you choices for making adjustments for artifacts that show up in your images on these contrasting edges. You can adjust the Red/Cyan for the longer wavelength artifacts and Blue/Yellow for the shorter wavelengths. In Figure 10-24, the Blue/Yellow fringe is exaggerated so you can see the Blue fringe appearing in the center of the image.

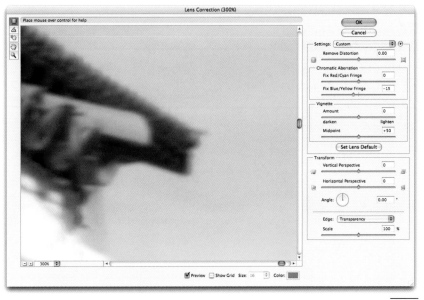

10-24

PRO TIP

You can zoom in on an area in the image by clicking the Zoom tool, or press Command/Ctrl and drag open a marquee around the area on which you want to zoom.

To make the adjustments to correct this kind of problem, zoom in on the image in the Lens Correction dialog box by clicking the Plus icon in the lower-left corner, or select a zoom level adjacent to the zoom percentage from the drop-down menu. Drag the sliders in the Chromatic Aberration area on the right side of the dialog box and you see a real-time preview showing the fringe disappear.

The other correction you find in the dialog box that can help with tonal corrections is the Vignette area. *Vignettes* appear as darker edges on your photos caused by poor lens construction, imperfections in the glass, poor flash coverage, and improper lens

shading. Again, these problems are more common with wide-angle lenses.

It's easy to detect vignettes. Just open the Lens Correction dialog box and drag the Darken slider back and forth. If you see the edges of your image come a little closer to the same brightness values in the center of the image, you can detect whether the edges are indeed darker than the rest of the image.

In the Lens Correction dialog box, drag the Amount slider back and forth to adjust the edge brightness (see Figure 10-25). Move the Midpoint slider to increase or decrease the shadowing or highlight along the edges of the image. If vignetting is a problem, you'll easily see the correction as you move the slider.

10-25

CHANGING DEPTH OF FIELD

The Lens Blur filter in Photoshop is an interesting tool for creating selective focus in a photo that is too sharp. You have some control when using this filter for things such as specular highlights, depth maps, blade curvature, and more. The Lens Blur dialog box has an extraordinary number of choices designed for changing depth of field.

Before you begin using the Lens Blur filter, you may want to create an alpha channel to isolate an area in your image that you want to remain in focus; however, using multiple channels is not something you can do with a single edit. You have a number of options for using a single selection. You can create a channel mask based on image content separating the foreground and the background. Another kind of mask you can create in a new alpha channel is a gradient that can help you define the depth of field. Additionally, you can add a layer mask to the duplicated layer and target the mask content for your Lens Blur effect. Something else you may want to do is duplicate your background to create a new layer and apply the Lens Blur to the top layer.

As with many new additions to Photoshop, the initial introduction of a feature can be a little klunky and lack some polish. We find that to be true with the Lens Blur filter. In some cases, you may find the filter doing the job of adding selective focus to be fine. This works when you need a single selection and a defined focal point where the blurred area can be managed using a limited amount of blur.

The problem with the filter is it can only provide you with this limited blur, even at the maximum setting. Furthermore, a single selection is all the filter will recognize. A gradient-type selection is only valid for limited image types, so don't try to use it for every image. You need to do some tests to see when this filter can help you.

We see the Lens Blur filter as a nifty new Photoshop feature that has a good start, and it can help you with some limited options for adding depth of field in a photo. To really take advantage of this filter, you may need to combine it with some other edits, as we show you in the steps a little later. We suspect that this filter will mature and offer more options in a later release of Photoshop, and hopefully, we'll see much speed improvement.

To experience using the Lens Blur filter, first become familiar with all the settings you have in the Lens Blur dialog box. When you choose Filter ⇨ Blur ⇨ Lens Blur, the Lens Blur dialog box opens. On the right side of the preview window are the settings adjustments shown in Figure 10-26. Before moving on to using the filter, look at the Lens Blur filter settings. Your options include:

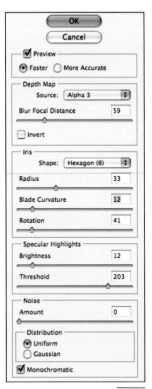

10-26

> **Preview.** This filter runs slow. If you have selected the Preview check box, you gain the benefit of seeing in real time the effects as they are applied. However, as you move each slider in the dialog box, the filter refreshes the image preview, and it can take some time to complete each setting you make in the dialog box. You can turn the Preview off, make all your adjustments, then turn it back on to preview the image. The filter runs much faster this way. Plan on toggling back and forth by selecting and deselecting the Preview check box as you work with the settings.

The radio buttons below the Preview check box offer you two options. Select Faster to see the screen refresh faster; select More Accurate to see a closer rendition of your effects when they get applied to the image but at much slower screen refresh.

> **Depth Map.** If there's any magic in the Lens Blur filter it has to be in the Depth Map section. The channel masks you create before opening the Lens Blur filter can be used as a Depth Map where the white accepts the lens blur, and black in a mask remains in focus. From the Source drop-down menu, all your alpha channels and layer masks are listed. You can select a mask, then move the cursor into the document and click where you want the focal point to be. However, you can select only one channel or mask for applying the blur in a single edit.

Custom Depth Maps can be created from a number of different kinds of masks. You can use gradients of all kinds, paint in noncontiguous areas in a channel mask or layer mask to create a blur within or outside the painted areas, create selections from image content and save the selections to an alpha channel, or use a layer mask. The options are endless. If you accidentally create an inverted mask and the depth of field is reversed

from what you expected, you can remain in the Lens Blur dialog box and click the Invert check box to inverse the mask. We take the image in Figure 10-27, create a radial gradient in a new alpha channel, and apply a Lens Blur. Using just the Lens Blur filter, you can see the effect in Figure 10-28.

> **Blur Focal Distance.** Click anywhere in the image and the Blur Focal Distance slider jumps to that area. You can change the blur distance by dragging the slider left or right or by clicking in the image.

> **Iris.** This option matches a camera's diaphragm, and the Shape drop-down menu provides you choices for the kind of diaphragm shape you want to use. Depending on the shape you use and the blade curvature, the highlights in the image change, either becoming more circular or more polygonal.

The Radius slider determines the amount of blur you want to apply. Move the slider back and forth to decrease or increase the blur amount.

> **Specular Highlights.** Specular highlights are the amount of light reflection you see on an object. The size and characteristics of the specular highlights change according to the distance to the light source and the amount of light generated from the light source. As the size of the light source changes and the distance to the object is repositioned, the specular light also changes. Larger and closer light sources change the specular light to a larger size and into a more spread-out, diffused light. Moving away from the object with less light narrows the source, and it appears smaller and brighter. This kind of control in analog photography is hard to manage. Traditional photographers need to carry a variety of light sources in order to control specular lighting. The Lens Blur filter is a snap compared to shooting film and organizing your light sources.

10-27

10-28

> **Noise.** Noise can be applied in the Lens Blur dialog box to compensate for the smoothed-out details that result when applying Lens Blur settings and to minimize any color changes.

However, you have more control over introducing noise by finishing up in the Lens Blur filter and then creating a new layer in the Layers palette. You can use blending modes, masks, and opacity settings for the noise you introduce in the finished Lens Blur image with much more control than using the Lens Blur dialog box.

To use the Lens Blur filter, we took the photo you see in Figure 10-29 where we wanted to change the focal point to target the EMT, creating a more selective focus effect and some motion blur to add drama to the photo. Using the Lens Blur filter is a good start, but we need to combine the use of the Lens Blur with other more traditional edits. Here's how:

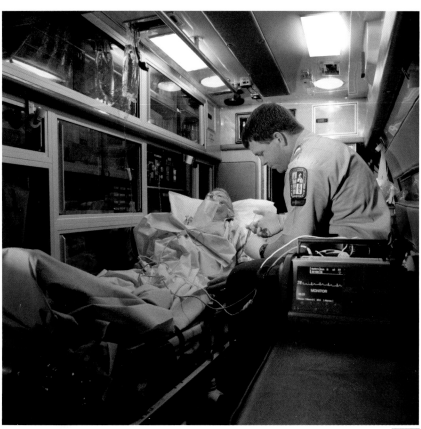

10-29

1. The first step is to create several selection masks. Start with a careful selection around the EMT guy. After creating the selection, save it to an alpha channel. We name our channel *EMT*.

Next, the far plane of focus near the back wall is created with the Rectangular Marquee tool. The EMT is subtracted from the selection. The selection is saved in an alpha channel as *far plane of focus*.

Next, a foreground selection is created. Create another selection using three overlapping marquee selections and save it as *close plane focus*. Again, the EMT selection is subtracted from the selection. Save the new selection as *close plane focus*. The three alpha channels created thus far appear in Figure 10-30. In the top-left quadrant, you see the RGB composite image. The top-right

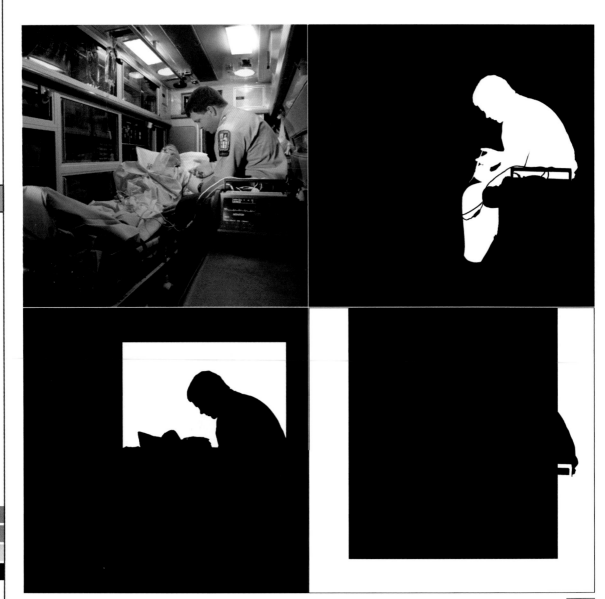

10-30

quadrant is the *EMT* channel, the lower-left quadrant is the *far plane focus*, and the lower-right quadrant is the *close plane focus*.

2. At this point, things get a little tricky. A medium plane focus is needed. To create another selection and save it as an alpha channel, load the *far plane of focus* channel, then add the *close plane of focus* channel. Invert the channel and save it as *medium plane of focus* shown in Figure 10-31.

3. For the final channel mask, load the *medium plane of focus* and paint it 50 percent gray. Then load the *EMT* selection and paint it black. This result is saved as the *blur target channel* selection, which is shown in Figure 10-32. As you can see, this channel blocks any blurring of the EMT, allows medium blur at medium distances, and the close and far depths (represented by the white in the channel) get a maximum blur.

4. Load the *blur target channel*, and create a new layer. The hope is that by blurring the layer, you can dupe it and add more blur, but it doesn't work here. Instead, we leave the layer in the stack and run the Lens Blur filter at default settings to create the blur shown in Figure 10-33.

5. After the filter does its best, move on to add more blur using the tried-and-true Gaussian Blur and Motion Blur filters. Use the lasso to create a rough selection in the lower portion of the image and feather it 200 pixels.

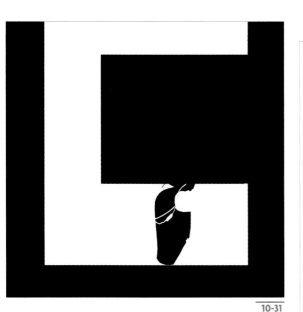

10-31

10-32

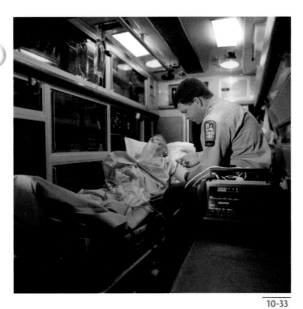

10-33

10-34

Create a new layer from the selection, then blur it heavily with the Gaussian Blur filter at a 50-pixel radius. Add a curves adjustment, and pull the white point to level 124. That adjustment darkens the foreground and adds depth to the image, as shown in Figure 10-34.

6. The final edit addresses the white lights in the ceiling of the van. We want them to glow to emphasize the drama in the photo. Use a Color Range selection on the background and target the white lights on the ceiling. In the Color Range dialog box. Sample the brightest point in the lights and move the Fuzziness slider to 75 to select the bright highlights. The selection is used to create another new layer. While the selection is active, click the Create a new layer icon in the Layers palette.

The new layer contains only the bright highlights. Use the Motion Blur filter (Filter ⇨ Blur ⇨ Motion Blur) and set the Angle to -16 and the Distance to

35 to add drama through applied motion to the lights. Change the blend mode for this layer to Screen to lighten the highlights. As the last edit, duplicate the layer again using the Screen blend mode to enhance the blurred glow. This layer just adds another application of the Screen blend mode to the image. The final layer stack appears in Figure 10-35.

10-35

The final result, shown in Figure 10-36, required the use of several complicated selections to target areas where we wanted to apply different blur filters to not only change the apparent depth of field, but to add a motion effect to the image. It's not as important to know the techniques we use to create the selection masks as it is to know what a tool like the Lens Blur filter alone can do for you. You may need to use that filter along with other filters and tools to create the precise degree of change to depth of field as you want.

10-36

With all the options I have for using Hue/Saturation and Curves, why would I want to use the Photo Filters?

If you go back in time to Photoshop 3, you would be able to perform just about all the corrections we've covered in this book using Layers, Levels, Hue/Saturation, and Curves. As Photoshop matured through time, the software engineers have added new features to help simplify color and tonal corrections for many users who have some confusion in regard to these kinds of corrections. Newer features such as Shadow/Highlight, Match Color, Exposure, Photo Filters, and Solid Color could all be performed using layers, and most often in the Curves and Hue/Saturation dialog boxes way back in Photoshop 3.

Many of these newer features are added to Photoshop to help you quickly and more easily make your edits to produce your final prints. Choose a method based on your familiarity with the tools you know. Just about any kind of edit you can make in Photoshop can be made using several different approaches. For the best methods, work with what you know produces the effects you desire. As new features are added to the program, it's always worth learning how to apply them in the event one particular feature helps reduce editing time and simplifies your editing workflow.

If you struggle with adding tints and making tonal corrections, the simplicity in using Photo Filters may help you. The more you know about Photoshop's capabilities, the more efficient you'll become in editing your photos. However, be mindful of when one tool is used and when another is used to create the kinds of color corrections you need to make in an image. It's just as important to know the limitations of a tool as it is to know what benefits you can derive from it.

When I use the Lens Blur filter, should I sharpen my image after applying the filter?

As a general rule, you'll want to sharpen images before you add any kind of blur effects. Unless you have a special circumstance where sharpening an intentionally blurred image is needed to produce some sort of defined edit, use the sharpening techniques we cover in Chapter 4 first. When using the Lens Blur filter, you'll want the focal point of your image to appear sharp while adding the depth-of-field blur from the Depth Map. If you try to sharpen after using the Lens Blur filter (or any other blur filter), you'll have a hard time masking the image to apply the sharpening in the area where the image needs to remain sharp.

When can I expect to see lens aberration?

If you use a good-quality lens on a DSLR camera, you'll find little to no lens aberration that needs to be corrected in Photoshop. If you use lenses at bargain-basement prices or you have a point-and-shoot camera, you may have problems where correcting lens aberration can help improve your image. If you use wide-angle lenses, run tests after taking photos with your new lens. Also, if you use a point-and-shoot with a variable zoom lens, take some photos at different zoom levels. Open the Lens Correction dialog box, and check your photos for lens aberration. You can keep a record of all lenses and focal lengths that need correction, and apply the corrections as needed.

To help you remember what lenses and focal lengths need correction, you can create an Action with a descriptive name according to lens and focal length and run the action when you open an image meeting the action criteria. You can record the settings for correcting the problem and have the action pause in the Lens Correction dialog box to observe the correction in case you need to refine it.

PRINTING

"All I can do in my writing is to stimulate a certain amount of thought, clarify some technical facts and date my work. But when I preach sharpness, brilliancy, scale, etc., I am just mouthing words, because no words can really describe those terms and qualities it takes the actual print to say, 'Here it is.'"
— Ansel Adams

Unless your photography is devoted completely to Web design, you'll eventually want to get all those images you spent so much time color correcting to a printed piece. With photography you have many printing options available to you. Your own desktop color printer is a likely candidate to output your creations as well as mini photo labs, commercial print shops, and service centers that offer large-format printing (see Figure 11-1). If per chance you want to create negatives or transparencies, you also have those options available.

To print your files to any source means you need to set up the file with the specific file attributes suited for your output device. This is particularly true when you submit files to vendors and when using online printing services. You need to be concerned about image resolution, file formats, the media source for how your files are submitted, and color profile use.

When you print to your own desktop color printer, you have control over all the print attributes. You lose this

control once you depend on a vendor to output your files. If you use a local imaging center that carefully looks over your file before outputting, you and your vendor can resolve potential printing problems before they happen. On the other hand, if you send your files to an online service or a discount outlet, you could waste a lot of money when files are printed as submitted and the files didn't meet the vendor's device specifications.

IMAGE AND CAMERA RESOLUTIONS

More than any other form of measure, *resolution* — when you talk about cameras, photos, and printers — is about the most confusing subject related to digital photography for many people. If you have some confusion regarding resolution, be aware of one basic fact: image resolution and printer resolution are *not* the same, nor do they need to equate to each other when printing image files (at least not in a one-to-one relationship).

In digital photography, you need to be concerned how the following devices handle resolution:

> **Digital cameras.** One of the major selling points of your digital camera is the resolution of the images it can capture. Camera manufacturers have added a little confusion to the subject of resolution. Camera resolutions are measured in total pixels of the images captured. A 6-megapixel camera, for example, captures images with roughly a total number of 6 million pixels. That number by itself doesn't tell you much when you want to print a file. Off the top of your head, it's hard to visualize the dimensions of your document and the file resolution needed to produce a quality print. The dimensions of the 6-megapixel camera translate to a horizontal resolution of 3072 pixels and a vertical resolution of 2048 pixels. Again, it doesn't tell you much unless your standard unit of measure is in pixels.

11-1

> **File resolution.** Granted, not a device, but file resolution is your second area of concern. Image files are measured in pixels and thus we often refer to a file as being *n* ppi (pixels per inch). The measure of most interest to you in regard to printing is what is the optimum ppi your printer needs to produce a quality print? That resolution might be 300 ppi or lower. The one fact that you need to remember is that in almost all cases related to almost all printing equipment, image resolution never needs to match device resolution. In other words, your Photoshop image doesn't need the same resolution as your printer is capable of producing.

X-REF

For an exception to this rule, see "Printing Black-and-white Photos" later in this chapter.

When it comes to file resolution, knowing the resolution alone is not sufficient information — especially when it comes to printing. If you tell me you have a 72-ppi image it could be a 42-x-36-inch image that could print a good quality photo print at 8 x 10 inches to 12 x 15 inches. If you tell me you have a 72-ppi image and the dimensions are 2 x 3 inches, you're lucky to get a quality print at ¾ x 1 inch. Therefore, be aware that image size, in terms of physical dimensions, is just as important as knowing the image resolution.

> **Device resolution.** Device resolution has long been a confusing subject for many photographers

and graphic artists. With a desktop color inkjet or a commercial inkjet printer, you can print at 1440, 2880, or as high as 5760 dpi (dots per inch).

Above all, realize that your file resolution does not need to match your device resolution; and in the case of inkjet printers, file resolution is several times less than the printer resolution.

Realizing you have three different resolutions to work with, the question then becomes, "What resolution should I use for my images to produce high-quality prints?" The one thing you can control is your file resolution. You have no control over your camera's capture in terms of resolution. You may have an adjustment on your printer to choose from two or more different resolutions. However, the real control you have is with your photos — but only to a certain extent.

When you first acquire a digital camera, one of the first steps to perform is to determine what size images you can reproduce on your printer. Here's how to do it in Photoshop:

1. Choose File ➪ New. In the New dialog box, select pixels from the Width or Height drop-down menus. Type the resolution of your camera for the Width and Height and set the resolution to 72 ppi as shown in Figure 11-2.

2. Click OK and a new document opens in Photoshop. Choose Image ➪ Image Size to open the Image Size dialog box. For either the Width or the Height, open the drop-down menu and select inches as shown in Figure 11-3. If your common unit if measure is centimeters make the selection for Centimeters.

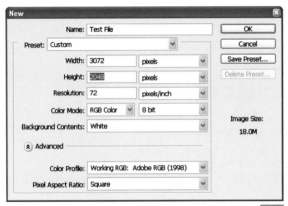

11-2

11-4

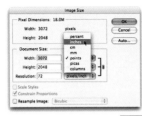

11-3

3. Type the *optimum resolution* for your printer into the Resolution field. The optimum resolution is the resolution for your file that is recommended by your printer manufacturer. For some help determining the optimum resolutions, see the next section "Printer resolutions."

Be certain the Resample Image checkbox is unchecked and read the values for the Height and Width (Figure 11-4). These values determine the maximum size you can expect to produce a quality print.

PRO TIP

Image resolutions can vary depending on the type of paper you use for your prints. High-quality coated stock photo papers require using resolutions higher than printing on matte and uncoated stocks. You may be able to drop the recommended resolution for your printer when using less than the coated stock photo papers.

4. If you want to determine area resolution — assuming you know the physical dimensions of your file and the resolution — simply multiply the width times the resolution and the height times the resolution. For example, if you have a file at 10 x 15 inches at 300 dpi, use the formula (10 x 300) and (15 x 300). The area resolution is 3000 pixels by 4500 pixels.

5. Another easy method for determining image sizes from your digital camera is observing the image thumbnails in Adobe Bridge. To be certain the image data appears in the Bridge window, open the Preferences dialog box by pressing Command/Ctrl+K. Click General in the left pane and then select Dimensions from the two drop-down menus as shown in Figure 11-5.

Click OK and the Bridge window reports the pixel dimensions below each thumbnail, as shown in Figure 11-6.

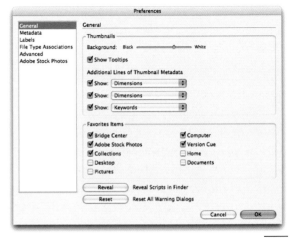

11-5

11-6

PRINTER RESOLUTIONS

All inkjet printers, laser printers, platemakers, and imagesetters print at a resolution. In most cases, the resolutions are variable and can be set by hardware or software. Some devices, such as dye sublimation printers, thermal printers, and film recorders, are continuous tone and don't print dots; however, these printers all have recommended resolutions for your image files to output quality images.

The popular Epson brand of printers from the low-end desktops to the commercial large-format printers have variable resolutions you can set when printing your photos in the advanced print settings. Epson printers come with resolutions ranging from 360, 720, 1440, 2880, and 5760 dpi. The most common printers in the Epson line take advantage of 360, 720, and 1440 dpi.

You can commonly find printers claiming two resolutions measuring the width and height of the prints. For example, many Epson brand printers claim 1440 horizontal resolution and 720 vertical resolution. Other models might have 2880 x 1440 or 5760 x 1440. Both of these values are important. We commonly define printers by commenting about the horizontal resolution. That value is important to know because it significantly relates to the size of the droplets plotted on the substrate. However, the vertical resolution determines the quality of your print. Theoretically a 2880 x 1440 print or higher would be ideal, but it's not necessary. A 1440 x 720 print gives you superb quality. Where you can benefit from higher vertical resolutions is in tonal transitions and gradients. For most people, however, you won't be able to tell the difference between a 1440 x 720 and a 2880 x 1440 print.

Print resolution is also related to print speed. If you print an image at 360 dpi, the printer spits out the finished piece in record time. Printing 1440 x 720 will significantly slow down the printing. A good trade off is printing at 720 x 360 where you can compromise a little quality for some speed. You may not want to print your final images at this resolution, but for tests, proof prints, and throwaways, this resolution setting works faster and prints with good quality. Furthermore, if you print on uncoated stocks or matte papers, you may often find very little difference between printing at 720 dpi vs. 1440 dpi.

As we said earlier in this chapter, image resolution and printer resolution are two entirely different animals. Your photos are made up of square pixels, the quantity of which determines your image resolution. In order to print a given pixel, the printer plots droplets or dots to form each pixel. Many droplets or dots can be plotted to form a single pixel. Therefore, as a general rule, you'll always find printer resolutions requiring much higher resolution values than your image files.

One important consideration to realize is that you can overburden your printer and actually produce inferior quality prints by attempting to print files with too high of a resolution. Higher-resolution image files take longer to print because more data is processed. Inkjet printers are not designed for printing higher-resolution graphics than the recommended sizes. Once you go above 400 ppi in your photos, the quality of your prints can severely decline and your print times will be much longer.

Speed is also a setting you can often make using the printer driver. If you have a faster setting, this option choice usually instructs the printer to print bidirectional. The paper feed is not affected, and you don't lose any quality or experience any undue problems if you opt for printing at faster speeds. It merely means ink is plotted when the print head moves in either direction.

PRINTING TO INKJET PRINTERS

Print settings vary according to manufacturers, and we can't hope to cover all printers in this chapter. We choose to discuss Epson printers because of their popularity and also because we both own several Epson printers. Many of the settings we address when discussing output to Epson printers should be similar to what you find with your printer driver. You may find some differences in nomenclature, but the settings should be quite similar once you find them in your printer driver's advanced settings dialog box.

PRO TIP

If you own a different brand of printer or use a service that uses other printers, what's important to know reviewing this section is the process involved in printing your files. Regardless of what type of printer you own, be aware of when a color profile is used and how color is either managed or not managed. You may have different checkbox selections and menu commands, but the process will be identical for any printer printing your photos.

Over the last few years, at least half of many service provider troubleshooting tech calls coming from clients have involved problems with accurate color output from Epson ink jet printers. We're not talking about subtle changes between monitor and printer, but huge monstrous color changes on output prints. As it turns out, almost all the strange output results originated from just one minor error when setting up a file to print — that being when and how to manage color.

We've come up with settings that will work well for you to get accurate results without stress or frustration. Just remember to use the settings exactly as described. When used with the proper settings, you can achieve superior results with either desktop or professional printers.

AUTOMATIC PROFILE SELECTION

When you install your printer driver, the installation utility also installs a number of color profiles. You can choose the profiles in the Print Preview dialog box and control all the printing using the profile provided by your printer manufacturer

You have a choice for how these profiles are used. You can choose to select the profile in the Print Preview dialog box, or you can choose an automatic method where the manufacturer created a no-non-sense process of automatic profile selection using your printer driver. The color profile is automatically selected when you choose the paper source.

The automatic method exists and we want to explain to you what goes on with it so you are aware, but we don't recommend you use it for your printing. Among other things, you really can't tell by looking in the Print Preview dialog box what profile you are using to print your file. In addition, you don't have a way to convert your working space color to the device profile for accurate soft proofing. But you should understand what goes on when the selection is made to be aware of some potential consequences.

The Color Engines in Photoshop, Colorsync, and the Epson Driver work in a similar manner, although they all show subtle differences when used to convert a file. For our first setup instructions, we use the Epson Color Engine and work with an unconverted file, letting the printer driver automatically select the color profile. Our unconverted file is a photo still in its native color space, such as sRGB or Adobe RGB (1998). Assuming your file is open in Photoshop and you've already sized your file for the target dimensions and resolution for output, here's how to print from the native color space, sRGB or Adobe RGB (1998):

1. First, choose File ⇨ Page Setup. From the Format for pull-down menu (Mac), select your printer (Figure 11-7). Make choices for the page size and orientation, and then click OK.

On Windows, choose File ⇨ Page Setup and click Printer in the Page Setup dialog box to open a second Page Setup dialog box. From the Name drop-down menu, select your printer as shown in Figure 11-8. Click OK in the second Page Setup dialog box to return to the first dialog box. Make your choices for page size and orientation, and then click OK.

NOTE

Notice that we first make a selection for the printer, and then make choices for the page size. Page sizes vary between printer drivers, and you need to make the choice for your driver first to see the supported page sizes for your printer. If you print to a custom page size, you need to select Manage Custom Sizes (Mac) or User Defined (Windows) from the Paper Size (Mac) or Size (Windows) drop-down menu to create a cus-tom page size.

2. Choose File ⇨ Print with Preview or press Command/Ctrl+Option/Alt+P. The Print Preview dia-log box opens as shown in Figure 11-9. The Print Preview dialog box you see in Figure 11-9 is very different than the Print dialog box you find when you choose File ⇨ Print or press Command/ Ctrl+P.

11-7

11-8

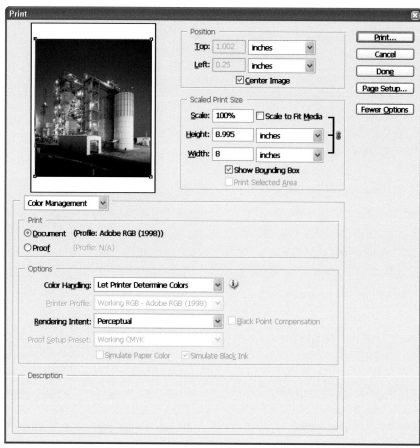

11-9

Always use the Print with Preview command because it provides you a preview of the file you are about to print as well as offering you a number of settings not found in the Print dialog box.

NOTE

When you choose File ⇨ Print with Preview, the Print dialog box appears. When you click Print in this dialog box, you arrive at another dialog box also titled Print. To avoid confusion, we refer to the first dialog box you open from the File ⇨ Print with Preview command as the *Print Preview* dialog box.

For printing files using the sRGB or Adobe RGB (1998) workspace while allowing the printer driver to automatically select the color profile, be certain to make the following adjustments in the Print Preview dialog box:

- **Document.** Select the Document radio button. Be certain to *not* select Proof. The working space color profile is shown adjacent to the radio button as you see in Figure 11-9.

- **Color Handling.** When using this method of printing, select Let Printer Determine Colors from the Color Handling drop-down menu.

The printer driver selects the color profile and gives you the best result for the paper selection you make. This method has fewer options to choose, making it a very simple solution for your printing.

- **Printer Profile.** This item is grayed out when you make a choice for having the printer determine the colors. Don't worry about selecting a printer profile here in these steps because the printer driver does so automatically when you select the media type.

- **Rendering Intent.** Open the drop-down menu and select Perceptual. Perceptual works well in this mode. You'll find shadow tones printing with a little more detail.

- **Position and Scaling.** Be certain to not check the box for Scale to Fit Media. If your image is larger than the paper size, exit the Print Preview dialog box and size the image for the target output in the Image Size dialog box. As a general rule, check the box for Center Image and your print is centered on the paper leaving you room for mounting if so desired.

3. After making settings choices in the Print Preview dialog box, click the Print button. A second Print dialog box opens as shown in Figure 11-10 for the Mac and Figure 11-11 for Windows.

4. Open the Presets drop-down menu and select Print Settings in Mac OS. On Windows, click Properties. After clicking Print Settings (Mac) or Properties (Windows), things get a little confusing because the different printer models will have different options. You won't see the same options identical in the low-end Epson printers as you have in the professional models. Some differences include the following:

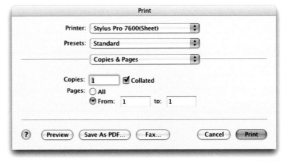

11-10

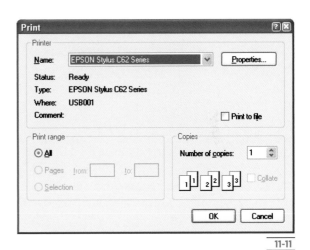

11-11

- **Professional and higher end desktop printers.** The Print Settings are shown in a separate Print dialog box as you see in Figure 11-12. The options you have here will work the same on the Mac as you find on Windows. The first option choice to make is to select the media from the Media Type drop-down menu.

From the Ink drop down menu select Color/B&W Photo. If you have a low-end model, your choices are either Color or Black. Choose Color if this choice is available.

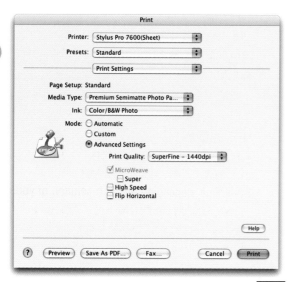

11-12

Click on Print Settings to open the drop down menu and select Color Management to open the Color Management dialog box (Figure 11-13). Check Color Controls in the Color management dialog box. This is very important and you need to be certain that this radio button is selected to ensure correct color conversion by the Epson print driver.

On Windows click the Advanced button. You may have a different menu choice to arrive at this dialog box for your printer model. If you poke around a little, you should find settings for Gamma and ink adjustments for the Mac (see Figure 11-14) or Windows (see Figure 11-15).

Click the Advanced Settings radio button and choose a Print Quality from the Print Quality drop down menu. For color prints on coated stocks choose the SuperFine – 1440 dpi setting. If you have higher resolutions on your printer using an equivalent to the SuperFine option, make that choice. On low-end models, your choice may only be Fine. Make this choice if you don't see a SuperFine choice.

By default MicroWeave should be selected for you. If you want to print faster, check the box for High Speed. Checking this option means your printer will print bidirectional and have no effect on your quality.

11-13

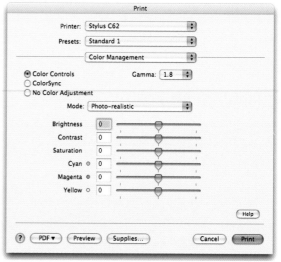

11-14

PRO TIP

DO NOT CLICK AUTOMATIC! If you click Automatic, you'll wind up double converting color and you're likely to see screaming magenta prints. This is one of the most common errors people make when printing on Epson printers.

EPSON Stylus C62 Series Properties

Main | Page Layout | Maintenance

Paper & Quality Options

Photo Quality Ink Jet Paper

Best Photo

Letter (8 1/2 x 11 in)

Orientation
- Portrait
- Landscape

Print Options
- Reverse Order
- Minimize Margins
- High Speed
- Black Ink Only
- Edge Smoothing
- Print Preview

Custom Settings | Save Setting

Online Support

Color Management
- Color Controls
- PhotoEnhance
- ICM

Gamma 2.2

Color Mode Standard

Reset Controls

Brightness +0
Contrast +0
Saturation +0
Cyan +0
Magenta +0
Yellow +0

Show this screen first

Basic

OK | Cancel | Help

11-15

The Gamma setting should match your monitor Gamma setting for correct print density. If your output print is too light or dark, make sure that the Gamma settings for monitor and output match. Leave the color sliders alone. If your monitor is properly calibrated, there's no need to make any adjustments for the ink saturation.

X-REF

See Chapter 2 for more detailed instructions for calibrating you monitor.

Select from the Mode (Mac) or Color Mode (Windows) drop-down menu and choose Photo Realistic. The Vivid setting should never be used. On lower-end printer models, you may only have a choice for Standard or Charts. Choose the Standard option if you have only these two choices.

- **Low-end desktop printers.** You follow the same steps for choosing the advanced Print setup dialog box (see Figure 11-11), but some of your settings choices will vary.

  Rather than having choices for Print Quality from a drop-down menu, you may have choices for the Quality type such as Draft, Text, Text and Image, Best Photo, and so on, or you may have a choice for Fine as opposed to SuperFine, depending on the resolution of your printer. Making choices here also makes your ink selection. Your color choice may be limited to only Color or Black. When printing color prints, you obviously need to select Color in the advanced print settings.

  All other adjustment settings are relatively the same as described for printing to high-end printers. If you do find an Automatic choice, be certain to *not* choose this setting.

5. Click Print. The printer gives a reasonably accurate output with these settings. With the higher end printer models, such as the Epson 7600, 9000, 9500, 10000, and so on, gray tracking is usually good to very good. Manufacturing tolerances are held very close on the high-end printers.

   With desktop printers, there is more variation. You might have a good low-end desktop printer, and the neutrals will match well. On the other hand, the factory worker who assembled your print heads might have been having a bad 14-hour day. If you see a consistent hue error in the neutrals, you can try tuning it out with the color sliders (shown in Figures 11-13 and 11-14), but a better way is to use a *viewing layer* described in the "Soft proofing files" section later in this chapter.

Using the Photoshop Color Engine

This method is the same as the steps used for the automatic profile selection, except you will decide what profile as well as one important difference related to your choice for color handling. We'll let the Photoshop Color Engine convert the colors on the fly and we use this method when we have a specific color profile we use to print to our paper. One important advantage of this method is the ability to view a reasonably accurate soft proof of the image on your monitor before printing. The reason we can do this is because we can select a specific profile for proofing our image. When using the automatic profile selection method, we can't select the profile because it's being selected by the printer driver.

The setup change for using the Photoshop Color Engine is in the Print Preview Window. All other settings are the same as described in the "Automatic profile selection" section. Follow these steps:

1. Choose File ➪ Print with Preview to open the Print Preview dialog box. In the Color Management Print area, click the Document radio button. In the Options area, select Let Photoshop Determine Colors from the Color Handling drop-down menu (see Figure 11-16).

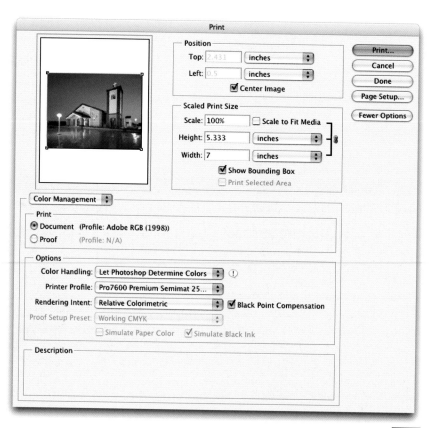

11-16

2. Now that you've selected Photoshop as your color handling engine, Photoshop needs to know what output profile you want to use for your print. Click on the Printer Profile drop-down menu and select your profile from the options. The profile, of course, must be matched to the output media you're printing on.

Setting Rendering Intent to Relative Colormetric is usually the best choice here, unless your image has very bright colors or many out of gamut colors in which case Perceptual will work better.

Be certain the Black Point Compensation checkbox is checked to reproduce rich blacks in your print.

PRO TIP

If in doubt about what Rendering Intent to use, check between the two rendering intents by selecting View ⇨ Proof Setup ⇨ Custom. To learn more about soft proofing, see "Soft proofing files" later in this chapter.

3. Click Print. Once again, your media setting must match the output profile you've selected. All other settings are the same as used with "Automatic profile selection" *except* for Color Management.

This time, use the No Color Adjustment setting as shown in Figure 11-12. There's a very important reason for this. Any setting besides No Color Adjustment results in the image colors being converted twice for printing. Photoshop converted the colors to the print profile in the Print Preview dialog box. When you click Color Controls or the ColorSync mode in the Color Management dialog box (see Figure 11-13), the printer driver thinks it's starting from scratch with the file and converts it again! Using the Color Controls setting will produce a light, screaming magenta print, and the ColorSync setting usually results in a screaming yellow print. If you get this kind of output result, try again and make sure all settings are correct.

Screaming Magenta Bias

Of Epson printer driver problems, the most common complaint is magenta prints and it's always the result of a single error during driver setup for printing. For reasons we don't fully understand about the Epson ink sets, either pigment or dye inks, a file converted for Epson output has a strong magenta bias. It seems that an equal mix of all the inks produces a green gray color. The magenta file bias when converted tunes out this green balance of an equal ink mix. That's why a double converted file always has a strong magenta bias.

To observe the magenta bias in a converted file, convert any small Photoshop file to an Epson output profile, like Photo Glossy Paper, for example using the Edit ⇨ Convert to Profile command. Next, select File ⇨ Save for Web. If you work with a large file and a warning dialog box opens informing you the image size exceeds the size the Save for Web command was designed for, just click Yes to ignore the warning. Since Save for Web isn't profile aware, the magenta shift comes through nicely in the Save for Web dialog box as shown in this figure.

continued

continued

PRINTING WITH A CUSTOM PROFILE

Printing with a custom profile is very simple. Just remember that you must use the profile with the exact same settings you used to print the test target when the profile was created. For custom profiles, you *always* use no color management throughout the output process.

Let us make this clearer. When you generate your test target for the profiling service where you may order a custom profile created for your printer, they require that you print the target without color conversions of any kind. The target has to reflect the actual colors generated by your printer from a known sample file with no modifications whatsoever for a known

11

Printing

printing condition and media type. The resulting profile tells the color engine exactly how to modify the output data to match the colors as closely as possible to your working space or a different previously embedded color profile.

For all this to work properly, the printer can't be allowed to modify the printing data in any way. All the work has to be done by Photoshop. So, assuming you have a custom profile ready to use, the setup is as follows:

1. Choose Edit ⇨ Convert to Profile. Select your custom profile from the Profile drop-down menu in the Convert to Profile dialog box.

Also in the Convert to Profile dialog box, set the Intent to Relative Colormetric (see Figure 11-17) and use the ACE (Adobe Color Engine) color engine. Make these choices unless you decided to use Perceptual intent when viewing your soft proof.

11-17

Click OK in the Convert to Profile dialog box, and your screen view changes on your monitor to create a soft proof of the file you are about to print.

2. Choose File ⇨ Print with Preview. The only other thing you have to adjust for this method involves the settings in the Print Preview window. Choose No Color Management from the Color Handling drop-down menu (see Figure 11-18).

We have our color profile reported in the Print section of the dialog box adjacent to the Document radio button. We converted the file to the printer's color space so we didn't want to use any other tool to manage our color. We just want the color used in the image to be printed without any color conversion. All the converted data is ready to go and the right choice here is No Color Management as you can see for the choice made in the Color Handing drop down menu in Figure 11-18.

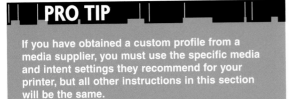

11-18

3. The remaining controls are the same as when using the options described in the section "Using the Photoshop Color Engine." Click Print and follow the same steps in the Settings and Color Management dialog boxes. Again, be certain to make your choice for No Color Management when you arrive at the Color Management dialog box.

Okay, so all this information has got to be confusing to you. To help clarify and simplify the rules described for the various types of profile usage, let us try to summarize what we've said so far:

> **Automatic profile selection.** This option is designed for novice users who want a simple means of printing without having to decide what profile to use. Use sRGB or Adobe RGB (1998), Let Printer Determine Colors, and choose Perceptual for the Rendering Intent. Click Color Controls in the Color Management dialog box.

> **Photoshop Color Engine.** You use this method when you want to make the profile selection yourself, but that profile is of a generic type created for printing to a particular kind of paper. You might have profiles you download from vendor sites that have created profiles for a line of papers like the Epson printers that print on Glossy Photo Stock, but you use other Glossy Photo Stock papers supplied by Kodak for example. You have an advantage for using this method and the next one listed below in that you can convert the color using the target profile and soft proof the image on screen. Let Photoshop Determine the Colors, and choose Relative Colorimetric for the Rendering Intent. Turn off all color management.

> **Custom Profiles.** Use this method when you create custom profiles for your printer and paper or

have custom profiles crated for you. If you receive color profiles from a paper supplier specific for your printer and the paper batch, also use this method. Use No Color Management throughout the print process.

If you carefully follow the directions for the three different printing methods we've described here, you'll have predictable, easy printing from your Epson Printer or other printer models having similar settings adjustments. Your ink and media savings alone will pay for this book in no time!

SOFT PROOFING FILES

One small step in your workflow that can help you save both time and materials is soft proofing your files on your computer screen. Assuming you have your monitor calibrated as we described in Chapter 2, your monitor should provide you an accurate view of what the colors will look like when using a color profile.

SOFT PROOFING IN PHOTOSHOP

Photoshop's built-in proofing options provide you with selecting different profiles and viewing the results on your monitor without converting color. You can easily shift between color profiles in a single dialog box while observing the results in real time.

To soft proof an image you choose View ⇨ Proof Setup ⇨ Custom. In the Customize Proof Condition dialog box you have options for:

> **Preserve RGB Numbers.** If your file is in RGB color mode, you have this checkbox for preserving the simulation for how the colors appear without being converted to the color space of the output profile. If you work with a CMYK image,

the menu description changes to Preserve CMYK Numbers and does essentially the same thing. You can use this checkbox to toggle on and off printing with a selected profile.

> **Device to Simulate.** From the drop-down menu, select the color profile you want to soft proof.

> **Rendering Intent.** Choose the Rendering Intent from choices in the drop down menu.

> **Black Point Compensation.** As a matter of default, use the Black Point Compensation option in all dialog boxes offering this choice to produce rich blacks in your output.

> **Simulate Paper Color.** This option simulates a much-less-than-brilliant-white appearance similar to many papers. Not all profiles support this option, so be careful if you assume that, when the check box is enabled, it provides you an accurate view of the way your file will be printed.

> **Simulate Black Ink.** If your printer prints very dark grays and not true blacks, checking this box simulates that appearance according to the profile you select in the Device to Simulate drop-down menu. Not all profiles support this option either. In using both the Simulate Paper Color and Simulate Black Ink options, run some tests to see if your profiles accurately support these options.

Here's how to soft-proof your print jobs in Photoshop:

1. We're going to use the Photoshop color conversion engine here and let the Photoshop generated soft proof give you a reasonably accurate display of previewing any color or tone variations to be expected from your output device.

Open a file you want to print in Photoshop. Choose View ➪ Proof Setup ➪ Custom to open the Customize Proof Condition dialog box (see Figure 11-19). From the Device to Simulate drop-down menu, select the color profile you intend to use.

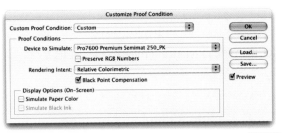

11-19

2. If you wish to compare the differences between your default view and a proofed view side by side, open a duplicate window by selecting Image ➪ Duplicate. Leave one image in standard view. Select the second image to make it active and choose View ➪ Proof Setup ➪ Custom to open the Customize Proof Condition dialog box.

NOTE

By default, your working CMYK space will be pre-loaded into the dialog box.

PRO TIP

When you create a duplicate view of an image window an annoying warning dialog box opens. To duplicate a window without having the annoying dialog box open, press Option/Alt and select Image ➪ Duplicate.

3. Be sure to check Black Point Compensation, and *do not* check Preserve RGB Numbers. You can click the Preview button on and off to see the changes to your file more clearly. You can also toggle between both rendering intents, Perceptual and Relative Colormetric, to see which you like best. Relative Colormetric is usually our first choice for best color accuracy.

4. Be certain the Preview checkbox is checked and you see the colors change on your image in the document window. Open the Device to Simulate drop down menu and select another profile. You can select any number of profiles and observe the color changes directly on your monitor. Click Cancel if you don't want the soft proof view to appear when you return to the document window.

We attempted to simulate a soft proof and present it here from screen captures. The CMYK profile we have to use for this book won't allow showing the dramatic screen difference because of the gamut limits of CMYK. We fudged the files a little in the CMYK soft proof mode to provide you with a realistic simulation for what we are seeing on our monitors.

The file on the left in Figure 11-20 is our standard monitor view simulated as close as we could get it here on this page. The file on the right is the soft proof view.

11-20

VIEWING COMPENSATION LAYERS

Suppose you've worked diligently to keep your system tight. You recalibrate your monitor regularly and run new printer profiles on a regular basis. You're working on a big deadline job and notice that your printer outputs have unexpectedly drifted off color. What you see on your monitor appears like the image on the left in Figure 11-21; yet when you print the file, it appears like the image on the right in Figure 11-21.

You reopen your monitor calibration check file and it appears normal. Something seems to be causing the printer to suddenly lose its careful calibration. Maybe the fresh ink cartridge you just installed isn't quite up to the color tolerances you usually expect and it's thrown off your calibration. Or perhaps the roll of new media is not quite right. Or maybe you haven't had time or money to purchase a good custom profile for the unfamiliar media your client is demanding you use for a particular job. It's 10 p.m. and the job is due in the morning.

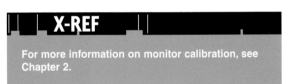

X-REF

For more information on monitor calibration, see Chapter 2.

Getting the output color right by trail and error can get expensive and you'll probably miss your deadline. If you are an amateur home user, all the fun goes out the door when your Christmas photos look far too green or red. There is an easy solution to the problem. It won't replace having a tight, well-calibrated system, but it will make your outputs far more predictable and save on time and wasted material.

Even if the profile is off, the main goal at this point is having a monitor view that matches what will come out of the printer so you know what it will really look like when printed. It's not a good idea to intentionally readjust your monitor color settings to match a bad profile. Everything else will be knocked out of kilter, and it's easy to forget to reset back to the proper settings again.

The best way to work around the problem is with a *viewing compensation layer.* The concept is simple and won't affect your careful monitor calibration for the rest of your workflow. Here's how it's done:

1. Reopen the file you've just printed, if it's not still on the screen. Duplicate the file by choosing Image ⇨ Duplicate. With the duplicate image window active, choose View ⇨ Proof Setup ⇨ Custom and select the profile you used to print

11-21

your file and click OK in the Customize Proof Condition Setup dialog box.

2. Now, place the *bad* output hardcopy close to your monitor in your viewing area so you can easily see it while working on your files.

With the duplicate file (the one you are viewing with your proof setup) active, open the Create a new fill or adjustment layer drop down menu and select Curves.

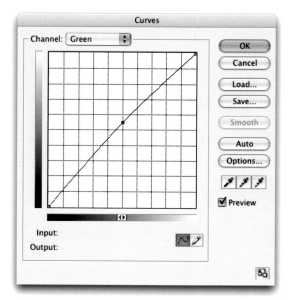

11-22

With the Curves layer open, make your best guess at the observed color shift on the output print, and correct it until the monitor view *matches the print you just made that has the color shift*.

You may think we're working backward here, but follow along.

Our example has a simple green bias and the move of the green curve shown in Figure 11-22 matched the screen view to the output print.

Great! Now both monitor view and print look lousy! The important thing is that the monitor matches the print.

3. Now, make a second curves adjustment layer following the same procedure as Step 2 and name it *Profile Correction* or any name that will allow you to remember what you used it for. Select the Background layer and the new layer appears between the Background and Viewing layer as shown in Figure 11-23.

11-23

With the second adjustment curve open, match the screen view back to the original file view, which is still open on the screen — again you're working on the duplicate file using the proof setup. If you find that overall density of the image view is too light or dark after the color correction, use the RGB composite curve adjustment to get it to match.

For our file, a simple downward pull of the green curve brought the monitor view back to a fairly good match to the original file on the left as shown in Figure 11-24.

11-24

4. If you follow these steps precisely, you'll notice right away that the correction curve was the exact opposite of the viewing curve.

Now that the profile correction curve is completed, we are ready to run another print and see how close we match our original file. Here's what to do. First, save the file, so you don't lose the viewing and correction layers. Next, turn off the viewing layer by clicking on the eyeball icon to the left of the layer. The file, in this case, will have a magenta cast. Don't worry, that's supposed to happen. And now, you flatten the image, and the viewing layer is discarded.

PRO TIP

It's a good idea to keep the file handy if you plan on printing other files with the same problem profile and media combination — we'll explain more about that a bit later.

5. On the flattened file, choose Edit ⇨ Convert to Profile and select the color profile you use for this output from the Profile drop down menu. Print the file using the same print attributes you used for the first print you made.

Here's what you've done so far. You adjusted your screen view to match your output. So far you flattened layers which discarded your Viewing layer, but you saved the file with the viewing layer so you can easily choose File ⇨ Revert to get back to it. With the image on screen corrected for your printer, you print again to get another print. All you actually did was to intentionally introduce an inverse color bias to the file to neutralize the original color shift out of the printer. The output was too green, so you fed the printer a file that was too magenta, in the same proportions. Hence what you saw on your monitor was not the view you wanted, but because the printer outputs with a color shift, you compensated for that shift to bring the color back to where you want it. The viewing layer allowed you to do all this without a lot of guess work.

You might find that the correction is a little too strong. That's not uncommon, because the monitor has so much dynamic range. It can fool the eye when making the viewing layer. If the file is overcorrected, just reduce the opacity on the correction layer. We usually find that a 75% setting works best, but experiment with different values until you achieve satisfactory results.

6. Run another test. If the resulting print comes close to the expected output color and density, you've found the correct curves adjustment and opacity setting. To make further printing faster and easier, you can now use your *correction* layer as a last step before converting to the problem profile. The nice thing about adjustment layers is the fact that you can simply drag the layer from one file to another. File resolution doesn't matter a bit as long as there is no layer mask used.

11-25

PRO TIP

If you are planning to use the correction layer repeatedly, duplicate your file containing the adjustment layer, and downsample it to a very small file of, say 500K. That way, the layer is always available and little precious RAM is consumed by keeping the file open. When you save the file, name it for the profile you're correcting.

In some cases, the correction needed can be far more difficult to figure out. Profile errors in many cases are nonlinear. That means that the color shift is not equal across the tonal range of the print. There might even be a color crossover, meaning that the highlights have a color shift different than the shadows. It can be very difficult to precisely determine the needed correction.

Let's view a different profile error outcome. Let's say you produce a print and it comes out looking like the image shown in Figure 11-25.

The print is way off color but it also has other strange anomalies. Notice that the dark tones in the parking lot have a red shift, and the cloud highlights are taking on a cyan cast. The lighter building elevation colors look greenish, which confirms a cyan bias in the light tones. This is the signature of a color crossover. Any old timers from the chemical processing days will recognize this kind of color problem. We are dealing with red shadows and cyan highlights.

This kind of problem can be very difficult to correct by guesswork, so we need a guide to help us. We'll make a test file that contains a gray scale. As we explain in Chapter 5, neutral colors are the easiest to judge for color shifts; and gray is the easiest of all, since it has no hue of it's own to confuse the issue.

Here's how you go about correcting for a color crossover:

1. First make a duplicate layer by dragging the Background to the Create a new layer icon in the Layers palette. You don't want to mess up the original file, so work on a new layer.

2. Next, place a grayscale across the bottom of the image by first selecting the Rectangular Marquee tool in the Tools palette or pressing M on your keyboard. Then, drag open a rectangle marquee across the bottom of the image as shown in Figure 11-26.

11-26

3. Press D on your keyboard to set the default fore-ground and background colors to black-and-white respectively. Press X on your keyboard to set the foreground white and the background black — do this to just simply create a gradient moving left to right. Select the Gradient tool in the Tools palette. In the Options bar click the Linear Gradient tool (first tool appearing on the left in the Options Bar). Be certain the Opacity slider is moved to the far right and reads 100%.

Create a gradient dragging left to right inside the selection making certain to start and stop the gra-dient at the left and right edges of the selection. At this point your duplicate layer should look like Figure 11-27.

4. With the gradient completed, turn it into a grayscale by choosing Image ⇨ Adjust ⇨ Posterize. When the Posterize dialog box opens, type in **21**. The gradient will change to 21 separate gray patches by order of density as shown in Figure 11-28.

11-27

5. Press Command/Ctrl+D to deselect the marquee rectangle and select File ⇨ Save As to open the Save As dialog box. Name the file something like *Test File* or something else you'll remember easily and click Save.

11-28

6. Set up and print the test file exactly as you did for your first file. Our test print file looked something like Figure 11-29.

The cyan/red crossover is very easy to see in the new test print with the gray scale. Just as we described in the previous steps, place the new test print next to your monitor and create a curves adjustment layer in the test file and name the layer *Viewing*. At this point you should have the Curves dialog box open.

11-29

Tuning out a crossover is a little different than fixing an overall cast. You need to create a nonlinear correction in the red curve for this file. Start with the viewing layer. Notice that the highlights are cyan. This means they need more red in them. The shadows have a red cast and we need to reduce the amount of red in the dark tones. The correction in the red channel will have an S shaped curve to make the correction.

The grayscale seems to be the most neutral near the center. (This can vary, depending on the particular profile error.) Select the Red channel with the Curve dialog box open, place an anchor point in the highlight area right on a vertical grid line. Move the anchor point downward until the highlight cyan tint seems to match your test print — just get this adjustment in a ballpark view for now. Our adjustment was made as shown in Figure 11-30.

7. Next, place an anchor point on the lower quarter tones of the red curve, and move it upward until the red tint matches your test print as close as possible. Go back and readjust the highlight anchor point if needed. You might find it necessary to move your anchor points a little closer or farther away from the mid point of the curve, but just play with it until you achieve the best visual match to your test print. Our final curve adjustment is shown in Figure 11-31. If you got it just right, your monitor view now looks just as awful as the print you just made.

8. Now it's time to create the correction curve layer. It's not as hard as making the viewing layer, because you use the viewing layer as a guide. You simply make an opposite curve adjustment. Create the Curves adjustment layer and name it *Correction* or other descriptive name of your choice.

Place anchor points on the same grid reference lines that were used in the Viewing layer you created earlier in the first series of steps in this section.

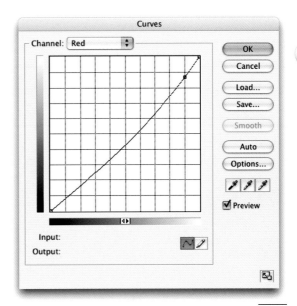

11-30

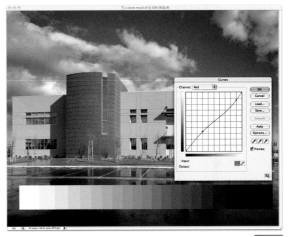

11-31

Once you have the anchor points plotted, use the arrow keys to move the anchor points in the opposite direction as was used in the viewing layer we created in Step 2 in the first series of steps in this section, until the gray scale looks as normal (neutral) as you can make it. Don't worry about turning back pages to see Step 2 in the last steps, just take a look at Figure 11-32 and see what we did with the Curves when adjusting our file. Notice we moved both Curve points only vertically.

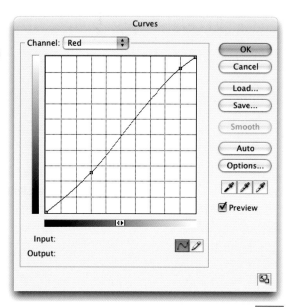

11-32

Convert the file to the profile used when you first printed the file and print using the same print attributes used when you obtained your first print. Once again, if the file is overcorrected, adjust the opacity on the correction layer. After all that work, be sure to save a low-resolution version of the correction file, with all adjustment layers intact, for later use if needed.

The image with our gray scale now looks like you see in Figure 11-33.

9. Turn off the viewing layer in the layers palette before you print the file in which case your monitor view won't represent the final color you'll get from your output device. Choose Image ⇨ Duplicate to create a duplicate file. Be certain the *Viewing* layer is turned off and flatten the image.

PRINTING BLACK-AND-WHITE PHOTOS

If you print black-and-white photos to your inkjet printer, the first line of reasoning needs to be along the lines of how much printing you do and what kinds of resources you want to dedicate to your black-and-white output. If you print an occasional black-and-white photo, you won't want to invest time and resources to set up a dedicated workflow for black-and-white reproductions. However, if your work is primarily black-and-white photography, you'll want to invest in equipment and software dedicated to reproducing black-and-white photo prints.

Let's take the first scenario where you print an occasional print to your desktop inkjet printer. The first question that comes to mind is, "Do I convert to grayscale and print from grayscale mode or do I print RGB files?" To answer this question, take a look at

11-33

what the masters of black-and-white photography did when working in the analog world. Ansel Adams, for example, redeveloped his prints with a toner to obtain the rich tones in his prints. He used a sepia toner to create a warmer look and he used a selenium toner to create a cooler look in his prints.

Your desktop printer responds in the same manner as using toners in the lab. As a general rule of thumb, you'll find printing RGB files will produce better black-and-white prints especially for those desktop inkjets supporting seven, eight, or even nine inks. When you have a printer with seven or more heads, you'll find neutral gray ink that will help you out when printing those smooth tonal gradations. Printers vary and your best bet is to run tests to see what works best for you. Start with printing grayscale images in RGB color and see if the prints are coming out to your satisfaction.

To add more richness to your prints and better tonal gradations, you can add a toner effect much like Ansel Adams did. As a matter of fact, Mr. Adams just might be impressed with the ease of using a Photo Filter in Photoshop.

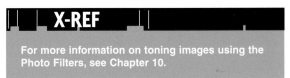

For more information on toning images using the Photo Filters, see Chapter 10.

DEDICATED BLACK-AND-WHITE PRINTING

If you're a serious black-and-white photographer and you create art prints, you'll want to do much more than print an RGB image to your desktop color printer, especially if your printer is not well designed for black-and-white printing. You'll find the best results come from either dedicating a printer to black-and-white photography or acquiring a printer that is designed for both black-and-white and color printing and acquiring special software tools for profiling and printing.

On the hardware end, be certain to investigate what printers support inks that are either designed for black-and-white printing or color inks that work well with black-and-white prints. The Epson 2200 and 2400 models are great desktop printers that support using the Ultrachrome color inks that produce impressive black-and-white photos. These printers support printing sizes 13 inches wide that can accept cut sheets of 13 x 19 inches or roll fed paper for longer than 19 inches. The 2400 model is an eight-jet system using three black inks — the inks are all pigmented inks. Epson also has a number of profiles for glossy, matte, and fine art papers for black-and-white printing.

If you deviate from ink sets supplied by your printer manufacturer and use third party inks designed specifically for black-and-white printing, you can void your printer's warranty. If you find third party inks work better for you, you should consider setting up a dedicated printer for black-and-white photography. Fortunately, the 2200 and 2400 model Epson printers are priced between $500 and $900 U.S. making your equipment investment affordable — especially if you are selling your prints.

On the software end, you have at least one excellent developer that provides software tools for black-and-white photography. The QuadTone RIP (Raster Image Processor) is a shareware product selling for $50 as of this writing. For a low-cost investment, you receive the RIP that requires TIFF-formatted files, custom profiles, and tools for adjusting tones in your images. The product is a single download available at www.quadtonerip.com.

If you use a service provider for oversized prints, you'll want to search out those providers that have dedicated machines for printing black-and-white photos. Many oversized inkjets may not match the quality of the newer line of desktop models without using a product like QuadTone. If a provider purchases special ink sets for black-and-white photos, they won't want to change inks back and forth and will need to dedicate one machine for black-and-white only. Try to turn your vendor on to QuadTone if you do a lot of business with them and they'll thank you for helping them produce quality black-and-white prints with little effort.

PRINTING 1-BIT LINE ART

A bitmap file in Photoshop terms is a 1-bit file having one of two values — black and white. The term bitmap here is very different than the bitmap file format that can save 24-bit color images as .bmp. You might have occasion to shoot some copy work of art that has no gray tones. Logos, emblems, insignias, and so on, might be examples of 1-bit files containing no gray tones. In Photoshop terms we usually refer to these files as bitmaps or line art.

When it comes to printing these files you have some resolution and printing requirements that deviate from the general guidelines we've covered for printing files. This is particularly true for printing files for press on imagesetters and platesetters.

The guideline you should use for these kinds of files is *image resolution = device resolution*. Therefore if you intend to print to an imagesetter having resolutions of 1200, 2400, and 3600 dpi, you should print your files (or have them printed by a service provider) at the device resolution. Above 1200 dpi is really overkill and you don't need to worry about matching the 2400 and 3600 dpi resolutions. But you should theoretically have a 1200 dpi 1-bit image to print 1200 dpi on an imagesetter or platesetter. If you were to print the same file on a 600 dpi laser printer, your file should also be 600 dpi.

If you print 1-bit images to inkjet printers the best solution for you is to convert your files to grayscale and create a little anti-aliasing on the artwork and type by using a blur or drop shadow. Without a little anti-aliasing, the bitmap graphic is likely to appear with jagged edges. If you composite images having line art, you need to size the line art graphic to the resolution of your color or grayscale image. For example,

adding a logo for a poster. Never size your print file to the resolution of the bitmap graphic.

PRINTING FOR PRESS

When you prepare files for press you have an entirely different scenario then when printing to continuous tone devices such as inkjet printers. Whereas an inkjet printer produces a continuous tone print, offset press produces prints with dots. The relationship between your image file and the number of dots printed by an imagesetter or platemaker is something you need to consider when handing off files to graphic artists or print shops. In addition, there are some other factors you need to be aware of when preparing photos that will eventually be printed on offset press that include:

> **Halftone.** A halftone screen or the term *frequency* or *halftone frequency* is used to describe the lines per inch that are printed. Halftone frequencies are measured in lpi (lines per inch). As an example, older newspapers were commonly printed at 85 lpi (today many newspapers are printed at 100 lpi). The dots are larger than dots used for magazines and books that use 133 to 150 lpi. Because of the absorption of ink being so much greater on newsprint stock, the dots need to be larger to avoid *plugging* that creates a mass of black ink. The dots from these printed pieces can be seen with the naked eye. Halftone screens of 133 and higher have much smaller dot sizes that are generally not seen with the naked eye and appear to be continuous tone.

The reason halftone frequency is important to you when preparing files for press is that there exists a relationship between image resolution and halftone frequency. As a general rule you can inquire from a print shop or graphic artist what halftone frequency will be used to print your photos. When you have this number multiply it times two. Therefore, if preparing a photo for a newspaper printing at 85 lpi your image resolution needs to be 170 ppi (85 x 2). If preparing a photo for a quality magazine that may be printed at 175 lpi your image resolution should be 350 ppi.

Unfortunately, the math is a general guideline and not always precise. You can't go wrong by multiplying frequency times two, but that much resolution is not always needed. You can safely save files with image resolutions of 225 ppi for 150 line screens and find no discernable differences in the printed pieces. All depends on the image content and the kind of gradations you see in your files. As a safe guideline use frequency times two and you can't go wrong.

> **Color mode.** Offset press prints are printed in process color (CMYK). You may or may not be asked to convert your RGB images to CMYK color. If your print vendor or graphic artist client asks you to provide files in CMYK, you need to perform the conversion in Photoshop as the very last edit you make. You should inquire about color profiles and request a profile if the print shop has a custom profile they use with their equipment. If you aren't given guidelines for profiling use the US Web Coated (SWOP) v2 color profile that comes installed with Photoshop. The SWOP in the profile name stands for Standard Web Offset Printing.

Many graphic artists use layout programs such as Adobe InDesign where they layout a document using RGB images — even layered native Photoshop images in RGB mode. When the file is printed, layers and transparency are flattened and the images are converted to CMYK at print time. If you are requested to convert to CMYK you can convert your working space to the color profile used for offset press by choosing Edit ⇨ Convert to Profile. In the Convert to Profile dialog box select the color profile used by the print shop as shown in Figure 11-34.

> **File format.** Save your photos as TIFF format. Select File ⇨ Save As and choose TIFF for the format. Click Save and the TIFF Options dialog box opens as shown in Figure 11-35. When this dialog box opens, be certain to click None for Image Compression. Do not save any of your photos using any kind of compression scheme when preparing files for press. In many cases your compressed files will print black only and nothing will appear on the Cyan, Magenta, and Yellow plates if you save files with compression.

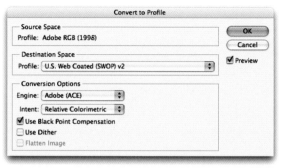

11-34

11-35

USING OUTPUT OPTIONS

Photoshop has a number of output options you can use for assigning other attributes for printing your images to both inkjet printers and when printing files for offset press. You can make choices for printing color bars, crop marks, emulsion, assign custom halftone frequencies, and more.

1. Choose File ⇨ Print with Preview to open the Photoshop Print dialog box. In the Print dialog box open the drop down menu under the image preview and select Output as shown in Figure 11-36. When you choose Output and the More Options are in view, you see a number of different attribute settings that can be assigned for your output.

2. Check the items you want to appear in your print. In Figure 11-37 you can see the results of checking all the check boxes except Interpolation, Emulsion Down, and Negative. If you print files to your desktop color printer for iron transfer materials or print to large format printers that use mylar, LexJet or translucent material (similar to Duratrans), you'll want to use the Emulsion Down setting. For all composite color prints leave these items off.

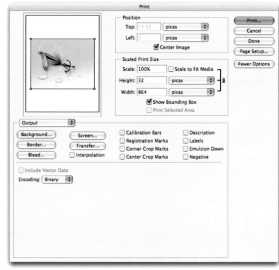

11-36

Fishing Lure CO05.tif

11-37

As you can see in Figure 11-36 the crop marks, registration marks, a border outline, calibration bars, and a description appear in the print.

3. If you rely on technicians to print your files at service centers, the technicians will take care of all the printing controls and you needn't worry about any of the settings in the Output Options when printing files on offset press. However, if you send your files to a service center for output on large format inkjet printers you may want to control one setting appearing in the Output Options.

If your file needs to be trimmed after printing and you have no clear defined border on the image, the technicians would ideally print your file crop marks using the Output Options. Unfortunately, busy shops can forget to print your file using this setting because most of their Photoshop files are not printed with crop marks. Having crop marks or a border insures you that the service center personnel know exactly where to cut your print. Rather than rely on the vendor to add crop marks or a border, you can submit your file with a border. This is especially helpful when you have white areas at any of the corners of your print where it may not be clear to the finishing personnel as to where your print needs to be trimmed. Such an example is shown in Figure 11-39 after a border was added.

To add a border, don't use the Output Options because these settings are used at the time of printing your file. A much easier method is to add the border in Photoshop. Press D on your keyboard to return to default colors. Press X to switch the colors to white foreground and black background.

Select Image ➪ Canvas Size to open the Canvas Size dialog box shown in Figure 11-38. Open either the Width or Height drop down menu and select Points. Add 2 to 3 points to both the Width and the Height text boxes.

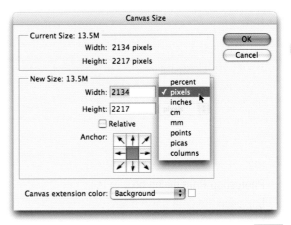

11-38

In Figure 11-38, the canvas size was 2134 and 2217 points. We changed the Width and Height to 2137 and 2220 adding 3 points to both the Width and Height. After we clicked OK in the Canvas Size dialog box, the image appeared with a black border (see Figure 11-39). This file can be sent to a vendor instructing them to trim the final print and cut off the border.

11-39

Paper and Inks

One great concern photographers have had when printing to inkjet printers has been with the archival quality of prints. In the early days of the inkjet printers you were lucky to get a life span of 6 months before your prints started to fade — a condition not acceptable by any photographer. As research and development progressed with inkjet manufacturers the inks have greatly improved.

Many inkjet printers support two kinds of inks:

> **Dye based inks.** Dye inks were the first to appear for inkjet printers. The original inks had very poor archival qualities but they printed more brilliant colors than the pigmented inks. Today dye based inks have much better archival qualities, and they still print more brilliant colors than the pigmented inks but the gap is rapidly narrowing.

> **Pigmented inks.** Pigmented inks have much longer archival longevity than the dye based inks. When they were first introduced the heads on inkjet printers tended to clog and the colors were not close to what the dye inks could offer you in terms of saturation and brilliance. Newer pigmented inks flow easily through the heads on inkjet printers and the color saturation has been greatly improved. They remain as the ink with the best archival quality where manufacturers claim more than 100 years of life.

With the proliferation of so many different inkjet printers for consumers and pros, the printer manufacturers and paper suppliers developed an incredible array of different substrates. Most common are the photo quality papers that appear similar to photo papers used by photo finishing labs. In addition to a variety of different coated stock photo quality papers having different paper weights, you can find specialized material such as mylar, canvas, watercolor, LexJet, adhesive, matte, translucent, etc. The list is long and you have an abundant number of choices.

Ideally you should have a color profile for each paper you use. Papers have, among other things, different absorption responses that affect the color saturation. Be certain to make the proper paper selection recommended by the paper and/or printer manufacturer when you print to any paper and be prepared to run many tests.

Using Service Providers

For printing to your own printer, you make choices for your inks, papers, and you control the color profiles used when printing. If you use a vendor, you rely on your vendor to inform you of what's needed on your end to print your files and what they have available to output your photos in terms of the materials used. When using vendors you have several different choices. You can take your files on a media source to a local photo-finishing center; or if they have available an FTP site, you can FTP or e-mail files to your vendor. You can use low-cost vendors such as FedEx Kinko's centers where you can use self-serve machines or large discount warehouses such as Costco to take your files or upload to their servers. Another option for you is using Kodak EasyShare Services provided directly from within Adobe Bridge where you can submit images and have prints and bound picture albums mailed to you.

Using photo finishing labs

Local photo finishing labs generally charge more money for outputting your files. Online photo finishing services are generally less expensive. The advantage you have with the professional labs is that they typically have qualified color specialists operating their photo printing equipment. If you use a local lab, you can generally bring your files in on just about any type of storage device.

Photo finishing labs use machines like Fuji Frontier, Agfa, Noritsu, and a number of other similar machines that output your images using a photochemical process similar to analog print making rather than inkjet printing. Many labs rely on their commercial equipment suppliers for color profiles that can be found on vendor Web sites that you can download.

If you have a relationship with a lab and any influence with the owner, you should investigate the kind of profiles they use. If they rely on profiles from the manufacturers, you might have them inquire about creating custom profiles — especially if you find color shifts between your images and their prints. If you do enough work with the lab, they should look into some low cost solutions for getting their output right. Sophisticated labs have color calibration equipment and may have a wealth of information to help you obtain the best results. It's always a good idea to spend a little time with the technicians and pick their brains for some valuable information.

If your lab tells you to use either sRGB or Adobe RGB (1998) they no doubt got that recommendation from their commercial vendor. You might do a little inquiry and ask if they have looked at custom profiling. Of course everything depends on what works. If you find your images are coming out exactly as you see them on your monitor (the wish of every digital imaging editor), then you needn't make a fuss.

USING SELF-SERVE AND DISCOUNT CENTERS

Self-serve and megastore outlets offer you the best prices and the poor custom photo finishing labs can't really compete with the prices of their finished prints. One reason these stores can offer such low prices is that they don't spend as much money on labor. You're not likely to find high-end qualified color technicians at these stores.

Color profiles for many large outlet vendors are found on the company's Web sites. You can be certain that the color profiles hosted on their Web sites are most likely provided by the commercial equipment vendors.

The individual stores in a chain are not so likely to have custom profiles created for their machines. And, with digital imaging, it's always so easy to blame you for the color shifts. We all too often assume anyone behind a counter working a machine knows more about the color handling of the equipment than we do.

If you use a discount store and walk in, be certain you save your files to the right media and save in the format acceptable to the service outlet. The self-serve machines and service outlets generally take your camera's media cards or CD-ROM and they may not have support for Zip, USB, or FireWire devices. Additionally, most vendors require JPEG images. This means you need to copy all your photos to your hard drive, edit them in Photoshop and save as JPEG (use the best quality settings with the lowest compression). Then you need to copy the final JPEG images back to a media card and walk them in to your service provider.

For color profiling, try to use the profile recommended by your vendor. Here's how:

1. When you prepare a file for a vendor using their profile, choose Edit ⇨ Convert to Profile to open the Convert to Profile dialog box shown in Figure 11-40.

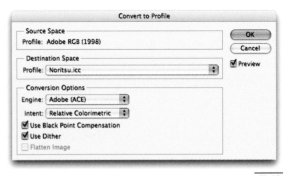

11-40

X-REF

For information on installing printer profiles, see Chapter 1.

11-42

2. From the Profile drop-down menu, select the profile you downloaded from your vendor and installed on your computer.

3. Click OK and Photoshop converts your working color space to the printer's color space.

4. Choose File ➪ Save As to open the Save As dialog box shown in Figure 11-41. Be certain the checkmark is enabled for embedding the profile and the profile matches the machine that ultimately will print your file.

5. Select JPEG for the format and click Save. Photoshop opens a second dialog box where you can assign the attributes of your JPEG file compression that opens after you click Save in the Save As dialog box. Move the Quality slider to the far right side (12) as shown in Figure 11-42.

6. Click OK and your profile is embedded in the JPEG file and ready to send to your vendor.

USING ONLINE SERVICES

Online services are available from Kodak EasyShare as an Adobe Photoshop Service you activate from within the Bridge window. This service enables you to upload images to the service where they are printed and mailed back to you. It's convenient and you don't have to leave your office or home to receive your photo prints.

The Kodak EasyShare Service is convenient for people who don't have the time to visit photo labs and when you happen to be on location traveling. You can order prints from anywhere in the world and have your prints waiting for you when you return home.

1. To use Kodak EasyShare, open Adobe Bridge and view the photos from within the folder containing them. Before you begin using the service you need to properly prepare your files. Kodak EasyShare requires JPEG files for the file format and the recommended color profile is sRGB. If your files use another profile, the first pane in the Adobe Services wizard informs you that the files use an unrecognized color profile which may not print properly. Notice the warning in Figure 11-43 just below the text "Provided by Kodak EasyShare Gallery."

To open the Kodak EasyShare wizard, select the files you want to print in the Bridge window and choose Tools ➪ Photoshop Services ➪ Photo Prints. The first pane in the wizard opens where you make a choice for creating a new account or using an existing account (see Figure 11-43).

11-41

11-43

Select Prints to Order					Order Summary		
Order single or double prints of all the photos.	4 x 6"	☑ Singles	☐ Doubles		Show Current Promotion >>		
	5 x 7"	☐ Singles	☐ Doubles		Qty	Item	Price
					2 -	4 x 6" prints	$0.30
✓	4 x 6"	$0.15	1	$0.15	1 -	8 x 10" prints	$3.99
✓	5 x 7"	$0.99	0	$0.00	1 -	16 x 20" prints	$17.99
✓	Wallets (4)	$1.79	0	$0.00			
✓	8 x 10"	$3.99	1	$3.99	Sub Total		$22.28
✓	16 x 20"	$17.99	0	$0.00			
✓	20 x 30"	$22.99	0	$0.00	Privacy policy >>		
✓	4 x 6"	$0.15	1	$0.15	Terms of use >>		
✓	5 x 7"	$0.99	0	$0.00			
✓	Wallets (4)	$1.79	0	$0.00			
✓	8 x 10"	$3.99	0	$0.00			
✓	16 x 20"	$17.99	1	$17.99			
✓	20 x 30"	$22.99	0	$0.00			

11-45

Send prints to the following people (Use the checkboxes to indicate selections)		Order Summary		
Address Book		Show Current Promotion >>		
		Qty	Item	Price
People Add New Address >>		4 -	4 x 6" prints	$0.60
☑ Ted Padova 555 Sky Road , Ventura, CA, 90000 (default address)	Edit>>	2 -	8 x 10" prints	$7.98
☐ Barbara Obermeier 555 Elm Street , Anytown, CA	Edit>>	2 -	16 x 20" prints	$35.98
☑ Don Mason 555 California Avenue , Bakersfield, CA	Edit>>			
		Sub Total		$44.56

Why are some of my addresses grayed out?

11-46

2. If you have an existing account, click the Sign In link in the top right corner of the first pane and a log-in pane opens as shown in Figure 11-44. Supply your log-on ID and password to log in. If you haven't created an account, fill in the fields on the opening pane to create a new account.

3. Regardless of where you are with the log in, click the Next button after filling in the log in information or if you created a new account. You arrive at the first step in your order process as shown in Figure 11-45. In the Step 1 Customize pane in the wizard, you specify the print sizes and the number of prints you want. Fill in the blanks and click Next to move to Step 2 in the order process.

4. Step 2 provides you with options for ordering prints to be distributed to a list of recipients. You can add to a list of recipients in the Step 2 pane by clicking on the Add New Address link shown in Figure 11-46. If you want to order the prints for yourself, your address is derived from your log on information.

If you want to ship prints to other parties, click Add New Address and the Add Address pane opens as shown in Figure 11-47. Complete the information in the Add Address pane and click Next. You are returned to the Step 2 pane where you can check the check boxes in your list of recipients if you want prints to be sent to multiple parties.

Log In		Not a member? Join Now
Email Address *	ted@west.net	
Password *	••••••••••	
	☑ Remember my password	
	Forgot your password?	
* Indicates a required field		

11-44

Please enter a phone number.	
Add New Address	
First Name *	Don
Last Name *	Mason
Address 1 *	555 California Avenue
Address 2	
City *	Bakersfield
State/Province *	CA
Zip/Postal Code *	999999
Country *	United States
Phone 1 *	661-555-5555
Email	DMason5849@aol.com
* Indicates a required field	

11-47

5. After identifying recipients, click Next and you arrive at Step 3 — the Summary pane. Your order appears summarized along with the shipping and handling costs as shown in Figure 11-48. Review the summary and click Next to proceed with your order. The next pane asks for billing information and the fifth pane opens where your files are automatically uploaded. Upon completion of the upload a confirmation is reported back to you that the files have been received and the order is in progress.

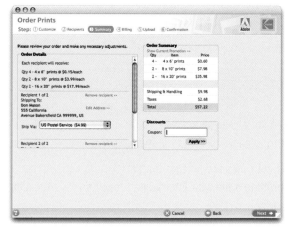

11-48

Q&A

When I print a photo from Photoshop, I have an option for scaling the image to fit my paper. What's wrong with using this print option?

If your file is larger than the media size, you are overburdening your printer with unnecessary memory and it will take longer to print your file regardless of what printing device is used. When you print to desktop color printers you can actually output files of much inferior quality compared to properly sized images if the sizing to fit the paper exceeds the maximum recommended printer resolution.

If your files are smaller than a 1:1 ratio and you size the image up in the Print Preview dialog box, you will be printing a file with interpolated resolution. The quality of your print can be much degraded if you upsize the file too much.

For best results be certain your original Photoshop image is edited and saved at the actual output dimensions.

If my camera can't take a picture for the size print I want, what can I do about getting a larger size print?

If you need to upsize your file you can try to use a third party product like Genuine Fractals as we mentioned in Chapter 1. Photoshop CS2 has much improved algorithms for upsizing images than earlier versions and you may find some images providing satisfactory results for display prints. If you do upsize a print and submit your file to a service provider, be certain to ask for a small test print and look at the results carefully before ordering a large oversized print.

For trade show booths and large displays, you might look into the types of oversized inkjet printers your service provider uses. Some inkjet printers such as Colorspan DisplayMakers require much less resolution than Epson and other inkjet printers. Whereas Epson printers require images to be 300 ppi as a general rule of thumb, the DisplayMaker printers are optimized at 150 dpi and you can often get good results with 100 dpi files. The lower resolution requirements mean you can size your images larger without interpolation.

I've followed all the steps recommended for printing my files but they still come off my printer with very bad color.

Assuming you have nothing going on with your software and method of printing you can have problems at the hardware end of your workflow. All inkjet printers require some maintenance most of which can be performed by utilities installed with your printer driver. Use the software maintenance utility that came with your printer and check for cleaning and test print options. Run a cleaning for your printer and print a test print that shows you how all the jets are firing. If your printer isn't firing all jets, you'll definitely see some color problems on your prints.

As a preventative maintenance operation, be certain to print a file off your printer every few weeks when the printer is idle in your office or lab. If you have long periods on nonuse the heads on the inkjets can dry up preventing a smooth continual flow of ink. When you look for purchasing printers, check the manufacturer reports on the life of the inkjet heads and recommendations for the frequency for making prints as a preventative maintenance operation. Some printers can tolerate very long times between prints without heads clogging while others can survive only very short times between prints without heads clogging.

What happens if I buy a new paper and I don't have a printer profile for that paper? How should I print my files?

The first thing to do is search the printer manufacturer's Web site and see if profiles exist for your printer and the paper you use. If you purchase a paper from a paper supplier, search the supplier's Web site for profiles available for download. Paper suppliers such as Ilford, for example, host profiles for their papers and many popular inkjet printers. If a profile doesn't exist from either the printer manufacturer or the paper supplier, try a third party profile developer such as Dry Creek Photo (`www.drycreekphoto.com`).

A good standard of practice is to first search printer and paper suppliers for the papers and profiles they support. You may find profiles created for your printer by a paper supplier and wish to make your purchases through the supplier rather than your printer manufacturer. In other cases you may find your printer manufacturer has created profiles for your printer and their new lines of papers. The bottom line is you should see if profiles exist before making your paper purchases.

If you purchased a paper before searching for profiles and you can't find a profile for your printer and the paper in question, try using the method we described for printing with either the sRGB or Adobe RGB (1998) workspace and let the printer determine the colors. If your prints are not satisfactory and you know the files have been edited properly, your last effort should be to have a custom profile created for the paper you use. We recommend Dry Creek Photo, but you can search the Internet and find other sources for creating custom profiles. If the color shifts are reasonably linear (even all over), you can use the viewing compensation layer method described in this chapter as a work around until you can get a quality profile for your media.

My desktop color printer uses CMYK inks. Shouldn't I convert my file to CMYK before printing?

Virtually all inkjet printers use CMYK inks and many printers use additional variations of CMYK inks such as light magenta, light cyan, and so on. Most of the inkjet printers prefer RGB files to CMYK especially those printers having more than four ink cartridges for the primary CMYK inks. If your printer likes CMYK files, it should be so stated in the user manual for your printer. If you aren't certain what mode your file should be before printing, check you manual. If you don't find enough information in your manual, search the Internet for specific recommendations for the color mode of your files for your printer. Of course as another measure, plan to run many tests to see what color mode provides you with the best output.

If I don't have a dedicated black-and-white workflow, how do I print my occasional black-and-white photos?

Try to find out if your printer manufacturer has created profiles for black-and-white printing. Be sure to use the paper for the profile and print your photos from Photoshop using the method for letting Photoshop determine the colors. If you can't find profiles for your printer, then use the method we described to using canned profiles.

If you find that your conversion to grayscale produces any unwanted color in your images, use the methods you like for the conversion, then flatten the layers and choose Image ➪ Mode ➪ Grayscale. Any color in the image should be stripped out. Since you have used other methods for converting to grayscale such as Hue/Saturation or the Channel Mixer, you won't disturb the grayscale adjustments when using the menu command to convert to grayscale. After converting to grayscale, choose Image ➪ Mode ➪ RGB to convert back to a color image and print your file. If you want to add a little color tone to your image after the fact, use a Photo Filter as we described in Chapter 10 and then print your file.

PRO GLOSSARY

Action: A series of recorded steps in Photoshop that can be played back to produce identical editing results much like a program macro.

Adobe RGB (1998): A working color space developed by Adobe Systems to represent a wide gamut of RGB color.

Barrel distortion: A lens defect that causes straight lines to bow out toward the edges of an image.

Bitmap: In Photoshop terms, a file that has only two color values — black and white. In terms of a file format, bitmap (.bmp) is an image format capable of saving 1-bit, 8-bit, and 24-bit images.

Bit depth: A value associated with how much information is available for displaying or printing each pixel in an image.

Cache: A hard drive area where information is stored to help shorten the access of viewing files and launching editing components of a software program. When using Adobe Bridge, a cache is used to store image thumbnail previews and metadata.

Camera Raw: A file format used with digital cameras where all the data is captured by the camera's sensor and post-processed when opened in a Camera Raw conversion tool. During conversion settings adjustments can be made for white balance and various image attributes.

Cathode-ray tube (CRT): A monitor like a television set that uses a picture tube emitting red, green, and blue colors.

Channel mask: A selection made in Photoshop and saved to an alpha channel.

Charged Coupled Devices (CCD): A camera sensor or scanner may be comprised of these tiny sensors used to capture a photo. This technology uses more energy than the CMOS technology being favored now by many camera manufacturers.

Clipping: Cutting off or deleting certain tonal values typically when either capturing an image with a digital camera or scanner or when adjusting the brightness values.

Color Noise: Noise in a photo that is often found in the dark areas and has a color component. (*See also* Noise.)

Color Profile: Data files used to convert color between devices such as a digital camera, computer monitor, and printing device.

Color Space: A mathematical description of colors representing a range of visible and printable colors.

Colorcast: An unwanted aberration of a color appearing in an image that needs to be corrected to produce a print with true color.

Complementary metal-oxide semiconductor (CMOS): A camera sensor used in digital cameras to capture images using less energy than the CCD chips.

Continuous tone: A smooth range of tones in either a color or grayscale image. When referred to in the context of printing, continuous-tone prints appear without visible dots.

Chromatic aberration: A color fringe along the edges of objects caused by a lens focusing different colors of light in different planes. Most common occurrences are with wide-angle lenses.

Curves: One of the primary adjustment tools used in Photoshop to change tonal values along a range of 256 gray levels. (*See also* Levels.)

Demosaiced: Stores image data in an interpolated file producing images in a larger file size. (*See also* Mosaiced.)

DisplayMaker: An oversized inkjet printer provided by ColorSpan that prints high-quality files from image resolutions as low as 100 dpi.

DNG: Digital Negative. Adobe's effort to bring the various Camera Raw formats to a standard format. (*See also* Camera Raw.)

Dots per inch (DPI): Often stated as the equivalent of PPI (pixels per inch). Although slightly different, it is commonly used as a synonym definition of PPI, which is a measure of image resolution and often used to describe printer resolution. (*See also* Pixels per inch.)

Downsampling: Reducing the number of pixels in an image by interpolation using one of several methods for calculating the result. The most common method used in Bicubic. (*See also* Upsampling.)

Dye-sublimation: A printer that employs a process that uses heat to transfer dye to paper. These printers are continuous-tone devices. (*See also* Continuous tone.)

EXIF: In terms of metadata storage, contains noneditable information related to the camera capture such as camera used, file size, date, f-stop, ISO speed, and so on. (*See also* Metadata.)

Exposure Value: A value given to all combinations of shutter speed and aperture settings; commonly referred to as EV. (*See also* F-stop.)

Film plane: An area inside a camera where the individual frame is positioned during exposure. In digital cameras the film plane is at the camera's sensor.

Film recorder: A device used to print files to negative and transparency film in RGB format.

Filter: Adapters that remove or block certain wavelengths of light. In Photoshop terms, filters are used to change image brightness, color, and density as well as recalculate pixel values.

F-stop: Relates to the aperture size when shooting a photo. A small value represents a larger opening. Large numbers represent smaller openings of the aperture. The larger the f-stop number, the greater the depth of field. (*See also* Exposure Value.)

Gamma: A mapping of tonal values within a perceived color space. The standard uniform perceived space is commonly accepted as gamma 2.2.

Gamut: A subset of colors within a color space or within a printing space. (*See also* Color Space.)

Grayscale: A Photoshop color mode having variations of gray pixels only with the absence of any color.

Halftone Frequency: Measured in lines per inch (lpi). Used for all files prepared for offset press. The lower the lpi value the more visible the dots in the printed files.

Haloing: An unwanted fringe around pixels often found in high-contrasting areas.

Histogram: Illustrates how pixels are distributed by graphing the number of pixels at each tone point along a 256 linear path.

Hue: Representation of a color within a color spectrum. Adjusting hue changes the color.

Imagesetter: A printing device producing halftone images and exposing them with a laser beam on resin-coated (RC) paper or negative film.

Infrared (IR): A nonvisible light spectrum above 700 nanometers. Typically, digital cameras have blocking mechanisms to block out all infrared light.

Inkjet printer: A composite printing device using four or more inkjets to plot dots measured in picoliters.

Interpolation: Artificial creation or redistribution of pixels through mathematical calculations according to a method prescribed by an algorithm.

Joint Photographic Experts Group (JPEG): A file format standard approved by an international standards committee capable of compressing image files using a lossy compression scheme.

Lab: A color mode where the brightness values are represented in the Lightness channel, and the a and b channels contain all the color information.

Levels: A dialog box where you can make adjustments for changing tonal range and color by changing values in highlights, midtones, and shadows. (*See also* Curves.)

Line art: In Photoshop terms, a 1-bit image having two tone values — black and white.

Liquid crystal display (LCD): A thin, flat display made of a number of color or grayscale pixels arrayed from a light source. (*See also* Cathode-ray tube.)

Luminosity: The intrinsic brightness of objects. In Photoshop terms, it represents the brightness values in an image.

Megapixels: The number of pixels measured in millions of pixels.

Metadata: Information about an image file stored within the image. Metadata can be used to define certain image attributes such as date, color space, resolution, camera used to capture the image, f-stop, ISO speed, and so on.

Moiré: An unwanted pattern of wavy lines or disarray of pixels.

Mosaiced: Stores data in an image file from original captured information in a noninterpolated format. (*See also* Demosiaced.)

Noise: Random extraneous pixels that diminish image detail. (*See also* Color Noise.)

Pincushioning: The opposite of barrel distortion where straight lines bend inward. (*See also* Barrel distortion.)

Pixels per inch (PPI): Usually used to define a measure of image resolution. (*See also* Dots per inch.)

Platesetter: Used by print shops to output digital files directly to printing plates.

Posterization: A condition where there are jumps in the tonal curve resulting in visible artifacts.

Resample: Changing the physical dimensions of an image without interpolation while maintaining the same number of pixels in a file.

Saturation: The amount of density applied to a given color.

Soft proof: A monitor preview for a document as it is likely to appear after printing.

sRGB: Officially termed as sRGB IEC61966-2.1 in Photoshop CS2. This is one of the two most common working spaces used to edit Photoshop files.

Tonal range: Range of gray tones along a linear path of 256 values.

Upsampling: Changing the image resolution through interpolation by mathematically producing more pixels via an interpolation method, the most common being Bicubic interpolation. (*See also* Downsampling.)

Unsharp mask: A filter that increases intensity of contrasting areas to provide the illusion of making images sharper.

Vignetting: A flaw in a lens that creates a defect in the image where the outer edges and corners appear darker than the center.

Working Space: The color space often used as the color model used when working on images in Photoshop. Typically, the most common two working spaces are Adobe RGB (1998) and sRGB. (*See also* Color Space.)

index

383

continued

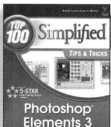

...all designed for visual learners—just like you!

Master VISUALLY®

Step up to intermediate-to-advanced technical knowledge. Two-color interior.

- 3ds max
- Creating Web Pages
- Dreamweaver and Flash
- Excel VBA Programming
- iPod and iTunes
- Mac OS
- Optimizing PC Performance
- Photoshop Elements
- QuickBooks
- Quicken
- Windows Server
- Windows

Visual Blueprint™

Where to go for professional-level programming instruction. Two-color interior.

- Excel Data Analysis
- Excel Programming
- HTML
- JavaScript
- PHP

Visual Encyclopedia™

Your A to Z reference of tools and techniques. Full color.

- Dreamweaver
- Photoshop
- Windows

For a complete listing of Visual books, go to wiley.com/go/visualtech

Visual®
An Imprint of ⊕WILEY
Now you know.